KAYAKING
THE FULL MOON

KAYAKING THE FULL MOON

A JOURNEY DOWN
THE YELLOWSTONE RIVER
TO THE SOUL OF MONTANA

STEVE CHAPPLE

HarperPerennial
A Division of HarperCollins*Publishers*

A portion of "River's Edge" was originally published in the *San Francisco Examiner*'s Sunday magazine, *Image*, as "Fathers and Sons."

A hardcover edition of this book was published in 1993 by HarperCollins Publishers.

HarperCollins books may be purchased for educational, business or sales promotional use. For information, please write: Special Markets Department, HarperCollins Publishers, Inc., 10 East 53rd Street, New York, NY 10022.

First HarperPerennial edition published 1994.

Designed by Alma Hochhauser Orenstein

The Library of Congress has catalogued the hardcover edition as follows:

Chapple, Steve.
    Kayaking the full moon : a journey down the Yellowstone River to the soul of Montana / Steve Chapple. — 1st ed.
        p.   cm.
    ISBN 0-06-016876-5
    1. Yellowstone River—Description and travel.   2. Kayak touring—Yellowstone River.   3. Yellowstone River Valley—Description and travel.   I. Title.
    F737.Y4C43   1993
    917.86'30433—dc20   92-54742
ISBN 0-06-092507-8 (pbk.)

94 95 96 97 98 ❖/CW 10 9 8 7 6 5 4 3 2 1

Once again,
to that mountain girl from Ipanema
and her two boisterous sons.

Acknowledgments

There were many along the river who helped us. Their stories are in large part this book. But special thanks are due Ray and Jo Ann Yardley, who assuaged our eccentricities; Stephanie Cavaroli, whose charm and competency buoyed us; Dana Jones and William Masters at Perception-Aquaterra kayaks, who parted the waters; Bill Parks and Willy Accola at Northwest River Supply, who kept us afloat; and Dave Strobel and Mike Garcia at Northern Lights, who offered calm advice to the uncalm. A host of family members shared their memories—Dorothy, Alex, Persis Chapple, Janet Chapple, and Margaret Chapple Christensen; and Robert and Fred Balsam, among many others—though their memories should in no way be held responsible for the author's own. Bitsy Vogel taught us about spiders. Jean Hartung offered common sense.

A number of research organizations and individuals provided materials, among them: Sister Dorothy Hanley, historian of St. Vincent's Hospital; Nathan Bender, director of Special Collections for the Renne Library at Montana State University; the Montana rooms at the Bozeman and Billings Public Libraries; Dan Himsworth of the Federal Soil Conservation Service; Richard Ellis of the Montana Department of Fish, Wildlife and Parks; Ken Barrett, Dan Gleick and Dan Gaillard of the Greater Yellowstone Coalition; and Sandy McIntyre of the Montana Wilderness Society.

Kent McCarthy and Karen Kuhlman, Randy Hayes, George Arconas, and Ruby Bell offered hospitality even while their homes were being invaded.

Terry Karten of HarperCollins shepherded the expedition from afar with kindly forbearance, while Ellen Levine provided gracious clout.

But for these friends, we might be up a creek without a paddle.

Contents

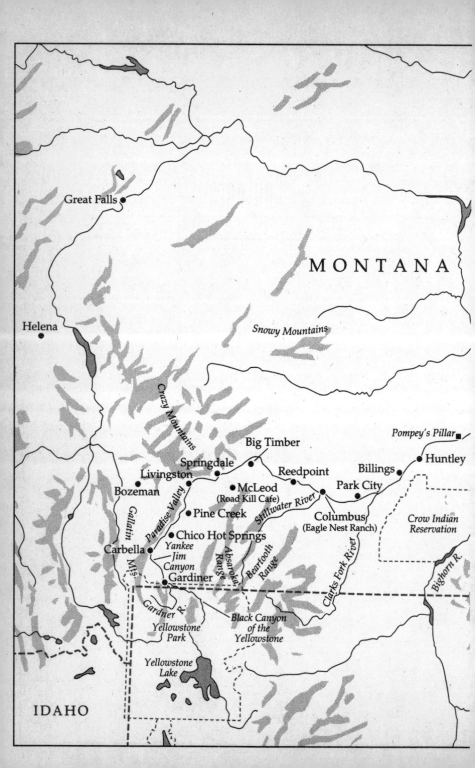

MOUNTAIN

The Moon When All Things Ripen: August 25, 1991

WE STOOD AFTER MIDNIGHT under August's full moon and watched in terror as a spruce log the length of a white-water kayak tumbled out of the Gardner tributary and slid, rolled, floated, and bobbed along the main Yellowstone eighty feet below us. Sometimes the spruce log disappeared into a suck hole only to erupt from the current a few seconds later. Once, the big log tumbled end-over-end in swollen rapids colored hog brown by the rain of the previous three days. There was no sound, no splash-splash from the cavorting log, only the constant electric rush of white water over granite far below.

My wife, the Brazilian, turned to me on that high bridge overlooking the upper Yellowstone, and we laughed. She was holding Jack in his Snugli, and I was holding Cody in my arms, both boys fast asleep. Ours was nervous laughter then, not anxious, strictly defined because, after watching the antics of brother log, we understood without speaking that it would be impossible to kayak this river we had come so far to run. At least not without a few days of local training. No way would we paddle it tonight, under the full moon, our original intention. Even under this clear moon the log kept disappearing from view. And I was afraid we would, too, if we jumped on that current.

But what a moon! It was so fat, it seemed to be dripping white lard and smiling at us at the same time. The Cheyenne call the August moon the Moon When All Things Ripen. Across the river to the east, the Moon When All Things Ripen lit up little, huffy, tree-covered Buffalo Mountain, in the Absarokas. Behind us in the Gallatins to the west, the light of the moon ricocheted off vainglorious Electric Peak, that grand edifice of chert and granite that towers over the upper Yellowstone in the same way that Emigrant Peak dominates Paradise Valley beyond Yankee Jim Canyon, twenty miles downriver, in the same way that limitless sky ironically defines the prairie Yellowstone, four hundred miles away.

It was a moon that stopped time and made hearts fly. But no amount of candlepower could have induced us to kayak the river that night.

Eventually, we would run, wobble, paddle, dunk, slalom, and swim our way down the river's 671 miles. It is a gorgeous piece of wetness, the Yellowstone, the longest free-flowing river in the Lower Forty-eight. While the vista of the Colorado is obscured by Los Angeles smog, the Columbia can no longer sustain salmon, the Sacramento is corseted, and the Arkansas and the Missouri are tributes to hydroelectric wet dreams from an earlier era, the Yellowstone still sings through canyon and prairie pretty much as heard by Lewis and Clark, the Cheyenne and the Crow.

We turned away from the Yellowstone and installed the boys in their car seats. We looked over the bridge once more. The drop of the river here is steep, as big rivers go. The spruce log was long gone. A great horned owl jumped from a clump of sage on Rattlesnake Butte, the rocky plateau that marks the park boundary a quarter mile upriver from the bridge. The owl flapped lazily across to Bear Gulch, where the road leads to the reopened gold mine at Jardine. The owl held something that wriggled in its talons. It was too far to see what it was. Deer mouse? Leopard frog? The bird flew upriver, around the bend, into Yellowstone Park and the river's high Black Canyon, which soon becomes the Grand Canyon of the Yellowstone. The Grand, with one 308-foot waterfall, is steep indeed.

As a young man, my father used to guide dudes on horseback to Yellowstone's Grand Canyon. This was long ago, in 1911, my father having been born in 1893, an interesting fifty-five years ahead of me. In those days, the wild places in America were many and dangerous. Yellowstone Park belonged to the grizzlies, and at the end of the day's travel my father hung the meat over tree limbs with ropes, a ways from camp, and each night he built the campfire high. There are still a few grizzlies in Yellowstone and downriver, and many more black bears. We shall build our campfires high, as he did, although today America's demons are human, and urban.

My desire to write *Kayaking the Full Moon* really began on the streets of San Francisco. After leaving Montana to attend Yale, I moved first to Boston and then to the West Coast, where I lived for ten years, got married, and fathered two boys. Many times I thought of changing our pace of life and moving back to Montana, rediscovering my roots in the process; but the ease, comfort, and culture of San Francisco, as well as business affairs and perhaps natural laziness, kept me from making any drastic changes.

It was a small, and perhaps not uncommon, urban incident that finally pushed me to act. One morning in the spring, I noticed something in the gutter in front of Record Hardware across the street from Washington Square Park, in San Francisco's charming North Beach, where we lived. The little family was on the way to the playground. The little something was a spent hypodermic needle.

In Montana, my father died of old age. He never locked the doors to any of his houses. He always left the keys in the car. On summer nights like this one, he would open the window wide and think nothing of it. In San Francisco, I once opened the window wide on a summer night. Two junkies climbed through it. There was a fight. My arms were cut. It took a year of physical therapy to restore them. Like many country exiles, I have learned to live with city crime, with homeless people nodding out on the benches beside urban playgrounds, with the tragedy of AIDS, and with pollution, too. Many mornings I have drawn a finger across the edge of the closed window in the boys' room and noted the soot that had somehow filtered in from the busy street outside. Like many of us, I had grown very tired, too, of the superficial and fundamentally un-American status-seeking of the past decade.

But it was too much, that spent hypodermic in the gutter.

Perhaps the United States was a gentler place when my father guided those dudes through Yellowstone Park. Perhaps it just seems that way now that I am the father. Certainly, however, my parents did not have to worry about bloody syringes in the gutters, nor anywhere else. The Old Man used to instruct me on things like the importance of not letting the tread wear down too far on a set of automobile tires, mountain roads being very rocky. But after that morning in San Francisco, I found myself instructing the Old Man's grandson: "Never pick up little tubes with needles sticking out one end."

As I held my toddler on his Fisher-Price tricycle, I made up my mind. I had been too long in cities. It was time to go home, to Montana, to this river, the Yellowstone, which tells the story of the West. I kicked the hypo to the curb. Gently enough.

This journey down the Yellowstone, then, would also be a homecoming.

In 1892 my grandfather, Dr. Henry Chapple, made a thirty-six-hour sleigh ride in a Christmas blizzard to deliver a ranch woman's baby. After the procedure, without tarrying, he turned round for home and his own holiday dinner. I wanted to know more about that ride, and that man. My grandfather died when he was thirty-nine years old. One of his brothers, Charles, a druggist, often invited Plenty-coups, chief of the Crows, and Plenty-coups's wives, to lunch in his front yard, when Plenty-coups visited Billings. The Absaroka Mountains, named for the Absaroka Indians (*absarokee* means "children of the large-beaked bird"), were once Crow lands, as were Yellowstone's valleys, all the way to the Dakotas. Not now. The lands became "reservations," and the reservations successfully shrank to accommodate first Washington and the War Department, and then the interests of Montana's miners and stockmen.

Plenty-coups brought the Crow into a strong but ambiguous alliance with the whites, a relationship that lasts to this day. In his autobiography the old chief talks of skewering Blackfoot prisoners on lodgepole pines until they "danced," yet he lunched in my great-uncle Charley's front yard.

One of Charley's sons, Charles, Jr., invented the incubator for premature children, which is something that changed the world. I wish I could say the same for myself. Uncle Charley, Jr., also had five wives, one more than Plenty-coups had, though Charley's were serial. He gave the royalties from his inventions to the Philadelphia Children's Hospital, where he was senior physician, and to the University of Pennsylvania. This was a Montana thing to do. In the America of our time, people who invent things such as incubators do not give the rights away. They incorporate and sell stock.

A Montana cousin of mine captained the submarine that torpedoed the first Japanese ship in World War II. He was made an admiral for his efforts, though he once told my mother (at a party where everybody was pretty potted) that he was just a hired killer, though a damn good one. Old uncles Will and Ed rode with Buffalo Bill Cody in Europe as fake Cossacks. Later, Ed became the territorial judge of Hawaii and Will became a playwright in Connecticut. Other uncles and cousins found gold or oil, sometimes a lot, and just shut up about it.

Montana is a good place to be alone by yourself and never want company. There is a ranginess to the place that reaches into the mind. All in all, my forgotten relatives made up a hardy crew—with the women perhaps a bit wilder, as we shall see.

Montana used to impart a kind of strength that led one—forced one—to do well, or at least to do right. The Code of the West, this used to be called. It used to be this country's code, too, and this summer I sensed the country was striving to recover it, to get back to where it belonged, or where it thought it belonged. Americans—romantic and idealistic—are always on a journey down some shining river.

And that is probably to the good. We are not such a cynical outfit. As a people, we increasingly crave meaning for our lives. This is one reason the West holds such allure for those outside it. In the West it is easy to understand your place in the realm of river, mountain, and sky. These three will last; you will pass on. From this constant epiphany, you gain perspective. You may even learn to laugh at yourself, always a tonic. It is a strong myth—that life takes on meaning when lived upon a land palpably more grand than oneself—because there is some truth to it. Off-river, I wanted to get my hands on some of that truth.

And then there were the boys I used to know, men now. What had happened to Johnny Woodenlegs? I had heard he was back in Lame Deer on the Cheyenne reservation. His great-grandfather was Wooden Leg, who, at the age of eighteen, had acquitted himself with honor in that centennial year of our lord, 1876, helping to best George Armstrong Custer's troops at what in 1991 was officially renamed the Battle of the Little Bighorn. Old Wooden Leg had carved the strange yellow beard off the face of one Lieutenant Cook, taken it on a stick to his lodge, and dangled it before his mother, who at first shrank back, and then agreed: such a new type of scalp might be strong medicine, indeed.

Johnny Woodenlegs and I used to play basketball together in

Billings. He was arguably the best player on the Lincoln Junior High Colts. I was unarguably the worst. He had fought in Vietnam while I had opposed the war. Wearing a uniform resplendent with medals, Johnny had shaken former president Bush's hand in Helena. On top of his head, Johnny had worn his great-grandfather's headdress.

I wanted to visit with the old girlfriends, as well, those who hadn't lit out for civilization. And I would meet them, nicely, my family and theirs getting together in hot springs and typically western joints such as Wong's Village down by the river in Billings.

I was getting to be that age when a man wants to look himself over. I wanted to have a rip-roaring good time. I wanted to remember and forget at the same time. I also wanted to search out the memory of that Old Man, my father, who died when I was eighteen.

High on that bridge over the upper Yellowstone, just outside the park that bears the river's name, we fired up the Trooper and drove through the little river town of Gardiner, named after Johnston Gardiner, a trapper from the 1830s. "Uncle" Joe Brown found gold at the mouth of Bear Gulch in the winter of 1865. Buckskin Jim Cutler found more gold twenty years later, but he got in such a row with the postmaster over ownership that the Northern Pacific refused to put in a spur road, isolating the place for another twenty years.

Nobody was feuding the night we retreated from the Yellowstone. Gardiner was asleep. We pointed car and kayaks north toward Chico Hot Springs Lodge, thirty miles away.

The river was in shadow as we drove. But in that transcendent light, it was not at all hard to see down Paradise Valley for miles and miles. Perhaps, I thought, we should switch from kayaks to horses. We would stay dry, and the horses would do the stumbling. But I knew this was an impossibility. No true Montanan really likes horses, as we shall see.

We started across the Yellowstone at Emigrant Bridge only to stop in the middle to watch the current braid endlessly around islands of willow and driftwood and smooth stones. After a while we turned off the engine and listened to the whisper of the water in the moonshine.

It hypnotizes, this river.

Chico Hot Springs

CHICO HOT SPRINGS LODGE, where we were staying while we quickly attempted to whip together the logistics for the expedition, is a restored cowboy/Victorian resort. There had not been enough time in San Francisco to plan extensively; in fact, we hadn't done much planning at all. The concept for the journey was all there, as they say in Hollywood, but the money came late. Yet we knew we had to be well down the river by mid-September or possibly encounter the early winter storms that had made wiser men of Lewis and Clark, Colter, Sanchez, and many other Montana explorers and river warriors who couldn't manage to get their paddles in the water before the water froze. Supplies, guides, maps, boats, food—all that would have to be done from Chico.

Luckily, Chico is a beautiful place to do anything, tucked in the shady pine notch between Chico Peak and Emigrant Mountain, a couple miles east of the Yellowstone. The lawns are green. Bourbon is served at the hot pool. Shetland ponies and farm animals run loose for children to play with. The breakfast buffet of bacon and eggs, melon, hash browns, toast, good coffee, juices, and blueberry, buttermilk, and whole-wheat hotcakes would fuel our efforts cheaply enough, since the dinners at Chico are ridiculously expensive unless you're willing to pay for game-farm fillets of elk and antelope—which we were from time to time. It was our duty on this journey, we decided, to eat well and converse with after-dinner guests wherever we might find them.

Built in 1900 over artesian hot pools, the original Chico Hot

Springs was a way station on the road to Yellowstone Park. In the winters of the 1950s, my family would often put chains on the car and slog up to this then-decayed resort. In those days, when snow had closed the airports and made impossible any quick escape to the south, mountain hot springs like Chico became our tropical vacation spots.

I remember my parents, or at least my mother, drinking Mountaintops (an old Montana drink in which warm bourbon is poured over ice water) in the lodge's common rooms, while children played board games all around. The more athletically inclined strapped on cross-country skis—those enormous, heavy, brown wooden runners then in use—for the glide down to the frozen Yellowstone. Chico Hot Springs was magical then. I wanted it to be magical now.

Chico's main building rambles on forever. It is a three-story green-and-white clapboard structure with six gables that front onto the lawn. The larger of the sixty rooms have baths. The rows of small cowboy rooms, as we always called them, share baths at the end of the halls. This is where the action used to be at Chico, on the third floor. Fishermen, cowboys, and wise party people of all descriptions would rent a couple of cowboy rooms for the weekend and invite their friends to bring along the towels. You could get drunk and dance as much as you wanted. No need to drive home, and the pools took care of any hangovers. The fishermen are still there, joined more nowadays by college students from Bozeman, Europeans on their way to Yellowstone, and wind surfers, who have taken one of the few unpleasant aspects of the Paradise Valley, its whistling and blowing wind, and made it into a tourist attraction.

I was pleased to rediscover that Chico's floors still creaked and that the oak and pine walls still smelled like a natural history museum. The long hallways all led to the pools. The big, warm pool is separated by a cement retaining wall from the smaller and shallower hot pool, beside the glassed-off bar. At night the sounds of country-western bands blast through. I have always loved swimming in the main pool as snow floats down, a legal George Dickel in my hand, though I hoped we would not experience snowflakes just yet. The temperature, after all, was still in the nineties, and Montanans were crying drought from one end of the state to the other, pretty much as they had every few years since the first Texas cattlemen drove their stock into the valley and on over to Miles City.

The hodgepodge of lobby, twisting corridors, blind hallways, swimming pools, dressing rooms, maintenance closets, and bar make for the kind of old-fashioned labyrinth a child memorizes long before his parents can figure it out. Cody, our blond toddler, was forever slipping out of our hands and disappearing down one dark hall or another. Then a parental shout would go up and we would race to the pool—the boy was only two, he could not swim. Sometimes he would be there on the deck, watching pasty white farmers with suntanned faces play horse with small children on their shoulders. More often than not, the farmers would be wearing their cowboy hats in the water. Twice, Cody walked fully clothed down the pool steps into water up to his neck. Though thin, he is tall for his age. But soon he discovered the bar, with its vintage jukebox and popular pool table. The little guy had a habit of stealing the white cue ball, which both-ered the players and drunks waiting to play, since they considered the cue ball necessary to their game. Ball and child were usually captured outside in the parking lot.

I knew my son was adjusting, making new friends, when I took him through the bar to the pool and he shouted, "'lo, Ed!" to a griz-zled old man in a flannel shirt who was busy racking the balls. Ed, along with half a dozen regulars nursing midmorning Rainiers, answered, "Howzitgoing, Cody?"

Truth be told, I had been in a lot of rowboats, rubber rafts, dinghies, sailboats, ocean liners, yachts, and a few canoes, but I'd maneuvered only two kayaks, off the Kona coast of Hawaii. They were ocean kayaks, which are open-cockpit craft with real keels, and they're very safe, a different sort of animal entirely from hard-shells. I had never paddled white-water boats anywhere, let alone down the upper Yel-lowstone. Ines, the Brazilian, my wife, was even less experienced than myself.

This confession made, I should say we had romantic will. We wanted to kayak the Yellowstone and so we were going to kayak the Yellowstone. Kayaking was the coolest way to go, closest to the water. Affirmative thinking, yes, but as a descendent of the state's first white pioneers, I liked to think I possessed that particularly western sense of often foolish optimism, which dictates that when challenged to do something, anything—clear 160 acres, withstand a –20-degree Liv-ingston winter, or run the rapids at hand—the true Montanan simply jumps in with a smile on his face and paddles. If all west Texas needs is rain, all we needed was a couple of kayaking lessons.

We had trouble finding a teacher in this part of Montana, especially since the season was closing. The guides at Beartooth White Water in Red Lodge were leaving for Jackson Hole. The clerk-professors at Northern Lights supply store in Bozeman were gearing up for the fall semester. Kayaks were pretty much a gourmet item in these parts. In the last year, wind surfers had descended from New York and Europe to practice on desolate little Dailey Lake, before they flew off again for the Oregon coast. Before the wind surfers arrived, dressed, to the local way of thinking, more for Aspen or Ketchum, fly-fishing had been the recreational sport of choice in the Paradise Valley, and for this most people used heavy, double-prowed Mackenzie boats, the furthest thing from a white-water kayak.

After dozens of calls made from the lobby phone, we finally found a rubber-rafting guide in Gardiner, whose real love was hard-shell kayaks. He was a small man with short legs yet very wide and muscled shoulders. His name was Mouse. We put Mouse up in one of the cow-boy rooms at the hotel, slipped him food from the buffet, and paid him by the hour. He supplied us with a spare Prijon Invader, a paddle, and a spray skirt, the confining girdle that forms a rubber seal between river and body so that, when the rapids crash into one's face, the kayak does not fill with water as in a canoe. The spray skirt is fitted first over the stomach. Then one climbs into the boat, and the skirt is stretched around the lip of the cockpit. We discovered that putting on the spray skirt and getting into the boat was a real chore in itself. But once in, you felt one with the kayak, as you might on a good horse or comfort-able mountain bike.

Chico's owner, Mike Art, a cordial, bearded Santa Claus of a man who used to own thirty-six men's clothing stores in the Midwest, gave us permission to use the warm pool one night for kayaking lessons. At ten, after all but a few swimmers had finished, we carried the kayaks through the crowded bar to the pool. They were playing Randy Travis on the jukebox and dancing a drunken Texas two-step as we walked through in our cobalt-blue wet suits and Nike water shoes. The door to the bar shut behind us. Steam rose in front of us. Randy Travis sounded muted. We were ready to be taught.

It all seemed simple enough and, of course, great fun, the big old warm pool with the fog wafting upward to Chico Peak, country-western sounds vibrating through the Plexiglas. Every few minutes, whenever the bartender opened his little window and handed forth another tray of iced bourbons in plastic glasses to the patrons in the hot pool, I would be distracted by the steam rising off their bodies but would quickly snap to attention as Mouse shouted: "Straight line! Straight line. OK, brace!" Piece of cake, I was beginning to think, as the warm waves from my efforts washed over the sides of the big pool.

We spent a lot of time learning to do the Eskimo roll, a nifty maneuver that rights the boat should rough current or a mistake turn you upside down. The basic technique is to sweep across the surface with your paddle, while you are still underwater, at the same time snapping the boat upright with your hips. The Eskimo roll is as important to kayakers as getting back on course might be to a race driver who goes into a skid while the stream of cars bears down behind. Yet Mouse seemed to minimize its significance to us. "It's something you pick up with practice," he shrugged. Or maybe we weren't listening well enough.

The next day, continuing our training, we put the boats into what must be the most placid stretch of the entire upper river, the gentle run from Emigrant Bridge to the Grey Owl fishing access. Here the river is wide, the drop slight. On the banks, cottonwoods and green irrigated fields of alfalfa flank the Yellowstone. A bit farther, on both sides, the snow-topped peaks of Emigrant, Cowan, Chico, Fridley, and Chisholm fly off the valley like white granite clouds.

We floated backward downstream, first Mouse and then myself, goofing, staring up at the lapis lazuli sky between the two mountain ranges. Paddling in a straight line was aided by the firm, shallow current. Now and then we inserted our paddles for correction, and we talked. There is a kayaking dictum among purists that calls for silence on the river so that one may hear the approaching rapids, but there was no reason for that here.

Mouse told me his real name was John Houston Prentis. His father had been a rodeo rider, and then a motorcycle racer, but after Mouse and his sisters were born, his father decided that hard-track racing might not be such a safe model, and he switched to kayaking. "He put me in a boat when I was ten. You could say I've been kayaking exactly half my life," said Mouse.

Actually, Mouse was not a talkative teacher. He kept his feelings to himself, except for one or two superstitions, such as believing that one must always load kayaks front end forward on top of a car. If the boat happened to point backward, it was bad karma. Earlier, thinking that I could help as we packed up at Chico, I had hefted the seventy-pound hard-shell onto the roof rack, and I had it pointed in the wrong direction. Mouse became very upset before he laughed. Kayaking is not as safe a sport as, for instance, golf, and kayakers often seem to draw on their more primitive instincts for protection.

After we had spent an hour conquering the river and building false self-confidence, Mouse asked me to try to pause in the slow water over a sandbar. I sculled backward, half-cheating by digging my paddle into the gravel in order to hold the tippy little Prijon.

Mouse wanted to see what I had learned about crossing eddy currents. Below the sandbar, about a quarter mile from the Grey Owl takeout point, the river suddenly narrowed and dropped about four feet down a bend to open up nicely a hundred yards farther on. The swirl of rapids that composed the bend was the kind of water I had fly-fished a thousand times before. Mouse wanted me to swing wide in the quickening current after the drop-off, and then cross to the right over the big eddy to the inside bank. This is called an eddy turn, one of the fundamentals. Mouse talked about paddle left, paddle right, and I moved my shoulders to create muscle memory as he sketched aloud what I should do. He stressed that I should shift my weight after the current finally turned my boat around and I was facing upstream, or I might dump.

He added: "If you do go over, and you can't make your roll, just hold your hands up like this." Mouse cradled his paddle in his palms, his fingers and thumbs gesticulating upward toward Chico Peak. "And I'll swing by and pull you up." This was the one thing that had bothered me the night before in the Chico pool when I had asked Mouse, "What if in the real river, I can't right the boat?"

I remember thinking as I launched myself back into the current that my face was already sunburned from the perfect September day.

I dug the paddle in once, twice, left-right, perhaps too deeply, and the current whipped me around the bend. The river dropped. The back of the kayak fell onto the rocks of the shelf. The boat fishtailed. I righted it. My muscles tightened all over. Clearly, this was not the Chico pool, and I had two hundred feet to go. I hunched over the front of the boat, for stability. I tried to breathe regularly but

I could only hold my breath. A wave slapped over the front of the Prijon and crashed into my glasses. I kept paddling to the midline of the current, and then it was time for the turn to the inside bank. I was scared. I paddled too hard. In a second I was upside down in the Yellowstone.

The beauty of the spray skirt seal, which kept the river outside, now turned ugly. I was trapped inside the cockpit. Underwater, some rocks scraped my helmet. Mouse had said to hold up my hands if this happened. Be serious! Without thinking or rolling, I tried to thrash my way out of the spray skirt like a fat lady fighting for air at a department store sale. My face broke the surface. I could breathe. Then the current again fishtailed the boat, which was still upside down, and my head was underwater once more. This time my right shoulder banged against the bottom. That should have hurt but I didn't quite feel it. I was still trying to break the seal of the spray skirt. My head came up again. I twisted but could not execute a roll. I saw Mouse paddling seriously toward me, and then I was under water again. Suddenly, the current rushed me to shore, and I could touch bottom with both hands and wriggle out.

No problem. Here it was shallow enough to hold the boat easily. I wasn't hurt, hadn't swallowed water. But I was angry with this Mouse. As if I were supposed to hold my hands up and float downstream like a water-logged banana or the armless hand that thrusts up the sword of Excalibur from the lake and this Mouse character would float by in the seconds before I drowned and help me do the hip-shake-baby to right the boat. I was as pissed as any fool who thought he could pay for Yellowstone river skills with a San Francisco check and a night in a resort pool.

"Hey, you forgot everything," said Mouse.

I was right to be mad at him and at myself, too. I insisted on walking the boat back to the head of the rapids and launching again, so that I wouldn't remember the turn as a defeat. This we did, but the taste of fear, and the distaste of not trusting one's guide, lingered.

Later, to a Livingston friend named Jo Ann Yardley, I explained what had happened that day. She told me that she had once attended a funeral for two eighteen-year-olds who had died in a car accident. My friend had been deeply saddened, but the kids in attendance, the friends of the dead, had flipped out, crying and acting numb.

"Young people don't understand anything about dying," said my friend, a mother of two. "They can't imagine it could happen to them and when it does, they can't handle it. You better get an older guide, some river person who has seen someone they know drown in the water right in front of them, or maybe almost chucked it themselves."

And she laughed.

Yellowstone by Air

THE NEXT DAY, we decided to step back and take a better look at what we were in for. We hired a plane and a pilot and went up to twelve thousand feet.

There is a landing strip at Chico: the road leading into the place. I wonder how many other resort driveways are lined by orange wind socks. One morning, early, Cody had already found somebody to boost him up on the Shetland pony he had named Brownie. Then we heard him screaming. We rushed to the door. He was yelling in delight. A plane was landing. A couple of cowboys who worked maintenance had put up two-by-four barricades at both ends of the driveway to stop ground traffic, and a single-engine Beechcraft swooped down. The plane made a screeching-of-rubber, bump-bump landing a hundred yards from the door to our room. I went back inside and finished shaving.

The Beechcraft was going to be in use that day, so we drove to Paradise Flying Service to hire another plane. I was afraid of going up in a single-engine plane. I peppered Frances Hodgkinson, the woman in charge, with nervous questions about the company's safety record, the unpredictable winds in Paradise Valley, what would happen if the single engine conked out, and more. Mrs. Hodgkinson, a precise yet gentle woman in her sixties, reassured me. She called for a pilot's weather report, a service prepared daily and constantly updated, and allowed me to listen to it. Her husband, Duane, stood by.

Duane, I learned, was to be the pilot. He was a small, calm man about seventy years old who talked more like an engineer than a wilderness pilot. In fact, for many years Duane had been a research engineer for Lockheed, near Sunnyvale, California. He had worked on the design of the Polaris missile, all the while operating a small airport near Santa Cruz, in the low coastal mountains. Duane had flown single-engine liaison planes in the South Pacific during World War II, and he had barnstormed before that. I had expected some fake mountain man with a pint of Jack Daniel's in the map compartment. Instead, we got a man with forty-eight years of flight experience. I wrote out a check. I made no jokes about the date, which was Friday the thirteenth.

As we taxied down the short runway, Duane handed us big cauliflower earphones with little pencil mikes. The cockpit noise was too loud for normal talk. The Cessna took off very smoothly, and in a few seconds we were one thousand feet up.

"I forgot my camera," I said.

"Let's go back and get it," said Duane. He sounded like my high-school calculus teacher, Barney Myers, one of the most patient people I have ever known.

Below us, semitrucks ambled along Highway 89. Chico Lodge looked like a Victorian cottage. Duane immediately banked to the right and set the plane down in front of the hangar. To Duane, going back for the Nikon was like turning the car around in the driveway. As I climbed back over the struts a second time, I thought that now was my chance to change my mind. It was still Friday the thirteenth. But I closed the door and strapped myself in. Wham! We were two thousand feet above Paradise.

The first thing you notice from the air is that a far more ancient river bed extends from one side of the Paradise Valley to the other. The old bed comes right up to the sides of the Absarokas on the east and the Gallatins on the west. This makes the contemporary Yellowstone River resemble a blue thread of hair dropped onto an immense yellow braid. From two thousand feet, the alluvial swirls and tracks of the ice-age Yellowstone are plain to see under a modern blanket of alfalfa, hay, and blond buffalo grass. They say that the valley is called Paradise because of the buffalo grass, which between the two mountain ranges was so nourishing, and the shelter was good enough, that cattlemen coming up from Texas felt they had reached paradise. Their herds could be parked safely for the winter.

The next thing you notice are incongruous swatches of color.

Thousands of acres have been put into pool-table-green alfalfa. These fields are circular, however, irrigated by enormous steel wheel systems twenty feet high, which "walk" along the ground propelled by the pressure of the water inside the piping. Here and there are puddles of aquamarine blue—large swimming pools. They look strange, out of place, orphans on the prairie, but throughout the thirty-nine-mile-long valley are mansions in the center of gentlemen's ranches. The owners fly in for a few weeks or months in the summer. There is one patch of lima-bean-green—a tennis court. It sits alone, unconnected to house or grounds. (I imagined some Antonioniesque cowpunchers rolling up long after midnight in a beat-up pickup and playing a quick game of tennis with fluorescent tennis balls in the moonshine, wearing Tony Lamas in place of Adidas.)

Until you reach Point of Rocks, eight miles south of Emigrant Bridge, the river is flat and wide. West of Point of Rocks, an old volcanic vent has created rounded, flowing hummocks, something like a giant horse blanket slung over a stepladder. Chalk cliffs hem the river nearby, and the cliffs are topped by columnar basalt, which resemble regular rows of dirty black teeth.

At Carbella, four miles south of Point of Rocks, the Absarokas and the Gallatins almost touch, just as they do at the north end of the valley, at the entrance to the cowboy literary town of Livingston. This sheer rock canyon of granite and dark, banded gneiss is named after Yankee Jim, an old coot who operated a toll road into the Gardiner gold mines. The Yellowstone is at its deepest in Yankee Jim, sixty to eighty feet during spring runoff. Yankee Jim is the most frightening stretch of soup on the river. This is where people drown. Even large Mackenzie drift boats have flipped over here and been sucked down and held by the current against underwater boulders. One rapid is called Boxcar because part of a train is said to have fallen into the gorge and was never recovered. I could not look at Yankee Jim without thinking what it would be like to shoot the gorge.

At the mouth of Yankee Jim is a delicate, arched, wrought-iron bridge. The dirt road over the bridge leads up Tom Minor Basin, where great numbers of spruce and pine logs, mixed with tropical hardwoods, were crushed and tossed fifty million years ago, moved helter-skelter by a great volcanic mud flow. Many of these trees are now petrified. From the air they look like half-broken pencils jabbed into tablets of naked rock.

As we flew south, the flanking mountains were so high that the Cessna did not climb above them until the far end of Yankee Jim. What mountains! Mt. Cowan, near Chico, is 11,205 feet. Mt. Delano, next to Cowan on the north, is 10,138. Emigrant Peak, next to Cowan on the south, is 10,691. Facing them across the river are Blackmore at 10,196, Sawtooth at 9,449, and Electric at 10,992. These are not the largest mountains in Montana. In seconds we would see those.

Duane motioned with his hand. Far below, at Corwin Springs, was a herd of captive elk, fenced in a pen. The elk looked tiny, like Lego pieces. Across from them were the buildings and sod-covered bomb shelters of the Church Universal and Triumphant, a New Age millennial group of several thousand devotees. I was surprised by the number of structures and their size. Big vent pipes stuck up from the underground shelters. The church, which had bought the old Malcolm Forbes ranch, was preparing for Armageddon, as it had been for some years. Most of its members were from southern California.

Then with a pop of sunlight we were above the peaks.

Suddenly, perspective was possible. The mountain ranges—Gallatin, Absaroka, Beartooth—were simply eruptions from a vast high plateau, an altiplano that stretched from Billings to West Yellowstone, from Bozeman to Cody, Wyoming. Several hundred miles beyond West Yellowstone, too far to see, was Salt Lake City. However, we noticed that the shoulder of the plateau changed at the extreme southwestern corner from forest green to a flat expanse of desert orange.

The immense plateau was like a calm, flat fist. The knuckles were the mountains. The back of the wrist was an endless forested plain. The fist's blue veins were the rivers of Yellowstone Park, first the twisty cobalt Lamar and then its tributaries—rushing Soda Butte Creek and passive Slough Creek—and then, farther south, the Yellowstone itself. Everywhere were old men's liver spots—the brown, ragged patches left by the great park fire of 1988, which burned an area the size of Connecticut.

It was not an angry fist, however. Cortés once described Mexico as a piece of paper crumpled by a mad hand and thrown to earth. For all the jagged, bare-knuckle mountains erupting from the Beartooth Range, the whole expanse still looks like a hand in repose.

Over Gardiner, we caught sight of the tallest mountain in the state, Granite Peak, 12,799 feet. It was probably fifty miles northeast of us. Nearer and almost as high was Mt. Inabnit, named for my sister-in-law Janet's grandfather, a Swiss immigrant bank clerk who preferred scaling mountains to shuffling papers.

And then right below, twelve thousand feet down, was the suicide run of the Yellowstone's upper canyons, Black and Grand, miles of churning white froth, unthinkable water for paddling. But we would meet several anonymous kayakers who had poached the swirling stretch in between the two canyons. It is illegal to kayak the Yellowstone in the park. That is why we were beginning our journey at Gardiner. But the technically courageous sometimes try. They are dropped off at night and sleep beside their boats until dawn. If they and their boats survive the run, they are picked up after sunset.

The canyons of the Yellowstone were formed when the tectonic plate underneath shifted and cracked. This fault line climbs over Lower Falls, 308 feet high, and Upper Falls, 109, and then mends. Suddenly, the river is placid, meandering through tall grass. It is drinking water to moose, elk, and buffalo, bands of which we could see. Then, it rolls out of Yellowstone Lake itself. The lake sits at 7,733 feet, higher than most mountains on the East Coast. It is the largest high-altitude lake on the continent.

As with the Amazon and the Nile, the source of the Yellowstone is a trickle of melted snow. The rivulets roll down Yount's Peak seventy miles southeast, in Wyoming, until they course across Two Ocean Plateau into the southeast corner of the lake, where most people assume the river really begins.

Two Ocean Plateau is a place I like to think about. My father would stop the car at Two Ocean Creek, and we would spit and watch which way our spit floated. Pacific or Atlantic? Spit in the ocean. It was wonderful, at age seven, to imagine what happened to those amber gobs.

Two Ocean Creek captured the imagination of a lot of people. Here, in the 1850s, the old mountain man Jim Bridger opined that the water ran so quickly it heated the stream bed through friction. This explained why steam rose up from the edges. You could cook a trout without taking it off the line, too. In Two Ocean Creek. Just swing the fish into one of the steam cauldrons. Then as now, this was actually possible. Nobody believed Bridger, though, and so he invented a few tall ones to spite the doubters.

In Yellowstone Park, said One-Eyed Jim, a hunter he knew had once taken an easy shot at a close-up elk. Hunter missed by a mile. Shot again. Missed. The elk was almost on top of him. Shot a third time. The bullet came back at him! What had happened, you see, said Bridger, was the bullet hit a mountain of glass—obsidian—and had come caroming around. What's more, the elk was not an easy shot. He was twenty-five miles away. The refraction was wrong.

Bridger must have also seen the petrified trees of the Mesozoic. But he expanded a bit there, too. He said he had seen petrified grass, sagebrush, and robins. In fact, the raspberries had hardened into rubies and the snowberries into diamonds, and the birds sang petrified songs, and his horse had been so surprised by it all that she jumped across the Grand Canyon of the Yellowstone, with Bridger on top, which posed no problem for horse or rider, however, since gravity in this part of the park was petrified, too.

Bridger tells some of the best lies the country has ever heard. You have to like a man who doesn't mind being called a liar, even when he knows he's telling the truth.

The great high plateau that we are circling with Duane in the Cessna used to be the territory of the Crow Indians. In 1868 the government mapped out the Crow "reservation" as the land east of the Yellowstone in the Paradise Valley all the way to the Little Bighorn and a bit beyond, south to Wyoming and north along the long stretch of the Yellowstone, which doglegs east at Livingston in what was then called the Great Bend. This was territory as big as Massachusetts, Connecticut, and Rhode Island combined. Some of the most beautiful land in the world, I think, land my non-Crow family considered theirs for generations, recent generations.

For reasons I want to discover downriver, the Crows did not often venture into Bridger's strange land, which is below us now. However, one man who did, a friend of the Crows, was John Colter. For many years Yellowstone Park was known as Colter's Hell. He had been to the Pacific with Lewis and Clark in 1805–06, but he, for his own reasons, did not want to return to civilization. He signed on with Manuel Lisa's fur company, and one winter, holed up in a two-sided cabin against a recess in a canyon wall where the Clarks Fork spills out of the Absarokas into the Yellowstone, he "became bored."

Many, perhaps most, people become bored after a long winter in Columbus or Billings, towns now located on either side of where that flimsy lean-to must have been. But these people do not sling on a thirty-pound pack, take out snowshoes and a buffalo gun, and walk five hundred miles, alone, in the dead of winter, to the Shoshone River in Wyoming, ask directions from an encampment of surprised Crows, then amble on up the Sunlight Basin into what is now Yellowstone Park, survey the largest frozen high-altitude lake on the continent, turn around, and walk down the Yellowstone River another three hundred miles, all the while still alone. That's ennui.

I wonder what it must have felt like to come over Two Ocean Pass almost two hundred years ago and watch the steam rising off the hot pots at the edge of Yellowstone Lake. Did Colter ever stand, hands resting on the barrel of his big flintlock gun, as Old Faithful erupted before him in a column of water "as large as my body, as high as the flagpole in Virginia City," the way Bridger accurately described the experience in the days, fifty years later, when nobody believed his stories?

In 1807, Colter paddled up a creek just to the northeast of the park, near the Gallatins. (We could see the crests of the Gallatins that morning from the windows of the Cessna. They looked like a spiked hairdo—wondrous, green, regular.) On a river near what is now Bozeman, Colter and his companion, John Potts, were surprised by Blackfoot Indians. Colter understood the ritual. He held up his hands. The Indians stripped him of his clothes. But Potts panicked and shot one of the Blackfeet. The Indians blanketed him with arrows. Then they pulled his body onto the bank, chopped it into pieces, and threw the parts in Colter's face.

The Blackfoot leader had a game in mind. He set Colter loose, with a head start. Colter was still naked but now he had a chance. He managed to outrun all but one man. Legend has it that this Indian hurled his spear at Colter from close range. Colter twisted, the lance missed, and the spearhead broke off. Colter plunged it into the man's face. Just then the rest of the band caught up to him. Colter managed to run on. Finally, he dove into a river, probably the Madison, floated downstream, and hid under a pile of driftwood that had lodged against the bank. Then he walked back to the fort on the lower Yellowstone. When he arrived, his joints were swollen. His feet were bleeding. Nobody recognized him. They believed his story about the Blackfeet, but did they believe his tales of geysers and boiling mud pots?

Colter was a man who usually got along with Indians. He loved the country and its people. Yet everything went wrong near Yellowstone. Colter is a bit of a metaphor. He had once traveled with the Crows in a party that had been surprised by Blackfeet; the Blackfeet identified white, American trappers as allies of their tribal enemies, and they usually killed mountain men on sight.

Colter's Hell was too far out of the way, too remote even for Indians, even for Lewis and Clark, who never ventured this far upriver, certainly for most trappers and miners, and for all settlers. But those wild stories of petrified bird song and columns of boiling water would not die.

In 1870 a group of pioneer Montanans decided to form a party to open up the region. They were interesting men. Henry D. Washburn had been a general on the Union side. Nathaniel P. Langford was one of the civic minded who formed the vigilante committee that hanged Henry Plummer, the sheriff of Virginia City. Plummer and his corrupt gang of highway robbers had preyed upon the gold miners.

But it was the misfortune of expedition member Truman C. Everts, former U.S. assessor for Montana, that captured the public mind of that time. His horse became lost in an area of fallen trees, and the next day the horse ran off. Everts himself was then lost for thirty-seven days. He dined on two small snow birds, some minnows, and thistle roots. Soldiers could not find him. He was located by two mountain men, lured by the $600 reward. When they found poor Everts, he was stumbling around with a burning branch in his hand, presumably for starting fires, talking to an imaginary companion.

I like this next part. Everts was rescued, all right, but the assessor's digestive system had been clogged by too much fibrous thistle root. Two days later another mountain man happened by with a remedy: a pint of bear grease emetic.

The first real scientist to visit Yellowstone was Ferdinand Vandiveer Hayden, a wild fellow who on an earlier trip up the Missouri and down the Yellowstone had discovered teeth of the Troodon and Palaeoscincus, the first dinosaurs ever to be described in America. This was in 1854, five years before Darwin published *Origin of the Species*. Hayden would be out alone on the banks of the Yellowstone chipping away at fossils, while Cheyenne and Crow fired away at each other. So the Indians gave F. V. Hayden a name: the Man Who Picks Up Stones While Running. A good name for a paleontologist in flight. The Indians thought this founder of modern geology was crazy and, therefore, holy. He was not to be killed.

Ferdinand Vandiveer Hayden figures again in our story a bit later, but for now we must leave him downriver, clutching dinosaur teeth and mollusk, his favorite fossil, to breast.

It is time to land.

We looked long at the white water in Yankee Jim Canyon as we followed the river north, and then we were at the hangar near Emigrant, across the river from Chico.

Preparations

L<small>ATE THAT NIGHT IN OUR ROOMS AT</small> C<small>HICO,</small> Cody awakened with a dry, whimpering cough. His forehead was hot. His fever seemed high. My notes say it measured 103.6. His screams woke the baby.

Strange that when explorers plan their expeditions to the unknown, they seldom factor in the unexpected. Nine very different world citizens start down the entire length of the Amazon in 1987. It never occurs to any of them that they may all soon be at each other's throats. Perry packs for the North Pole. Does he remember the right boots? Columbus sets sail for China. He does not anticipate the Americas. Amoebic dysentery, snake bite, grizzly attack—downtime is always left out of the equation. Adventurers are optimists, or else they would stay home in front of the VCR, dogs upon the ottoman. Certainly, no modern adventurer remembers to remember that a toddler might be felled by flu. We did not sleep well.

Next morning we drove the boys to the Park County Clinic, in Livingston. The clinic is cantilevered over the Yellowstone, within yards of the Ninth Street Bridge. Before we carried the children inside, we stood and watched the river swirl through the cement pilings. We had been told that this was one of the most dangerous spots on the Yellowstone, because the bridge is set at an angle to the flow. Which two pilings to scoot through depended on water level and time of year. It was important to choose the correct chute.

There was no wait inside the clinic. Clerks and nurses were courteous—we were not in the city. But Cody had some bad flu. Both boys had infected ears. Little Jack was listless, as well, with very dry skin, hardly his normal self. It was a moment of reckoning for adult adventurers.

After our idyll at Chico, we had imagined that we would begin tent camping. This would be the proper way to proceed, pitching blue-and-yellow dome tents beside the river, as the whisper of the rapids lulled us to sleep night after starry night, bidding us forget crime, traffic, rude behavior, and the miscellaneous bad hysteria of city life.

I recalled a hot summer day in Billings long before moving out of Montana when my family watched in bathing suits as summer hail crashed down upon the cars. By the beginning of dinner, snow was falling. We listened to the warning voices of our grandmothers. The record for temperature variation during a twenty-four-hour period in Montana—and the nation—was set on January 23, 1916, in Browning: ninety-eight degrees, from forty-four above to fifty-four below.

If it would be foolhardy to proceed downriver in dome tents with lanterns hissing nicely in front, what would we switch to? Where we would be going, there were not a lot of hotels like Chico Hot Springs Lodge. With trepidation, we decided to rent a recreational vehicle.

This proved difficult, for insurance reasons, and expensive. We located a mobile home lot in Billings that was willing to rent us a self-contained unit for $225 a night, no break for long-term rental. Finally, after calling all over the state, we discovered in Bozeman a small operator named Gary Stevenson, who would rent a trailer and van at family rates.

Stevenson was a rangy bear of a man, six-foot-four, about sixty years old, with a very expressive face. The lines and muscles jumped and scampered about his cheekbones. Each of his eyebrows was the size of a small squirrel's tail. Whenever he explained something that was of vital importance to him and barely comprehensible to us, we would soon be lost in the hop and jump of the man's incredible squirrel-tail eyebrows.

For example, it seemed our Aristocrat Travel Trailer needed to be carefully leveled with struts and jacks before the refrigerator would work properly, since RV refrigerators are not powered by Freon, as are household refrigerators. This refrigerator was heated and cooled by a mixture of many chemicals (Stevenson named them all), and if the refrigerator happened to be even fifteen degrees off kilter (Gary showed us a little bubble level attached to the stove by a string, which when laid flat would indicate the success of our efforts) then the little demon Frigidaire would self-destruct. Explode? Detonate? Spew forth toxic fluids? What do Aristocrat Travel Trailer refrigerators do when they do their thing? Stevenson did not say. And we were already lost in those acorn-hunting eyebrows.

Stevenson was not Avis, though he was certainly more versatile. He was mechanic, clerk, cleaner, and sole proprietor rolled into one. He carried a grease gun in his back pocket. Before founding his recreational vehicles business, he had for twenty years parked B-52s at Strategic Air Command bases. He had also served as crew chief on countless nuclear-ready flights, and he played electric bass in an air force country-western band that toured Germany and England, where he had met his wife. He brought her back to the Four Corners district of Bozeman.

The refrigerator, the gas stove, the lights, the water holding tank and water pump, the chemical toilet, the various fuses and shutoff valves, the folding tables and beds and hidden latches and every other clever dumb gizmo—Stevenson explained in such folksy detail how RVs work that we could no longer bear to listen. It was a new world to us, and two and a half hours seemed an overly long time to enter a new world. We were impatient to return to the river.

The Aristocrat and accompanying Dodge Maxi Van seemed to us as complicated as a strategic bomber. Perhaps we should have noted that anybody the government selects to park its B-52s might find it easier to park a van and trailer combination than people who had never parked anything longer than an Isuzu Trooper.

But we were in a hurry that afternoon. Those first days, it seemed as if we were always in a snit to get somewhere, buy something, see some landmark, or paddle a pocket on the river. We acted just like people from California or New York (in Montana, they don't make much of a distinction). That afternoon, our concern was to pick up my sister Persis at Gallatin Field. Persis was flying in from Sacramento.

Before we drove to the airport, we stopped by Northern Lights to pick up new kayaks. Northern Lights is an outdoor supply store that sells state-of-the-art climbing, kayaking, and backpacking equipment. The store's building is a vaulted, wooden structure fashioned without the use of nails, screws, or metal of any kind. It looks like my idea of a Viking meetinghouse. A twenty-three-year-old kayak fitter named

Dave Strobel helped us to load the kayaks on top of our new Yamaha rack. He hefted the boats easily and tied the knots effortlessly. I offered him a Heineken from the cooler.

Dave said he had kayaked the Yellowstone many times. He told us the upper river would be "a piece of cake" this time of year. This struck me, because it was the same phrase I had used back at the Chico pool. Strobel smiled at our combination of Isuzu Trooper, Aristocrat Travel Trailer, and Dodge Maxi Van. "Yuppie Oakies on the Yellowstone," he offered.

We drove for the airport. The little expedition was expanding. We planned to have visitors fly in and float with us, and perhaps (fingers crossed here) help out with babysitting so that the parents could get on the river together. Ours was no ordinary expedition down the Zambezi, as I said before. But my sister Persis had been the only one to volunteer for the run down Yankee Jim Canyon.

A recently retired speech pathologist in the Sacramento school system, Persis, who had just turned sixty-one, wanted, I think, to prove something to herself. Running the Yellowstone for her had nothing to do with returning to Montana. She hated the place. She had left at eighteen and never looked back. Montana girls of the fifties did not light out for the woods, as Huck Finn once did, and a nineties woman might, being tired of gridlock. A Montana gal of my sister's vintage craved urban sophistication, eastern educations, and California cities. That the bloom was off the rose for each of these hoarfrosted American fantasies had not occurred to her, and probably never would.

My sister had been a sickly child. She suffered rheumatic fever, tuberculosis, and crossed eyes. The eyes had been corrected by a visit to the Mayo Clinic, the Minnesota hospital almost mystically preferred by Montanans with enough money to fly over, but TB and rheumatic fever cut as much as two inches off Persis's height, which even now, after six decades, was no more than five-foot-one. All these childhood maladies had also left her terribly feisty—at least this was the conclusion of her much younger brother.

Persis once told me that when she was thirteen, which would have been in about 1943, the family drove to the Festival of Nations in Red Lodge. Red Lodge is now a ski resort on the eastern slope of the Beartooths, but back then it was still a coal-mining town that liked to celebrate its ethnicity. While the parents were distracted by a parade squadron of miners in Serbo-Croatian dresses, she had slipped a carny guy two bucks for a loop-the-loop ride in his World War I barn-stormer. My father had been a pilot in that war, and he was livid when she landed. My sister was not to be chastised. She felt alive doing barrel loops while wearing a leather helmet in an open-cockpit single-engine plane, as thousands of gawkers stared upward. Feeling alive meant everything to a little girl who had thought she was about to die, on several occasions, over time, because everybody she loved thought she was going to, too. Die. Perhaps this had something to do with why she wanted to kayak the upper Yellowstone.

So we picked up Persis at Gallatin Field, in that snowy cup of mountaintops—Spanish Peaks, Tobacco Roots, Gallatins, Hyalites, Bridgers—called Bozeman. The place is named after John Bozeman, a Florida pioneer who abandoned his wife and three children and ended up promoting a trail through Crow and Sioux country to the gold fields of Montana.

Immediately we drove back to Livingston to buy provisions at John's IGA, a large twenty-four-hour market. It was about eleven at night. The store was almost empty. We bought a lot of things. Hormel ham, yams, bags of taco chips, black and red beans, a case of Classic Coke, Kraft campfire marshmallows, T-bone steaks, a leg of lamb, many flashlights and batteries, several twelve-ounce bags of French roast coffee, fishing lures and flies, cilantro and parsley, Gatorade and spring water (since the river was running muddy), Rainier and Heineken, Jack Daniel's, overpriced Napa Valley chardonnays, a box of Reese's Peanut Butter Cups and one of peanut M&M's, Cutter's insect repellent, a fly swatter, a red polyester sleeping bag for Cody, cheap socks, bell peppers and Newman's Own spaghetti, pasta, bananas and raw pistachios and good local bread, oatmeal, vegetables, a five-pound sack of baking potatoes and a five-pound bag of short-grain brown rice, really lots of diapers (small baby size, 10 to 18 pounds, and larger toddler size, 24 to 32 pounds, both in blue), milk, blueberry muffins, celery, cans of tuna, two cartons of eggs, bacon, butter, and orange juice. We filled that Aristocrat Travel Trailer. We did not want to starve. The river was too muddy to count on good fishing. We felt like mountain men.

The next day at lunch we picked up the nanny at the Livingston Bar & Grill. We were to have two nanny/helpers on the expedition. Geraldine was the first. Her parents drove her down from a small town several hours to the north of Livingston. Her parents were both naturally a little suspicious of sending their only daughter out with what they regarded as a California author. At the same time, they seemed glad to be rid of her for the rest of the summer.

We had had great difficulty securing any nanny at all. The nanny concept had not reached Montana. Women regarded Ines as something less than a Real Mother when she explained that she wanted someone to be with the kids while she kayaked. Men looked at me as if I had more money than I let on. This was exasperating. In San Francisco, an ad in the *Chronicle* always produced dozens of earnest replies from overqualified women and some men, too. People here thought we were weak, if not crazy. But to us, it was a matter of safety and convenience, and so what?

We inquired about town and at Livingston's two pulse points, the Owl and the Guest House Bar. When this did not pan out, we put an ad in the September 17 issue of the Livingston *Enterprise,* to run for a week:

HI—WE'RE LAUNCHING
family expedition down the
Yellowstone. We need large
house 1–2 months, $600 month;
experienced nanny $250/week
and Mackenzie drifter (lease) or
John boat (buy). PO Box 172,
Livingston, MT 59047.

We renewed the ad for two more weeks. We received no replies to the house ad, since, though the median price of a three-bedroom house in Park County was $40,000 in 1991, three movies were being filmed in the area that summer: *A River Runs Through It, Keep the Change,* and *Far and Away.* Production chiefs had long since snapped up every available rental for their actors and crews. Nobody wanted to lease a Mackenzie drifter, either. Mackenzies cost $2,500–4,000 and are easily sunk. We received three replies to the request for a nanny.

The respondents understood that we wanted them to look after our children in their houses while we traveled down the river. These women thought we would drive back to visit every few days. When we explained that they were to come along and help and perhaps have a fine adventure themselves, one turned us down, and the other two asked for a night to think it over. We called them. They said they were sorry. Their husbands would worry too much. The women were chatty, cordial, and unapologetic.

Geraldine had been secured through an agency that solicited Montana girls for work back east. In a few weeks Ines would read one of the agency's posters at the Road Kill Cafe in McCloud, where actor Michael Keaton and others keep ranches, that advertised for girls who wished to GO EAST, where they might work with GOOD FAMILIES IN NEW JERSEY (30 MINUTES FROM NEW YORK CITY).

Geraldine was subdued in the presence of her domineering parents. She was a tall, gawky girl, probably intelligent but devoid of charm. While her parents made small talk, she read a paperback, *The Silence of the Lambs*. We had our reservations. But we had no other prospects. The Brazilian was tense about Cody's health and about camping in a trailer. Persis, who after twenty-three years had been in Montana less than a day, and then only for my father's funeral, was in a hurry to hit the Yellowstone. She had been honing her kayaking skills on the American River near Sacramento. I, likewise, wanted to get the hell out of Dodge. End of September was pushing it in terms of Montana's weather, I knew, and our river skills did not yet fill me with confidence.

Ines drove the Trooper with Geraldine in front, Cody and Jack in their car seats in back. I followed in the Maxi Van with the Aristocrat in tow, loaded to the gills with provisions, and sister Persis beside me. The trailer tugged at the van like a kite in the wind. We cruised high over the blacktop on the van's softly bouncing pneumatic seats. At last we were rolling, south on Highway 89, returning to Gardiner, where the Yellowstone tumbles out of its park as brashly as a baby with a saxophone between its knees.

We drove into Gardiner a little after one in the morning. Nothing looked to have changed in the six days since we had surveyed the river from the town bridge. We turned into the first RV park at the north edge of town. We did not want to risk turning the long van and trailer combination around, although Stevenson had showed us how: backing left turned the trailer right, and vice versa. He made it look easy, but not so easy that we thought we would be able to do it ourselves the first time. The trailer park office, situated in a wooden shed at the top of a steep incline, was closed for the night. PICK A SPOT. PAY IN MORNING read the placard in the window.

We inched down the graveled incline to the flood-lit parking area, which lay on a bulldozed pad without trees, grass, or plants of any kind. The other RVs and trailers looked like big sleeping steel lizards. The bright lot overlooked a narrow swirling curve in the river. We could hear the rapids as we descended, and my mind was on securing the best view. The lot was all but full. Still, a perfect spot was open at the north end. Tired, and wanting to start the journey at the spot beside the river, we soon discovered we had driven the wrong way around the ring road. There was no way we could avoid backing up now. Persis and Ines got out to assist. I began to back up.

"Stop!" screamed my sister.

The trailer twisted off its hitch, and we heard a sick little crunch of metal upon metal. I got out to survey the damage. There was a fresh dent in the trailer wall where the hitch bar had scraped it, but our mistake was surrounded by three or four other such scars. We were not the only novices to hire one of Gary Stevenson's B-52 rigs.

The Brazilian and I did not speak. We were too weak from the flu, which we had caught from the boys, and we were discouraged. Persis was too tired. We stood for a few seconds staring stupidly at our predicament. A flashlight appeared. It was held by a man in rubber sandals and Bermuda shorts, no shirt.

"Want me to park your rig, folks?"

We did. The man was very friendly. This was Ted, a retired schoolteacher from Oxnard, California, who signed on each summer, like most of the regulars in the RV park, to work jobs in Yellowstone Park. He parked our van and trailer as easily as I might slide a slice of bread into a toaster.

We slept. I wanted to sleep as long as possible. Everybody but Persis was dog sick with this killer hot-weather flu.

At 6:00 A.M. came a loud banging under our heads. Persis and the ever chipper Ted were unbending our bent trailer hitch with a one-pound sledgehammer.

We could not get anything going in Gardiner.

The little town is Yellowstone's winter headquarters. It is populated by hard-drinking career park mechanics, outdoorsy students who clerk for the concession stores in Yellowstone or clear trails, and outlaw poachers. Professional poachers have called Gardiner home ever since Yellowstone Park opened. The modern crop sneak into the park at night to gather fresh elk antlers or to cut off deer penises with Gerber knives. Asian businessmen powder the elk horn and deer penis and sell it as aphrodisiac in Hong Kong and Taiwan. I also know an old ranger and his wife who gather up the town's stray dogs and feed them in the barn behind their house, since Gardiner is too small a place to have a humane society chapter. Helen's Corral serves burgers made from buffalo. At the Blue Goose, the pool table is professional. The Town Cafe sells Swedish Calculators, pieces of cardboard in the shape of your hand, with holes for your fingers. The big news of a few years ago was the hunter who shot two backpackers making love in their lighted tent pegged in the center of Bear Gulch Trail. The woman was on top of the man, the sheriffs determined, which created a large bearlike silhouette in the light of their lantern. The hunter claimed that the two were also making noises "like a grizzly." The hunter was never charged.

But Gardiner, Montana, is an amusing place only if you are in an amusing mood. We were sick. The town seemed desolate to us. The hills were long ago stripped to timber the mines in Bear Gulch. The wind whistled down from the park day and night.

We walked out on the bridge over the Yellowstone where we had watched that spruce log tumble from the Gardner River a week before. Our legs were a little wobbly from the flu. We had no guide, since Mouse was sick, too, and avoiding us, and we did not feel confident to begin by ourselves. We were not yet comfortable in our whitewater kayaks. To us, these darting little boats were like sports cars, with us in the passenger seat and nobody driving. Twice we saw young kayakers playing in the rapids below the bridge. They made it look easy. We climbed down and asked them to guide us through the town stretch. Nobody would do it. They recommended Northern Lights in Bozeman, where we had picked up the boats.

We did not have the energy to explore the town. We felt out of place in the RV park. Barren, though friendly, the place still could just as well have been located in Costa Mesa or Trenton. What was the point of our being here? I loved the bumper sticker on Ted's $30,000 trailer: IF GOD WASN'T A HOOSIER, HOW COME THE SKIES ARE BLUE AND WHITE? But this was not what we had come for. On the third morning, around dawn, there came a clattering of metal-tipped hoses, then the sound of a wrench twisting the cap off something, then a whoosh like all the toilets in Penn Station flushing at once. The people in the trailer next to us were discharging their sewage.

Ines was up on her elbow on the fold-down bed, trying to decipher the sounds. "RV life," she concluded, "lacks poetry."

Maybe we were doing something wrong. I don't know. But the kids were still sick. We were still sick. The nanny was up at night with a flashlight reading *The Silence of the Lambs* in her sleeping bag, and our toddler hated her. My sixty-one-year-old sister was up at dawn pacing the river, itching to get going. None of us seemed to be able to float downstream for long without turning over. Some things need changing.

The core problem, I decided, was one of beauty. We needed more of it. We scouted the territory and decided to shift camp downriver about twelve miles, to the mouth of Yankee Jim Canyon, to the spot called Carbella, where the delicate iron bridge arched over the river and the side road led to the petrified forest high in Tom Minor Basin. The campsite was part of the ancient river bed, here stony and covered with short yellow grass. Willows, juniper, and thin young cottonwoods lined the river. The place possessed a windswept serenity. We affectionately named it the Bush of Ghosts. Behind us to the east was Red Mountain; in front, across the river, Crystal Cross Mountain and Dog Tooth Rock (a mountain by any other name); and farther, due west, Eaglehead Mountain.

The Yellowstone was smooth at Carbella, if not exactly placid. We could practice in these waters, and we could keep our eyes upstream, on Yankee Jim Canyon. That would be good. Yankee Jim was the golden ball. If we could run the canyon, it would be smooth sailing, I hoped, all the way to the Missouri. The problem with our journey was that, naturally, we had to start with the Yellowstone in the mountains, and this was like learning to swim by jumping off the high dive.

We were so tired the first night at Carbella, we did not bother to make a campfire. It turned out to be the right thing. It was pouring rain as soon as the sun went down.

Sometime in the middle of the night, the toddler started screaming. "My foot! My foot! My foot!"

There was nothing wrong with his foot. It was a bad dream. But his screaming had awakened the baby, who was a sound sleeper. Now the baby was screaming, too. I comforted him in my arms. I noticed my flannel shirt was soaked from my fever, but my forehead was dry. Ines was trying to find some milk. We thought we had bought some during the day but now we couldn't find it. Ines fumbled to turn on the little gas heater. The babies screamed on. Ines tried Carnation powdered milk for Cody. He refused. She mixed in half a cup of Nestle's hot chocolate. He took it, and went to sleep. In my arms, the baby nodded off, finally. I looked over. Ines was asleep, too.

I was standing in the doorway of the trailer, naked now except for thick blue polypropylene socks. I had stripped off the soaked flannel shirt. I opened the flimsy aluminum door. In the moonlight, I could see the beautiful iron bridge, with the canyon dark behind. The three-quarter moon was reflected in the smooth water. I stared from the doorway. The sky was clear. The air was cold and wonderful. The rain had come and gone. Then I heard them, the coyotes. They were somewhere behind us on the slope of Red Mountain. They were yipping in a chorus, not at the moon, and not howling. They sounded, from the pace of the pauses, as if they were running, perhaps running something down, and there seemed to be several animals, perhaps half a dozen. They were loud, and to me, then, they sounded happy. I swung the baby in my arms. I was suddenly happy, too: the moon, on that rippling water. The fever had broken. I put Jack down. I lay down. Instantly, I was asleep.

The next day, Dave Strobel drove up from Northern Lights in Bozeman to be our guide. We began to learn the river on our doorstep.

Our laid-back new guide sat in his custom yellow French kayak like a cowboy on a low horse. He was a man at ease. All he needed was a Marlboro dangling off his lip, but any cigarette would have been quickly extinguished in the spray. Endlessly, we practiced tracking in a straight line, which is not as easy as it sounds since white-water kayaks have little keel, to make them as maneuverable as possible. We practiced ferry crossings, in which one paddles at an angle upstream across the current, and eddy turns, rodding down a rapid and then circling round as the current reverses direction at the edge of the eddy and heads back upstream.

The classic eddy turn had been my nemesis below Emigrant Bridge, with Mouse. One of the kayaking dictums that was being drilled into our thick heads was that you always lean downstream. The exception is for the eddy turn, especially in strong water. When the eddy swirls the back of the boat around and suddenly you are heading upstream, you must lean in the opposite direction. Exactly when the midline of your body passes over this riptide change in current, that is when you must shift your weight and lean the other way. Theoretically, this makes sense. You're going downstream, you turn right, the side current swirls farther to the right, so you bend the other way, since this is the way current and kayak are now proceeding. In practice, of course, this sort of thing is tricky.

After a few successful eddy turns, I leaned toward Los Angeles when I was supposed to lean toward Philadelphia, finding myself, once again, upside down in the Yellowstone. Strobel once told me that being upside down was not such an awful thing. He rather liked traveling upside down, on some rivers. Over on Idaho's Lochsa, the water is so clear that upside down you can see the trout swim by your face, and the eddy lines look like a Mountaintop drink. Strobel, I was beginning to realize, was not a man to panic quickly. Upside down, watching the fish swim by!

Even so, a good beginner in my place would have executed his Eskimo roll. Even a competent beginner would have pulled the loop at the front of his spray skirt and ejected like a fighter pilot over Nevada. I simply forced my way out, gasping like an emerging nymph. But it worked. I caught some air, discovered I was alive, and managed to grab one of my water shoes, which happened to be floating by just then.

"You have a talent for survival," said Strobel.

Ines and Persis were doing much better. They weren't fighting the river. It was too strong. I was paddling a kayak the way I used to paddle rubber boats and rafts as a kid. You sink your paddle deep in the current and pull your boat where you need to go. That is fine on a lake, but on a river with current, like the Yellowstone, it is best, as they used to say, to go with the flow. Poke at the river, paddle only when you want to correct course or change directions. The river is stronger than you. Acknowledge the fact.

The weather did not get better. It got worse. Still September, yet a storm moved in that laced the mountains a thousand feet above us with snow. At our level it rained a cold rain. "You're going to get wet anyway," Strobel would say as he accepted a cup of coffee in the shelter of the trailer.

Each morning, Strobel drove all the way from Bozeman, a distance of fifty miles. Then it was time to suit up. When we started, I had been skeptical of all this expensive, high-tech equipment. In our neon colors, we looked like robins in rut. But I was wrong. Properly dressed, we never felt the river nor the cold. On our feet we wore Nike water shoes over thick polypropylene calf-length socks. Polypropylene, like wool but unlike cotton, wicks away water from your skin. Above our feet, Farmer John wet suits with bare shoulders, covered by polypropylene uppers, then wool sweaters, and finally paddling jackets. These paddling jackets had an outer shell of rubber over Gore-Tex, with Velcro gaskets at the wrists, neck, and waist. You might drown. But you would drown dry.

In fact, in the chilly mountain mornings, the water seemed warmer than the air. After a number of embarrassing dumpings, everybody realized they probably would not die. You simply made your roll, grabbed your boat, and swam to shore. We were becoming hardened, beginning to act on instinct, which was Strobel's intention.

Whenever anyone asked about Yankee Jim, a few hundred yards upstream from our learning pool, Strobel would shrug and say: "Piece of cake, especially this time of year."

We also learned the rudiments of reading water. A patch of white water seen from upstream could be a normal rapid flowing merrily along in place. Or it might be a more troublesome pourover, water rolling over a submerged rock. Or it might be a suck hole. In Yankee Jim, certain holes were nasty. The current reversed directions, holding the boat while a reverse wave of upstream water curled over the sides until one managed to escape.

The second day at Carbella, Ines wanted to practice with the Colt .45 we had brought along. In San Francisco the pistol had been an urban safety measure, against humans. In Montana, Ines was afraid of bears. At first I said that I did not think bears would follow the river this far outside the park. I meant grizzly bears, since the smaller black bear is rarely a danger. But I thought again about this. Perhaps I was being falsely reassuring. I had hiked the trail to Slough Creek, north of Roosevelt Lodge, in Yellowstone, ten years before. I had considered more than once the possibility of bears that day. It was roadless country behind our camp at Carbella, up Red Mountain and over to the north edge of Yellowstone Park, a distance of about thirty miles, to Slough Creek. Grizzlies sometimes roamed that far in a day.

Later, I would talk with a Bozeman woman who had been mauled and bitten by a sow grizzly just over the mountains from Carbella, near Slough Creek. The woman's name was Sarah Muller. She was thirty-five. She had dark hair. She was not new to bear country nor to

Yellowstone—she had worked in the park for eleven summers. Muller was from Minneapolis, where she had worked for a company that put on rock concerts. She had seen the mountains only once before, on a ski vacation to Colorado. She loved the look. "I was sick of the city," she said. "I wanted an adventure."

Sarah Muller liked Yellowstone, camping out, hiking to work at dawn, clearing and maintaining the trails. It was ten in the morning, a warm day, becoming hot, August 1992, almost a year after we would leave Carbella. Muller was hiking down Buffalo Fork Trail, twenty minutes ahead of a friend who guided for Mountain Trails Outfitters. Her friend and the outfit's cook were on horses, leading a string of mules.

Muller crossed into a meadow covered with wildflowers. She remembers the flowers well. They were pink sticky geranium, lupine, cow parsnip, and bluebells. She sensed motion in the tall flowers. She saw a bear about forty feet away.

"I was hoping it was a black bear. It was pretty small. Then she heard me and stood up on her hind feet. I thought, oh, no, this is trouble. Then I heard two scared cries. She had cubs. I saw them next to her. I guess they had been grubbing for roots. I hadn't cut them off from their mother or anything, but she came for me immediately. She ran the forty feet. There was no tree for me to climb. You can't fight a bear. They are so strong. She wrapped around me. I tried to put my stuff sack in her mouth so she wouldn't bite me, but it didn't work. She came at me seven times. I looked her in the eye. People say you shouldn't look a bear in the eye, but I wanted to tell her: 'Don't do this to me.' But she wanted me.

"She lifted me off the ground by my elbow. I'm what you call a six-foot woman. I weighed 160 pounds then. I weigh less now, after the operations. I don't really know what happened. I hope to remember some day. It was so quick. The next thing I knew I was on the ground and she was gone. It was almost like a dream."

Muller's arm was fractured in two places when the bear lifted and shook her. "I have my biceps, not my triceps. My arm's pretty worthless." Seven ribs were broken. "I have an ugly scar above my right eye. My right eye is lower than my left, now. She bit into my brain through my sinus cavity. I don't have a sense of smell now. I have all these metal plates in my nose. I asked the doctor how many stitches, and he said, 'I lost track at a hundred.' I was so torn up."

Muller never curled up or played dead, but after a while the bear left her. Muller screamed for her friends, but they could not hear her. "The flies came to me pretty quick. They wanted the blood. That part of the trail has tons of flies. Over on Slough Creek, there's more mosquitoes."

After her friends caught up to her, the guide rode his horse to Roosevelt to call for the helicopter. The cook administered first aid. The medics decided the first Park Service helicopter was inadequate. A second helicopter, called the Life Ship, was sent out from Idaho Falls. The ride back to the emergency room in Idaho Falls took an hour.

"You know how helicopters vibrate? That hurt a lot. I was so thirsty, too. They don't give you water or ice chips when they know you have internal injuries."

The morphine in the hospital gave her nightmares. "One night I dreamed of dogs, I don't know why. Another night I dreamed of the bear. The worst was the night when I got up the courage to look at my face for the first time, at what the bear had done to my face. I couldn't sleep then. I stayed up with the nurses. I began to have creature dreams, creatures with one eye, or the eye staring out at me. They didn't give me morphine for my third operation. They didn't want me to have more nightmares. That was pretty painful, that third operation."

Muller considers herself an environmentalist. "I don't agree with everything, but I subscribe to *Buzzworm,* and the Nature Conservancy. . . . I never really had any problems with the bear as a bear. I was kind of mad at her. I am more paranoid now, you know, gun on one side, can of bear spray on the other, mace and cayenne pepper. Two hunters over by West Yellowstone swear bear spray saved their lives when they surprised a sow and three cubs feeding on a carcass. But maybe it just pisses them off, I don't know. The thing to do is make plenty of noise. Those little bear bells don't work. Get the big ones. Bears are like sharks. They are kind of dangerous animals. My body still hurts me, and it will for a long time, but I think I'm healing."

So there were dangers on the river, besides the river itself. For some reason, we never got around to taking the .45 out and practicing, at Carbella. I guess we were as afraid to look the mirror in the eye as Sarah Muller was.

Gardiner Town Stretch

AFTER TWO DAYS THE WEATHER CLEARED. We decided to start. We thought our river skills were passable, or at least testable. We drove slowly up the canyon road past Corwin Springs and the lands of the Church Universal and Triumphant to the bridge at Gardiner where not so long ago we had watched that old spruce log tumble and cavort.

The morning was sunny if cool. A storm would most likely pass over in the afternoon. We parked at the Yellowstone Park boundary, where the winter maintenance buildings sit, old and yellow, under a tall smokestack that looks industrial and out of place in the middle of the mountains. On the park side, the river is flanked by a cliff closely dotted with tar paper shacks and old log cabins, affording cheap rents with great views. At the bottom of the trail is a small abandoned water mill. The Gardner River was almost black from the rains. The Yellowstone was a lighter brown. They swirled together like ink into coffee.

We had made one important change from Carbella. I had ordered a rubber kayak, a Momentum, from the White Otter River Company in Ketchum, Idaho, to be delivered UPS overnight to Chico. The Momentum was self-bailing. A row of holes at the front of the flooring allowed a thin film of water to rush into the boat, flow along the sides, and empty from a series of holes in the back. This film of moving water stabilized the kayak, and, more important, the holes quickly drained the boat whenever quantities of water splashed over the sides and front. The Momentum's cockpit was open. There was no spray skirt. If you turned over, you swam, but there was little danger of being trapped, as in the hard-shells. Feet were to be tucked under the tubular walls. This provided a tight fit, something like good stirrups on a strong horse.

Unfortunately, United Parcel Service did not keep its guarantee of next-day delivery from Ketchum. We had to go with a second vinyl kayak, bought locally, which we christened the Rubber Duckie. The Duck looked like a boat carved from the Michelin rubber man—large, overly pneumatic, and definitely not self-bailing. Still, the Duck seemed a safer bet on the treacherous Town Stretch than did the white-water hard-shells.

The Gardiner Town Stretch is a fast sluice box of a ride. From the put-in point at the mouth of the Gardner River, the run is a straight shot for about two miles. The grade is steep enough that looking downriver one can see the slant of the drop. The river is wide, perhaps two hundred feet across, and broken by a jumble of rocks, suck holes, pourovers, and rapids of undetermined origin. Perhaps we should have been less afraid, but I don't think so.

I pushed off, and the different currents that were at odds with each other were soon at odds with me.

There were two bad rapids right at the start. They cut an expanding *V* of white water, one after the other, and I made for the top of the *V,* as Strobel, who was right behind (I hoped), had instructed. The Duck rose and fell with the waves, and I rose and fell with the Duck. It was like riding a trampoline in a flood, and as the trampoline rushed downstream, somebody sprayed a garden hose in my face, which at times seemed more like a fire hose.

The Rubber Duck proved not to be the most maneuverable of craft. As soon as the river's fire hose filled it, the Duck became an unwieldy bathtub, difficult to paddle one way or the other.

"Better bail," came a voice.

Strobel slid alongside.

"How can I bail?" I shouted back.

"Onshore," said Strobel.

I guided my bathtub to a grotto of rocks, where it bumper-carred into a boulder. I got out, water splashing up my wet suit, lifted one side, returned most of the water to the river, and launched again. I would do this five times on the Town Stretch. The Duck, I realized, offered only the illusion of safety. If you knew what you were doing, you were better off in a hard-shell kayak.

If you look up as you pass under the tall car bridge that bisects Gardiner, you experience a glorious second of vertigo, and then it's time to stop feeling that you're feeling so good, and paddle or die!

The two-mile run ends at what we decided to call RV Rapids, which was Elk River Mobile Park, that ode to Winnebagos and retirees we had abandoned for Carbella. At RV Rapids the river makes a sickening hairpin turn. Perhaps this was the RV park's revenge on us for slighting her and leaving.

The next half-mile is simple current. I paddled to shore and bailed out the water. On the bank, four pronghorn antelope picked their way up a narrow game trail. Antelope walk with a kind of jump, a hind-leg hike at the end of each step. They seem always ready to take off running. Antelope are primitive animals. They look like deer but they evolved millions of years earlier, in the middle Miocene. Their sandy hairs are hollow. Up close they look as if they are covered with millions of quills. Both males and females have horns. Their eyes are large, among the best in the animal world. They can see and sense movement for miles. But these four antelope were trapped on their cliff trail. They jumped and jogged, picking their way, half-frightened by our boats, half-distracted by clumps of gamma grass beside the trail, until we were around the next bend.

There, on the river, we surprised six harlequin ducks. Harlequins are exquisite, dark birds with circles of white around their eyes and white slashes down their necks. The ducks water-walked away. They took so long to lift off the river that it seemed they were leading us on. Where they rose off the water, the river turned roily once more. By now I was beginning to enjoy the rush. At least there were no hypodermics, as in San Francisco, on dry land. And then like a perfect finale came the worst part of the run, McConnell Hole, from the top.

I reached up with my left hand and twitched my sunglasses back and forth to defog them. I was wearing a duck-billed hat to keep the sun off my bald pate, but the hat was by now soaked, and the wetness somehow created a condensation that fogged the lenses so that I couldn't see what I was doing or where I was going. It didn't occur to me to toss the hat.

McConnell Hole took me to her breast. She tossed the Duck like a chickadee. It was glorious. I was shouting. When you are really frightened on a river, I had already discovered, the best thing to do is simply to whoop at the top of your lungs. Joyous noise somehow puts the body into equilibrium, and who is to hear, except the ducks?

The rubber kayak swamped but did not overturn. The current slugged it sideways onto the sandstone beach. I was done. That was it. The Yellowstone rolled on. I was alive. The four antelope hop-walked their way over the ridge. The harlequin ducks settled back on the river behind us. Adrenaline sizzled through me. Our journey had begun. Back home in Montana, I had been born again.

The Brazilian declined to run the Town Stretch, though Persis proved to herself that she was still only sixty-one. She took the Duck and bailed out but twice. Strobel was not impressed by our novice shenanigans. After all, nobody drowned. But I could see that he was intrigued that a sixty-one-year-old schoolteacher was caroming down the upper Yellowstone like some wet pneumatic billiard ball. In Montana, old folks generally keep to their RV parks.

That night we celebrated with a feast of cutthroat trout and native greens. Ines, Persis, and I walked around the rocky Carbella meadow with a single copy of H. D. Harrington's *Edible Native Plants of the Rocky Mountains*. We tried to match living forage with the delicate line drawings in the text. It was a difficult task. We especially wanted to find some common camass, a shallot-shooted plant that offers a supposedly delicious onionlike bulb and grows in this part of Montana.

"It has been reported," writes H. D. Harrington, "that many local Indian wars were fought over the collecting rights to certain meadows where camass happened to be abundant. The only drawback was that bulbs of the death camass often grew on similar sites and apparently were sometimes mixed in by mistake, often with fatal results."

We lingered over that last line, and decided to make do with cattail shoots (which, Harrington informs, are known as Cossack asparagus in Russia) and dandelion leaves, which anyone can identify. There were plenty of both at that time in Carbella meadow.

The cutthroat trout were much easier to corral. Cody and I picked our way under the willows that lined Rock Creek, which dumps into the river from the east, off the slope of Dog Tooth Rock. The gentle swirl formed by the confluence had created one of the eddies where we had learned to ferry in the cold rains a few days before. On the hike down from the gravel road, I picked up several small, reddish-brown pieces of petrified wood that reminded me of *ha'poa* lava from the Big Island of Hawaii.

I had a trude fly already at the end of my line. The trude is a bold attractor pattern. It doesn't imitate a specific insect. But if trout are present, they usually come up for a look. Rock Creek drops off a small gravel bar into the Yellowstone, forming several tiny streams. I flicked my trude here and there, but with no luck. I reached for my fly box, only to discover I had forgotten it. I guess my mind lay back upstream on the Town Stretch, and on Yankee Jim, which we would attempt tomorrow. I caught a couple of grasshoppers and skewered one over the artificial fly. This primitive offering worked much better.

Cody and I soon landed four cutthroat—a twelve-incher, a four-teen-incher, a fifteen-incher, and a ten-incher. Cutthroat are very beautiful animals. Black spots begin behind their eyes and become more common, like gathering rain, until, by the tail, they freckle the fins. Over the gill plates there is always a slash of sunset orange, which is how they came to be named. In fact, the black-spotted cut-throat is the Montana state fish. But, to put it politely, cutthroats, black-spotted or not, are gullible. The upper Yellowstone holds rain-bow trout, brook trout, and German brown trout. Only the cut-throat is a native and, like natives of many places and species, these were self-destructively naive, at least in their interactions with out-siders.

In a "catchability-recatchability" experiment once performed in Yellowstone Park, native cutthroat were found to be two times as likely to be hooked as were brook trout and eighteen times more eas-ily hooked than were the wily German brown. (When people asked my father how he had done on the east Rosebud, where we had a cabin, my father would sometimes answer like this: "Pretty good. Three browns." Yet that wicker creel would also be holding a nice mess of rainbows and "natives," which is what old Montana fisherfolk called cutthroats.)

I let Cody take the line in his hands and pull in the first cutthroat. Only two years old, he was enraptured. I figured there was not much chance the trout would unhook itself. Cutthroat are dumb as fence posts.

I had a funny thought as I watched my son cavort at one end of the line and the trout gambol at the other. They were both alike, in a way, both God's creatures, and each had something in common besides their short time on earth: their freckles. Cody has his own brush of spots across his nose and under his eyes, much like a cutthroat. The setting sun poked through the dirty-laundry clouds above Yankee Jim as I watched fish and child. I thought about my comparison and wondered what it would be like to be a fish. I imagined a toddler yanked to shore by a laughing fish on the bank, positions reversed—the boy with a hook in his lip, the fish standing clear of the water, beside himself with finny pleasure.

What is it like to be a fish? Better morphists than I have wrestled that question to the bank. "To get yourself into the mood of fishness," begin Varley and Schullery in *Freshwater Wilderness: Yellowstone Fishes & Their World,*

> imagine the following: you have no shoulders, neck, or chin. Your eyes, nose, and mouth are moved to the very top of your head. Your arms become shortened and re-form as small fins. Your chest cavity becomes three times as deep as it is wide, and one or more fins sprout along your backbone. Your legs join into one member, and their bones are replaced by a continuation of your backbone, which runs clear to your feet, which reshape themselves into a tail. By now you are uncomfortable standing vertically, so you lean over and slip into something more comfortable—water.

Conjuring the fish god.

The Indians of Yellowstone country did not respect fish, unlike Indians of the Pacific Northwest and the Shoshone to the south, who were derogatorily called the Fish-Eaters by the meat-eating Yellowstone tribes. Here, Indian lives were part of plain and prairie. Deities did not include a cutthroat trout.

My mind wandered back to a people who did respect fish, the Saxons, and to a line of Saxon poetry:

God made a song when the world was new
Water, water sings it through.

The sound of the mountain Yellowstone at sunset, its translucent rocky song, water rustling between reed and willow, water hissing over log, water crashing against boulder, water lunging downstream over small granite waterfall—water, water, everywhere. . . .

We ate well that night. A fish's tastiness has nothing to do with its gullibility.

Tomorrow, Yankee Jim Canyon.

Yankee Jim

WE PLANNED TO SCOUT THE CANYON in a rubber raft before making the descent by kayak. Strobel arrived late, something about a fight with his girlfriend on the way to the airport, but he brought a small, thirteen-foot commercial-grade raft fitted with an aluminum rowing frame. Dave was familiar with Yankee Jim, but to be even safer, we had hired Rowdy Nelson, a twenty-one-year-old local water man who for several summers had rowed the canyon for the Chico rafting company. By the end of the summer, the river had gotten too low and dangerous for commercial rafting, and Rowdy was now free.

We drove five miles to the head of the canyon and suited up. Dave discovered he had forgotten the pump. We spent two hours driving to Gardiner and visiting the bars that were open for the morning trade (which was every one: K-Bar, Blue Goose, and Town) until we found a chipper bearded river rat with a Rainier longneck in front of him who was willing to loan us the proper pump.

I was annoyed by the delay, but Dave and Rowdy are not the sort of people who become annoyed. Rowdy was a handsome character of near–movie star looks who wore open river sandals, neon surfing fashions, and shorts from Bali. Like Strobel, he was a very calm person. Nothing fazed him. I was beginning to realize that wild rivers did not necessarily attract wild people, but rather the opposite: calm people who at heart do not wish to be calm and are in search of the edge that danger brings.

Rowdy was from an old Montana family in the Paradise Valley, south of Livingston. His grandmother had recently sold their ranch on Deep Creek to Jeff Bridges, the actor, and though Rowdy considered Bridges "a good man," he seemed a bit unsettled by what had happened. Now he guided the river in the summer and planned to move in the fall to Whitefish, near Glacier National Park, where he would teach skiing.

Like Strobel, Rowdy is an artist on the river. Yankee Jim Canyon begins like a horror movie, deceptively nice, a flat stretch, birds chirping. But as you travel down that first half-mile of flat water, you can't help but notice that the river drops like an amusement park ride. You cannot see the rapids just around the first bend, but as you approach, you hear them, louder and louder. It's like the start of a roller coaster where you pull slowly up the track, knowing all along what must happen after you reach the top.

This first rapid is called Boat Eater. With the sad, slight smile he always wore, Rowdy explained that "you had to be a little careful with Boat Eater." Earlier in the summer his boss had been rowing a group of tourists. The man made the wrong approach. The long raft flipped. The tourists had had to swim for it. A nine-year-old boy was unable to make it to shore. They fished him out below Carbella, "kinda shaken."

I once bought some land in the Beartooths from a man who entered Yankee Jim with two customers in a johnboat, which is a flat-hulled, square-backed dinghy. The johnboat capsized at the start of the canyon, which would have been where we were, and only the man who sold me the land survived. I remembered what the mechanic at the Paradise Flying Service had said after Duane's Cessna touched down and we were talking about our reasons for returning to Montana. "Buddy of mine drowned there last month. They were in a Mackenzie drifter, fishing. Stupid thing to do, a Mackenzie in Yankee Jim." The big mechanic wiped his hands on an oil rag, and shrugged.

I was glad we had hired Rowdy because he looked like a kid who rarely did stupid things, at least when he wasn't on his own time. For control, Rowdy rowed backward. The current snapped and rose all around us. Only a few times did water wash over the transom or slap us in the face, but that was because Rowdy was good. It was not at all hard to imagine how folks who were not so good might get wet, in a different type of boat.

The next rapid is called Big Rock. "Try to avoid that one, OK?" said Rowdy, methodically pulling away from the suck. "If you can help it."

We looked back. Dave, who had been following in his yellow Prijon, was surfing Big Rock. The eddy is so strong that it crashes back upstream, and it's a lot of fun (if you are someone like Dave) to trap yourself in its queasy hole and ride the reverse wave upstream. Big Rock is a perpetual wave machine. A body can surf it forever, since the downstream current holds you in place, if you are good.

Dave noticed that we were looking at him. He took his Harmony black graphite paddle and tossed it a few feet into the air like a majorette at halftime. This meant the only way for him to keep the kayak from capsizing was to hold it with hip action alone, which he did, as white water splashed over him to the top of his helmet, on both sides at once, and also from the front, over the rock, at which point the five-foot paddle came down perfectly into his hands, and he pivoted to join us at the approach to Boxcar.

The train for which Boxcar Rapids is named is supposedly at the bottom, pinned by the boulders fifty feet down. The train spilled late one night in the last century when Yankee Jim was soused.

Boxcar is not a single problem but a long run of soup. If there were sandy beaches on both sides, kayaking there would look like fun—if you capsized, you could swim to the banks. But at this point in the canyon, the walls are inverted. They don't rise up. They rise down, like a stone pyramid stood on its head, on both sides. If you lose your boat, there is nothing to hold on to. You must swim, keeping to the center of the current, which is the strongest and most difficult part, for a mile or so. If you are brushed toward the rock walls, you will be sucked under.

"But if you have a life preserver?" the Brazilian asked Rowdy.

"The state requires 'em," Rowdy shrugged. "Probably better to be a strong swimmer, here."

About two-thirds of the way down the run there is a massive, sloping rock that is not as steep as the walls. We gave it an ironic, placid name: Picnic Rock. There was a C-2 canoe with a bashed prow wedged in a crevice of Picnic Rock. Up on the rock was a man in a bikini bathing suit. His knees and nose were bleeding.

"Y'OK?" shouted Rowdy.

The current was fast. Dave was now alongside the man in his elegant covered canoe. The man waved us off. He said something in German. In a second, in a hairpin cove a hundred yards downstream, was another C-2 full of Germans, a woman and a man, both wearing bikinis.

"Need help?" Rowdy shouted.

"No, no!" the man answered.

We looked upstream. Strobel was paddling backward, for the challenge. The first German was still bleeding, resting. The current tugged the sea rudder at the end of his C-2, threatening to whip the boat off Picnic Rock and back into the river.

Dave shot alongside us.

"Don't think they knew what they were in for," said Rowdy.

"Don't think so," agreed Dave.

I didn't sleep well that night. Around four, I scissored my body out of the folding twin bed and opened the trailer door. I stared out at the wide spot in the Yellowstone where Strobel had tried to teach us a few things. In that pellucid light, all the furniture of our little world was in focus: single cottonwoods scattered like palms, the line of willows at river's edge, river, swirl of river's eddies, and beyond, the flowing hummocks of lava, covered these millions of years by bunch and yellow gamma grass, and long beyond, still higher, the granite escarpment that stands like a jagged wall in front of Dog Tooth Rock, which rose as the last thing I could see to the west, closing off the night sky, a volcanic cone powdered with summer snow, reflecting back a pale fishbelly white in the Montana moon. It was as if I were looking through a camera lens.

I felt a distanced clarity. Behind on Red Mountain, the coyotes were with me, again, I noticed, and that made me smile. Coyotes are basically small wolves, and I made a mental note to check out the wolf farm that now existed above Paradise Valley, downriver. The government planned to reintroduce wolves to Yellowstone Park. Sheep and cattle ranchers were beginning to raise a cry, but what I wondered right then was, how would the coyotes take the news? They would be like little brothers who had had the run of the family farm for a long, long time, about 110 years, ever since the government had stopped paying a major bounty for wolf ears (around $15 in 1911), and now big brother was coming home, and big brother wolf was more of a taker than a sharer. The coyotes yipped on, unsuspecting.

Finally I scanned the canyon through the delicate arch of Carbella's iron bridge. It was almost dawn. I heard the door of the van open. It was my sister, fully dressed. She did not see me. I watched. Persis picked her way through the sage and scattered cactus to the river, and then, as I had, she stared long upstream, at the dark granite mouth of Yankee Jim. She was still staring when I softly closed the door.

We started at ten. Yankee Jim Canyon in kayaks was not the piece of cake Strobel had predicted, but it was almost the same thing, a piece of fear, since in our kayaks the journey was over so quickly you would have had to have learned nothing at all to have had time to be afraid.

What makes you feel so good on a run like Yankee Jim is that you must concentrate. You are forced to lash mind and body together. No time to think, worry, whine, plan, cavil, or speculate on anything that isn't about to hit you in the face or wash over the kayak's bow within sixty seconds, and that's stretching it.

I did not dare look to the left or to the right, but I still saw the inverted black granite walls flash by like curtains. The boat jumped up and down and I took shotgun shots of water in the face, but the point was to stay in the center of the current and away from the canyon walls. Staying dry at the edges was the mistake. It is a very powerful river, the upper Yellowstone. I enjoyed it.

At the end of the three major rapids is a flat run. Here an osprey hovered over three merganser ducks. There must have been some small fish beneath the ducks; I don't know that osprey prey on other birds. All four rose up as I crashed through. This reminded me of a time long ago when I was a child visiting San Francisco. My brother had been mustered out of Korea, alive, and the parents drove down from Montana to celebrate at the St. Francis Hotel, which fronts on Union Square. I liked to cross the street to the square and run through the crowds of pigeons that rose off the park like clouds of white handkerchiefs. For someone six years old, this was a feeling of strange power. And then I understood I must be safe on the river, because I was no longer concentrating on what I had to do in the present. And then I passed under the elegant metal bridge high above my helmet, and then came our campsite, and my family, who screamed from the bank.

My sister is very macho. Not so macho that she did not want to run the canyon without Strobel behind her but macho enough to want to push the current a bit. She made it through Boat Eater, but she decided to surf Big Rock as she had seen Strobel do behind me. Her kayak flipped. Persis flipped back, tried to roll, once, twice, but she was still mostly underwater. Strobel streaked toward her, his first piece of real work since we had hired him. But Persis was head to the sky by the time Strobel drew alongside, paddling furiously downstream out of anger at her mistake and also at what she saw as her overreaching ambition, I think. By that time, I had gotten out of my boat, and Ines and I could see from the cliff what had happened, but Persis never mentioned it, and Strobel had the sense to keep quiet, too. In my family, at least with the women, middle age seems to come late, if it is acknowledged at all, and at sixty-one Persis may have been entering a midlife crisis. I only hoped I would live that long.

McConnell

CAROMING DOWN YANKEE JIM WAS A HEADY EXPERIENCE. We had made it, and the glow carried into the afternoon. Ines and I decided to double back and paddle what Strobel had described as the flat water between McConnell and Corwin Springs, between the Town Stretch and Yankee Jim, on the land now controlled by the Church Universal and Triumphant.

However, as we made ready, a lashing storm quickly moved into the mountains over the canyon—we saw it arrive and settle in like an unwanted relative. Strobel had cautioned against being on the river in the middle of lightning. We waited until three, when the sun shone like an angel on fire, as if the storm had never been. We drove south toward the park with light hearts.

It was the Brazilian's first nonpractice time on the river. I took one of the long Perception Spectrum kayaks Strobel had brought us, and she picked the rubber Momentum self-bailer, which had finally arrived. We had come to regard the Momentum as the safest in our arsenal. My macho sister kidded Ines that this stretch was like a duck pond. I knew better, since I had counted six white-water runs from the Cessna, but I said nothing. I thought with a little smile: we left San Francisco to be free, and yet we were fast becoming anxiety slaves to this dangerous river. It was an irony that we seemed to enjoy, so far.

For the McConnell run we piled on the usual layers of protective gear and trapped ourselves under the spray skirts. Surrounded by cedars on a small bluff, McConnell sports a small sandy beach, from which we launched. I felt like a teenager at the prom as I bunny-hopped the boat into the water. The canyon light was delicate, softer than Caravaggio. We laughed at ourselves. The kayaks floated off gaily.

In thirty seconds we were caught in the first rapid. I let out a rodeo whoop to mask my fear. Behind, I heard Ines moaning almost as loudly. I didn't dare look back until the bottom of the run. Then I swirled the boat in an eddy turn and turned my head. Small haystacks splashed against Ines's shoulders and face, but the self-bailer instantly drained the water, and she paddled furiously toward me.

In a minute we were floating together in the flat water above the next drop. I could taste the brown river water on my face, clear and cold with a flavor of fresh mud. Unable to turn quickly in the rubber kayak, Ines paddled right into my hard-shell. We laughed at the collision. Our hands caught, and we started to kiss. I didn't dare close my eyes, since the boats were both drifting rapidly downstream. Out of the corner of one eye, outlined against the mountain, I could see one of those Yellowstone Park sea gulls that, a thousand miles from the Pacific, always seem lost. This fellow was wafting without wing movement among the treeless hills that crimp the river. Neglected by their pilots, both our boats abruptly dipped into the water. We broke away before we capsized. Every second the current was pushing us downstream, and now we heard the rustle of the next rapid.

I hunched over the front of my kayak, and the water crashed against my face. Were we fools to be here? Who knows? Another wave hit my face, and I had to look over my glasses, which certainly shortened my field of vision. Paddle or die! A reasonable motto when you can't see five feet ahead of the boat. But after a hysterical moment of instinctual leaning and bracing, we were in safe current again. ("I was totally scared," Ines would modestly admit later.)

The Town Stretch and Yankee Jim had required such concentration that it was only now that I had the time and space to ask myself if we were really prepared, after only a few hours of instruction in a resort pool and a few days alongside a smooth spot in the river, to be running the upper Yellowstone in the late summer, or any other time of the year for that matter. My answer was not reassuring: Hell, no!

But by then it was time for the next rapid.

Strobel had deigned to stay in camp for this stretch, which I guess was just too placid for the boy. The end of the third run had a nasty granite boulder jutting so wickedly into churning white water that it was like looking down into an old-fashioned washing machine. There was a pourover just below. Perhaps Strobel's standards were not mine. A swimming pool full of river water crashed against my face. Yes, my standards were lower than Dave's. I began to shout again in order to calm myself. (Ines was on her own.)

At that point I recalled that Dave had once been the youngest person ever to climb Yosemite's Half Dome. He and a friend had enrolled in some Outward Bound–type program in Bozeman when they were fourteen, and after some months of climbing little eleven-thousand-foot peaks in Gallatin County they had decided to drop down to California to hunt bigger game: Half Dome from the hard side.

And then I remembered Dave sort of chuckling about a pastime he and some others liked to engage in over on the Bear Trap section of the Madison, about forty miles due west of us this afternoon—the same river where John Colter found himself stripped naked while the Blackfeet threw Potts's body parts into his face, 184 years ago. This game, or maneuver, is called "endoing." The idea is to go over a precipitous little drop that flips your boat, only instead of panicking or praying to God, or simply dying on the spot, as I might be tempted to do, you keep going. You throw yourself behind the boat's sickening forward free-fall, and you tumble end-over-end like a Ferris wheel down the length of the run. This is the object. Endoing.

Endoing was Dave's idea of big fun. Now I understood why a thrashing current and a few swimming pools full of river water in the face were too boring to entice him out of camp.

And I'm sure the next rapid would have caused Dave to yawn, though it caused Ines and me to paddle hard for the west bank and quit. For this little roil on the river was a nasty thing. It did not look consistent. There appeared to be some underwater obstruction, a log or boulder, that was creating a suck hole on the surface for perhaps thirty feet. The waves did not remain stabile—somewhat like a row of hair curlers—but rather dipped and jumped erratically like cockroaches on a hot griddle.

On the other hand, the west bank was too shallow, a wide bar of small rocks that finally rejoined the main current with a small, lurching drop. Ines and I were next to each other at this point. We paddled, but the boats would not move. We were caught, and the water was very swift. It did not seem wise to climb out and push. One might break an ankle. We bunny-hopped. My hard-shell thunked and thudded, but I knew the damage would be only cosmetic. The sound of Ines's rubber self-bailer scraping against the rocks was more worrisome. If she tore a hole, one of the boat's tubes might collapse out in the main river, and she would lose all control.

There were no alternatives. We bunny-hopped. Small shoals of whitefish and cutthroat scuttled away from the prows. And then, miraculously, the boats dropped off the slight ledge and we floated free again.

Ecstasy! The sun was setting. Now the light was a Dutch master painting, soft and subtle. Forget the modern love for the harsh Caravaggio. The muddy river rushed, and it smelled like fresh bread. We could not get close enough to kiss again, but we were doing it. We were on the river. Fools of the expatriate romantic variety or not, we were in flow.

When we beached the kayaks at Corwin Springs, we rested for a few minutes, gathering the energy to carry the boats up the tall bank to the road. In our silence, we noticed a strange gurgle-bleating. We looked close but saw nothing. Then, far across the river, on the slope of the hill, we saw a herd of captive elk, the same Lego elk I had noticed from the Cessna. The noises were rutting calls, very plaintive they seemed to us then, coming from such major beasts. We laughed.

That night in camp, we ate the T-bones, with brown rice, and collapsed before the children did.

I was glad we were done with the upper Yellowstone.

Now I want to talk more about Montana and less about river anxiety, which, to be truthful, has just been unavoidable until now.

Six-Mile Creek: Hard Hunting

THE CANYON ENDED. The valley opened. We relaxed. September 21, a cold day. Instead of hammering the river again as we had done for weeks no matter what, we hung up our wet suits to dry, and went grouse hunting.

We were staying at a homespun bed and breakfast on Six-Mile Creek where we had become friends with the owner's two boys. Sons of a prosecuting attorney, the boys, ages fourteen and fifteen, had spent most of their lives in a wealthy suburb of Los Angeles until four years ago, when their mother had decided to parachute from her marriage into the Paradise Valley. Emigrant Mountain rose off their land, and the boys wandered over it as if it were their unfenced front yard. They collected medicinal plants and elk horn to sell, the way urban kids pick up aluminum cans for the deposit. They read books on how to dress out deer and which rifle ensured the flattest bullet arc over three hundred yards, .243 or 20-20 Swift. But unlike most boys who fantasize about these things, these two had stuffed their wilderness manuals into their backpacks long before dawn on the opening day of elk season and crept out of the house, boots in hand, as their mother slept surrounded by the little West Highland terriers she raised as a hobby. Then, within sight of their new home, they shot themselves a real elk.

During the school year the boys met the bus at 6:30 each morning for the forty-five-minute ride south to Gardiner, because their mother believed there were drugs in the Livingston schools. The older boy had a computer in his room and, behind the computer, a loaded Weatherby 30-06 big-game rifle with a Nikon scope. The rifle leaned precariously against the log wall. The younger boy kept a cockatoo and a tank of African cyclids, which he fed chopped elk meat, since he believed this was a better source of protein than pet shop fish food. Both boys walked around their carpeted log home with loaded pistols on their hips. Never can tell when a bear might come knocking, I guess.

In fact, a few weeks before our stay, a black bear had ambled onto the back porch to munch upon a little dead mouse the cat had abandoned. The boys from L.A., with their mother, snapped flash pictures through the plate glass of the breakfast nook before the bear nonchalantly retreated to a hollow log by the creek, a hundred yards upstream, where he settled in for a snooze under a juicy beehive. It was the opinion of the household that this bear would sleep in his hollow tree until spring.

Early on the morning of our hunt, we spent an hour driving around trying to buy some shotgun shells. At the Pine Creek Store I got into an argument with the owner and his wife, who, though they were not from Montana, I thought, took us to be interlopers because we insisted on steel rather than lead bird shot. Many hunters believe steel shot damages gun barrels, and this may be true, but it is also a fact that lead shot eventually poisons wounded birds, and lead pellets, insisted the boys' mother, must also cause brain damage to growing boys who inadvertently swallow them while eating the grouse she cooked.

The Pine Creek Store was a lead-shot-only kind of place. We bought lead. Two and three-quarters inches, number six shot. Funny the prejudices Americans hold dear.

We started up the mountain. Five hundred feet up, we could already see twenty miles north to the pinch point of the Gallatins against the Absarokas at Allenspur, where the valley ends and Livingston lies; and we could also see fifteen miles back to Carbella, over the coal and basalt cliffs that line the Yellowstone near Point of Rocks. Across the valley at the top of the Gallatins, it was snowing heavily. Below the snow a big curtain of black rain blew north for miles. But where we stood, high on the other side, the sun was shining like the cross of Jesus.

We crossed natural irrigation ditches that sluiced water off the mountain to the alfalfa fields below us, until we came to a tiny mountain marsh of cattails and short willow bushes. All of a sudden a snipe rose off the grasses beside the pond. Startled, I made two quick shots, but the bird was long gone. Snipe look like curlews, with a curved beak, and they're about the size of a small duck. They don't helicopter up, pause, and then fly off, as pheasants and grouse do. They get the hell out of Dodge, in a straight line of adrenaline, and you have to be good to bag them. I didn't care that I had missed. Snipe are a sport bird, not as good-tasting as grouse, and I don't like to kill anything I am not going to eat. (I hate big-game marlin fishing in Hawaii. Glorious creatures alive, dead marlin are often sold for cat food.)

When I swung that .12-gauge shotgun, I could almost see my father, in an old cloth overcoat over white shirt and knotted tie, a gray Stetson town hat on top of his head, executing that same shotgun swing across mountain country like this, correctly leading some other beautiful bird, escaping in a time long ago. He, too, killed only what he intended to eat. His memory was encoded in my muscles, and I sighed.

Bird hunting, if you don't have to hike too much, is an old man's game, one of those sports you grow better at with age, smoother, more instinctual, until perhaps your eyes start to go, and maybe your hands begin to shake. By the time I came along, my father no longer enjoyed hunting deer. He thought it was too easy. He stuck to birds, which meant pheasant, chukkar partridge, blue and mountain grouse, or ducks, which, to his way of thinking, were different from "birds."

I remembered the first time we went duck hunting together. It was at a very low-key hunting lodge in Mexico, I think Baja. Since nobody in the family ever got up much before nine if they didn't have to, it was awfully exciting to me to be in the lodge kitchen before dawn, listening to Spanish being spoken, nodding our heads yes or no and smiling thanks as the old cooks splashed Mexican coffee in front of everybody, even me. I would have been half the age of these boys I was with on Emigrant Mountain.

But I disgraced myself that morning duck hunting in Mexico. Nobody had told me the rules, since the rules of this ritual were made stronger by their being unstated. There were plenty of ducks sitting on top of the water in front of our Mexican blind, but nobody was shooting at them. I couldn't figure out why. Everybody was waiting for something. I couldn't figure out what. I was the most impatient of all. I wanted to prove what a good shot I was. Suddenly, two of those ducks water-walked toward us. They were fighting or shifting position, or bored or looking for minnows or something. I jerked up my little .410 JC Higgins and blasted them both, right there on the water, twenty yards off. Was I proud! Until the silence settled in, and I could see my father controlling his thoughts as he worked over what to tell me. The Mexicans looked away from the dead ducks, the birds' necks floating flat on the water; and the Mexicans looked rigidly away from us. They did not want anyone to be embarrassed. They did not want my father to shout at me. They did not want me to cry. They wanted good hunting. They wanted us to come back.

My father swallowed.

"Wait till they're flying next time, OK?" was all he said, finally, and then it was my turn to turn away, for a long while.

A man does not shoot sitting ducks.

On the rising slope of Emigrant Peak, snow storm behind us, sun on our heads, we walked in that prematurely fall morning in country so fresh we could smell the plants and the trees as if in a nursery. We had no dog. We were the dogs, taking turns poking at juniper bushes, at the tops of which blue grouse like to sun themselves, or stamping into snowberry patches and clumps of rose hips, guns to shoulder, ready for that shock of whirring wings that never ceases to startle.

We hunted seriously for an hour, but no grouse. Now we were at perhaps six thousand feet. The boys had pointed out four dead deer and two dead elk, so far. Coyotes got them, or poachers, or disease. It was ironic, encountering so many dead animals underscored how lush and untouched Emigrant Mountain was. There were a few long-abandoned homesteader shacks, roofs rotting on the ground. The boys had gone through the shacks with a metal detector. Today, the younger boy picked through shingles until he held up a pair of ancient black leather boots. Besides their own house, the only home we could see was an enormous gabled mansion sitting on an artificial lake far below to the southwest. This belonged to Al Giddings, the producer of underwater special effects for movies like *Jaws*.

Since the grouse would not cooperate, we hunted herbs. The younger boy had slipped on a sandstone ledge and gashed his hand a bit. He staunched the blood with yarrow, a furry little fernlike plant. The boys pointed out Indian tobacco, which they had dried and smoked, and natural spearmint and watercress, which lived in the icy rivulets that coursed off the mountain around us and in springs. The watercress was tart and wonderful. We ate handfuls of raspberries and examined chokecherries and rose hips, sage and wild dandelion. Whenever the boys found an elk antler or skull they put it on top of a fence post and discussed whether it was worth the effort to lug back down the mountain. They kept a bone yard under the house, for selling. I kept a gopher's tooth that I found. It was almost an inch long and curved back yellow and horribly like a crone's fingernail. If a gopher fails to chew down a tooth like this, it can pierce its brain.

Another thousand feet up, we reached an overgrown apple orchard. This was prime grouse cover, but again, no grouse. The boys were hungry and bored. We took bites out of the little apples, which were crisp and good.

Two pistol shots popped out and I turned. The younger boy was blasting away at an apple at the top of the tree.

"Let's shoot apples," he said. So we shot apples in the cold air.

Plunking apples the size of plums at twenty feet is some fancy shooting, but the boys were good and they laughed at the satisfying thunk the bullets made when they hit juice. I gently insisted that we stand so the bullets went up the mountain, not down into the valley. Whenever we crossed barbed-wire fences, I offered to hold their guns. These things are elemental, but the boys had no father in Montana to prompt them.

After another hour we had hiked to the level of the juniper line. I was sweating under my polypropylene underwear but my face was cold in the wind.

"Grouse hunting is hard hunting," said the older boy.

"Grouse hunting is not a popular sport in Montana," said the younger boy.

We laughed and started down. We took a different route, and behind a hill we came to a big rainwater pond surrounded by big ugly cows with udders and horns on their heads who were not at all happy to see us. In the center of the pond were half a dozen ducks. Instantly, the boys were excited. The duck season was open. But neither boy had licenses.

"Come on," said the younger boy, "let's go home and get some money from mom and go back to the Pine Creek Store and get some duck stamps, and come back!"

We were in the middle of nowhere, nobody around. Going home and coming back legal would take some time.

I smiled. "Would you consider shooting the ducks now, and then buying stamps when you get home?" I was testing them.

The younger boy was stunned. The older boy looked at me angrily. "Would you?"

I told them the story of how I had disgraced myself in Mexico on my first duck hunt. They laughed a lot at that.

We walked back skunked, though, still no grouse. The younger boy borrowed $20 from his mother and started off for the store for the stamps. I drank a quart of orange juice with the older boy, and we had hot chocolate, too. When we were done, he said, "I shot a grouse just up the creek two weeks ago. Let's try there."

As we walked up Six-Mile, five-inch trout smashed through the shallow water to get out of our way. They didn't dart professionally like little trout who had seen a lot of people walk through their territory. We passed the hollow log where it was predicted the bear would be in the winter. We snuck through the land of a neighbor who did not like people hunting on his property. We crossed a car bridge and doubled back toward the house. No grouse. We picked some more apples.

"Is that a grouse?" asked the older boy quietly taking the apple out of his mouth. He pointed with his apple hand. Thirty feet away a small stripe of black next to white looked unnatural in the yellow grass. The boy lobbed his apple in an arc. It landed a foot from the odd colors. The grouse jumped into the air. We shot at the same time. Maybe my shot was a tenth of a second quicker. The older boy was very polite. I think he wanted me to have the grouse.

We cleaned the bird with a penknife, and I put the wings on the back ledge of our car to dry and for good luck (but I think now that doing that was bad luck), and I put the cleaned and plucked grouse, which looked as white and fat as any chicken, into a plastic bag to marinate in white wine and a handful of a basil-herb mixture Ruby Bell had given us at the Beaujolais Cafe in Mendocino. Was that big-breasted bird tasty, grilled the next night.

Hard hunting.

Pine Creek: Good Mother Lizard

THE DAY BEGAN WHEN THE PADDLE HIT THE WATER.

The Yellowstone here was hardly the bow-thumping cascade of Yankee Jim, but the current was strong, and the eddies took off helter-skelter, twirling toward the bank like square dancers wearing full skirts. It was important to keep the Spectrum pointed downstream. I realized that the river was dropping rapidly, though smoothly.

After an hour I needed to stop. This can be a tricky procedure in a kayak. I floated farther, rounding several bends. Obviously, the need was not going to go away. My mind cataloged that, during and after breakfast, I had drunk two cups of coffee, a pint of orange juice, a swig of Cali tea (which we kept in a Jim Beam bottle—a sign, I thought, that we were becoming Montana-California hybrids, a little like the Snake River cutthroat, perhaps), and milk with the cereal. A veteran water man would not have been so squeamish, I am sure. He would never have bothered to leave the boat, at least in summer.

I began to check the shoreline for a good place to stop. For a while the bank was too high, the current too fast. I came around a corner, and above me in front I saw two great blue herons floating out of the trees to a side channel flanked on the riverside by an exposed gravel bar. The gravel bar looked like a good place to dismount, and I thought that afterward I might be able to investigate the herons. There was supposed to be a heron rookery on this run. I also decided I was hungry. However, whatever my reasoning, stopping turned out to be a mistake.

At the end of the gravel bar, the water dropped two or three feet, gathered speed, and rushed into a wall of granite boulders, which immediately forced the current to the left and around the next bend. To shoot the riffles without dumping, I would have to keep to the main current where haystacks would wash over the boat, and then negotiate a very hard and immediate left. If I did not swing left in time, there was a chance I would be turned sideways to the flow, capsize, and be washed upside down under the boulders, where I might be banged around. This promised to be an unpleasant experience, especially on such a beautiful day.

As I sat in the boat, half onshore and half in the water, I looked from the river to the mountains. Tall cottonwoods shivered lima-bean green beside the river. The canyons ribbing the foothills were dark with spruce and shadows. It was far more lush here than the Bush of Ghosts, that sagebrush moonscape around Carbella. Higher, on the north slope of Emigrant Peak, the aspens were turning that contradictory subtle shade of pale chartreuse that is so hard to get right even in good paintings.

I made my exit. The best way to step out of a kayak onto the shore is first to strip up the spray skirt, then lay the paddle behind the cockpit with one end on the bank. As you lift yourself out, you lean on the middle of the paddle. This keeps the boat from wobbling and you from falling.

By the time I had beached the kayak and stripped off the top of my wet suit in the dry, eighty-degree heat, the herons had disappeared. In the side channel, paddling in their place, were mergansers. As I set out a hunk of bitter Asiago cheese, sourdough bread from the Emigrant Bakery, and half a bottle of chardonnay from San Francisco, I kept my eye out for deer along the banks. The brushy cover looked good but it was too bright, too early in the day for deer.

The night before, we had been driving slowly south along East River Road near Deep Creek when a mule deer, spooked by our headlights, had jumped stupidly, straight at the car. I slammed on the breaks. This deer managed somehow, in midair, to arrest its course and dodge the lashed kayaks that jutted over the hood. The deer fell in a crumple at the shoulder of the road. We got out, ourselves stunned. The deer jumped up, seemingly unhurt, and leaped over a barbed-wire fence in the moonlight. We examined the car. Not even a dent. But scratched wondrously across the hood in a flower arabesque was the curlicue of the animal's hoof.

I was lost in the largeness of the landscape, the memory of the previous night, and the hypnotic rasp of the Yellowstone as it smoothed over the island's gravel bar. Slowly I was brought back to the reality of what the river held in store now that I had finished my lunch.

I packed the empty wine bottle in the bulkhead, and laughed. I realized, once again, I was afraid. I tugged on the spray skirt and started to pull up the wet suit. The heat felt good on my shoulders. I looked down at those dangerous dogleg rapids one last time. Maybe I should not have drunk the wine. But I got down on my knees and talked out loud to the mountains. In the full sunshine came a gravel bar epiphany: no reason to confront myself too much.

All I had to do was shove into the current and angle ingloriously over the gravel bar to the extreme left. For some reason, I had not noticed this alternate route before. Over on the far left bank I might have to scoot back and forth like a salamander caught in the mud, until the boat reached floatable water, but by doing so I would avoid the main rapids.

Done.

Like a navy in retreat, I paddled hard for the left bank. The rocks scraped the bottom of the kayak. The chassis wobbled. Then the boat was free, clear of the gravel ledge. In a minute I was downriver, and safe, enjoying once more that feeling of float. Killdeer called from the bank. A lost ruffled grouse bobbed strangely over the open sky of the river. I caught sight of an osprey, or fish eagle, eating a trout in the shallows. I was very lucky, I thought, to see an eagle at all. It was only the second one of the trip. Then I saw another one. Then I heard the rushing of another close rapids. This time I made sure to point the bow into the current and keep paddling. I was soon beyond the riffles. I made a note not to have lunch at the head of a rapids. Never give fear an opportunity to build. Jam through first, eat afterward.

It was turning into a hot, glorious morning, and the river, for a while, was easy. My mind wandered. I knew I was somewhere parallel to the actor Peter Fonda's ranch. This interested me not because of any flashback to Fonda's classic film, *Easy Rider*, but because I had heard there was a dinosaur dig going on near the ranch. This was a flashback not to the sixties but to the late Cretaceous.

The alluvial plain of the Yellowstone is dinosaur country. Some of the most spectacular beasts on display in East Coast museums happen to be *Tyrannosaurus rexes* from Montana. In recent years, the man who was leading the dig near Fonda's ranch, John ("Jack") Horner, curator at the Museum of the Rockies in Bozeman, had uncovered dinosaur graveyards composed not of lone *T. rexes* but of over ten thousand individuals. Some plant-eating dinosaurs evidently ran in placid herds, "the cows of the Cretaceous." This intrigued me mightily.

Like most people, I had always held to the *Dances with Wolves* view of what the plains of the Yellowstone were like before we—us white men and white ladies—arrived: that the grasslands were covered with countless herds of brown buffalo, so many that the members of the Lewis and Clark expedition were forced to wait for hours downriver for the animals to pass before they could proceed, and sometimes at night had to fire their weapons to keep from being trampled in their beds. But this vision of Montana, obviously, was fresh-painted. This morning I conjured not bison on the banks but, instead, giant, oddly shaped, scaly skinned, duck-billed *Maiasaura peeblesorums,* the "good mother" dinosaurs with which Professor Horner was revolutionizing the world's view of dinosaurs, perhaps our view of ourselves, and certainly my view of historical Montana. *M. peeblesorums* is now the official state dinosaur of Montana.

Used to be that these "terrible lizards" (that is what *dinosaur* means) were seen as cold-blooded monsters wobbling out of bad Japanese movies to climb New York skyscrapers and menace blond actresses from the Midwest. Mere reptiles. Cold-blooded predators. Some dinosaurs, however, like the *Maiasaura,* have come to be understood as closer to present-day birds, nurturing of their young, creatures of curiosity and, perhaps, even of feeling, possibly warmblooded—certain species at least—in short, animals no better and no worse than you and me, and a damn sight more reasonable. Dinosaurs never got around to poking holes in the ozone or barbecuing each other on the end of tank muzzles in Croatia. So far as we know.

I had never heard of John W. Horner before the summer we came back to Montana. But after visiting Northern Lights for supplies, I had stopped for a beer at Ira's on Main Street, a bastion of nouvelle cuisine that was either out of place in Montana or else a sign that this university town was becoming more like Ketchum to the south. But

Ira's was not yet open. I wandered next door, to an establishment called Bingo World.

Bingo World is open twenty-four hours a day. The walls are lined with video poker machines. The rest of the one big room is filled with thin formica tables where sat gamblers, aficionados, old people, sheepherders, . . . Who would want to leave home at three in the morning and come downtown for a few rounds of bingo? The mystery was compounded by the fact that there was nobody in the joint at all except for the clerk behind the bar, which was located beyond the tables.

This clerk's name was Sheila Coughlin. She told me she was in Bozeman to study dinosaurs. She was an undergraduate at Montana State University, and her "paleo" professor was Jack Horner. All her life, Coughlin told me, she had loved dinosaurs. Her father, who was a vice president of Citicorp, in New Jersey, had clipped *New York Times* articles for her, some of which told about an eccentric—to New York ways of reasoning—professor out in Montana who had unearthed dinosaur eggs and dinosaur babies, and was doing some new thinking.

Coughlin looks more like a fashion runaway than a kid bitten by dino-mania. She has short red hair, silver jewelry, and wears head-to-toe black. She told me more about Horner, that he had never graduated from college—in fact, he had flunked out seven times, and had no degrees at all save an honorary Ph.D. from MSU. It occurred to me, bathed in the fluorescent light of Bingo World, that it often takes an outsider to change, really change, the way we look at the world.

"Please, please be careful there," Horner warned me, his first words, "or you'll be in more trouble than you can imagine. Not only that, I'll have security escort you out of here. That is a very, very fragile specimen."

I had just entered Horner's office in the basement of the Museum of the Rockies and, in my effort to shake his hand, had inadvertently bumped against the blackened skull of a dinosaur that was lying out on a little coffee table, like some forgotten turkey carcass the day after Thanksgiving. In life, the dinosaur to which the head belonged was probably the size of ten or twelve Honda Accords. In fairness to me, the skull was hard to see, since Horner's office is so cluttered.

There were thousands of books and scientific papers strewn about on shelves, a terrarium housing a live iguana, a Macintosh SE, and several framed pictures depicting nonacademic subjects—one, for instance, of a leggy barmaid in a cut-back nightie clutching a six-pack of Rainier beer, and another, a very long and horizontal poster displaying all the products of the Rainier Brewing Corporation, from lites to ales. Rainier beer turned out to be veritable thinking fluid for Horner, in the field at least, and may well have contributed to his winning, a few years back, a MacArthur Foundation award. In fact, Horner once shamed Princeton University into giving his crew $10,000 by first asking Rainier Brewing for the money. I was hoping details would follow, so long as Horner didn't make good on his threat to ring up the guards.

"Fair enough," I replied, with purposeful calm. "So why is this skull so valuable right now?"

"Valuable? What do you mean?"

"Is that the word?"

"Well, it's one of two of those particular species extant in the world. All right? And it hasn't even been named yet. If it were one of ten I wouldn't want it broken. I mean, it took someone a year to prepare that. A year. A year of sitting down at a microscope and working full-time. OK?"

OK. So we got off to a good start, Horner and me.

Horner, who stands six-foot-three when he is not slouching around like a broken tennis shoe, collected his first fossil when he was eight, with his father, who ran a sand and gravel business in Shelby. The place is a roughneck oil town in north central Montana, serious dinosaur country. In 1977, out with his father again, in what is called the Two Medicine Formation, 261 miles almost directly north of our point on the river, Horner picked up a crunched bit of rock. The fossil turned out to be one of the first complete dinosaur eggs ever found in North America.

The next summer, Horner returned from Princeton, where he was working as a preparator. On a Sunday morning, he and digging buddy Bob Makela wandered into the Brandvold Rock Shop in the tiny Montana town of Bynum. The shop was dusty, located in an old church. When Marion Brandvold asked him to identify two pieces of bone, a femur, and part of a rib, Horner was immediately stunned by the size of the fragments.

The fossils were tiny, each only about an inch long, "smaller than I ever expected to see. . . . I didn't explode with excitement. I was in a rock shop where they sell things. I didn't want to seem overly excited because I didn't want the owner to think she had something that was worth millions of dollars. I looked at it, and I turned to Bob and I said, 'You're not going to believe this, but this is a baby hadrosaur.' And Bob said, 'Bullshit.'"

In the fossil record, baby dinosaurs were as rare as hen's teeth. Nobody knew exactly why. And without eggs and babies, it was next to impossible to make educated guesses about how dinosaurs really lived. But now, in this unlikely place, a window was opening on the late Cretaceous. Mrs. Brandvold drove the dinosaur hunters to the ranch where she had found the bones, and there, working with screens and a garden hose, the underfunded but increasingly excited partners unearthed what they felt could only be a nest of baby dinosaurs, the first such nest ever found. It was in the shape of a hollow bowl, about six feet across, with elevated sides. A salad of green mudstone held the skeletons of fifteen tiny duckbill dinosaurs (a type of hadrosaur).

From this and other diggings in the bone yard of what came to be called Egg Mountain, Horner changed the foundations of paleontology. Eggshell fragments in some of the nests led him to believe that the babies had stayed there for some time, that they hadn't simply hatched and crawled away as do other baby reptiles, such as modern crocodiles. Nearby, Horner unearthed the fossilized bodies of adults. From the proximity of the babies and adults, he guessed that the babies were being fed in their nests, much like baby birds. The structure of the babies' bones and evidence for their rapid growth led to the idea that these dinosaurs might well have been warm-blooded, also like birds. The theory that dinosaurs may have been warm-blooded had been tossed out before, most notably by Yale's John Ostrom and the University of Colorado's Robert Bakker, but they had often been working with statistical evidence from past digs. Horner had come up with fresh, concrete evidence. He named this new nurturing duckbill dinosaur *Maiasaura,* or "good mother lizard."

In his book *Digging Dinosaurs* (written with James Gorman), Horner provides an evocative description of what maiasaur nesting behavior might have been like in the Montana of long ago:

> Picture yourself on a plain, flat like the Great Plains, but a coastal plain. The sea is 100 miles away. Around you are numerous small streams bordered by dogwoods. There are vast flat expanses of something like

raspberry thickets. In among the nests the ground is beaten down from the tromping of large dinosaurs. . . . These are, let's say, reddish brown, with pale undersides. They are as long as elephants, but much thinner in body, and they move more fluidly, bobbing their heads the way birds do. . . . Sometimes you can hear them, bleating perhaps, or honking. If you move closer, you see that they are eating berries by the stream. At the nests they open their jaws wide and regurgitate the berries.

In the nests are newly hatched, foot and a half long, uncoordinated, squeaking baby reptiles. Their faces are flat. Their eyes are big. They are all crowded together and very noisy. They scramble over each other for the food their mothers bring them. . . . The dinosaurs show the kind of alertness and playfulness you would expect from lions with their young, or from wolves, or horses, because like those animals they have the high metabolism of warm-blooded creatures. Any feelings they might have, however, any primitive emotions, are impenetrable. To look into their eyes is to look into a lizard's eyes, or a bird's eyes, not the seemingly revealing eyes of the family dog.

Never one to view dinosaurs as terrible museum beasts, Horner has often deflated academic orthodoxy. In fact, the consuming question of many—Why did dinosaurs become extinct?—used to irk him so much he once displayed a rubber stamp that read, WHO GIVES A SHIT WHAT KILLED THE DINOSAURS?

But perhaps Horner's most controversial theory was that baby dinosaurs may have been cuddlesome.

"Jack posited that baby dinosaurs were, shall we say, cute," explained Jere Lipps, chairman of the Department of Integrative Biology and director of the Museum of Paleontology at UC Berkeley. "The idea is that these baby dinosaurs had bigger craniums and eyeballs relative to their other features so as to elicit mothering behavior in their parents. This theory has caused comment because, how do we know that cuteness means anything to a dinosaur, even if, to us, their neonatal bone structure happens to look cute?"

Horner was called on to provide authenticity to the script of *The Land Before Time,* a full-length animated feature with dinosaurs as protagonists that plays like a toddler's version of *The Magnificent Seven.* I asked Horner if the movie is authentic.

"Dinosaurs don't speak, and they don't speak English."

Horner had a sense of humor. It was cowboy humor, delivered

deadpan with just the eyes twinkling, to let you know he was joking. Montana humor.

In a way, it was a good thing I nudged that blackened redfish of an allosaurus head (or whatever it was) on Horner's office coffee table, since his tirade turned out to be the most rapid-fire speech I would get out of him during our time together. Chatting with Horner reminded me of the quip about the artist Edward Hopper, as recalled by his wife: "Talking with Eddie is like dropping a stone down a well, except that with Eddie, the stone never hits."

Except with Horner, the stone always hit. It just took a while to hear the splash. Here's the way it sounded:

To what do you attribute your obsession with dinosaurs?
[Pause] It's [much longer pause] hard to tell. I like being outside.
   [Pause that lasts half as long as the Jurassic] I don't mind getting
   dirty. [Short little baby pause] And I like a mystery. I like all kinds of
   fossilized animals. I've written papers about fossilized shrimp. But
   dinosaurs . . . [another Jurassic pause] I particularly like . . . [pause
   longer than the Cretaceous, which I think was longer than the
   Jurassic] because—because they're big and they're gone.

Horner smiles his trademark charmer. He half-bows his head and the mirth crawls shyly upward from his eyes. I ask him:

People have this idea of dinosaurs as being extremely stupid, right?
Yes.
Has that proved to be as inaccurate as the idea that dinosaurs are
   reptiles, lacking a nurturing instinct like birds?
How do you measure whether an animal is stupid or not?
Well, in the popular mind, people think of dinosaurs as vastly less
   intelligent than even rats or wolves or dolphins or other animals,
   and I wonder—
[Uncharacteristically jumps in] What does intelligence have to do with
   survival?
A certain amount, I imagine.
What?
If it . . . [interviewer now caught off guard]
[Pushing ahead] Does a cockroach have a brain? Is a cockroach very
   smart? They've been on earth for millions of years. Dinosaurs are

one of the most successful groups of animals that ever lived. Their group's duration is 140 million years. Your group's duration is 4 million years.

Right. So far.

Yes. Just so. It depends how you measure success. Just because you can build a skyscraper doesn't mean you're going to last more than another twenty years. Right?

Survivability is a big one in terms of respect for a species?

I mean, what are we doing here? Evolutionarily, we're gene machines, right? That's all we are.

Why did it have to be you who came up with these creative leaps, do you think? Was it luck? Was it being from Montana?

It's bound to be something. . . . In paleontology you have to be lucky enough to find something. But then you also have to be smart enough to interpret it. . . . Some people, like molecular biologists, take a very close-up view. And other people, like naturalists, a very distant view. I'd say a very good scientist can do both. So, when you find something, it's important that you not focus too much on the little problems, but that you're not out trying to tear the world apart with some kind of earth-shattering new discovery, either, because people who run around trying to find earth-shaking new discoveries often miss much of the most important data, which is sometimes very trivial.

So why is much of youthful America in the grip of dino-mania?

Horner almost licked his lips. He could have eaten lunch in the time it took him to reply. But I detected a smile somewhere behind his small, mammalian eyes.

They're big . . . and they're gone. . . . I think dinosaurs fill a really important niche. They allow us to use our imagination.

And there I was, still paddling down the Yellowstone, approaching Carter's Bridge now, preparing to use my imagination once more. I could see those duck-billed good mothers on the banks, covering the ancient Yellowstone's grassless valleys (grass had not yet evolved) like bison, their dinosaur bird heads bobbing as they munched on proto-raspberries and honked cries of warning whenever a shark-toothed *T. rex* prepared to lunch on a straggler. This full-fledged flashback hit me just above Front-of-the-Boat Rapids, as I would soon christen the run, since the white water flying into my face at this bend caused me to scrunch forward in the boat and beg for deliverance.

But first a bad wave slammed against my chest, and I was thrown backward in the cockpit. I kept paddling in this position, but it was unstable. My back was too high. The boat shuddered and started to fishtail. It was my fault, bad form (extreme fear does that to you), I knew I had to hunch forward. The water crashed into my face, and suddenly I could hear myself shouting, "Front of the boat! Front of the boat! Front of the boat!" And as soon as I heard my own voice, my body hunkered down over the front of the boat like a fly to a greasy pan. The haystacks were all over me, but now the boat was stabilized, and cutting through them. I was OK.

Front-of-the-Boat Rapids, the third rapids above Carter's Bridge, if you ever happen to find yourself up in old Montana.

It is at times like these that the mind wanders.

Point of Rocks

WE DROVE BACK TO POINT OF ROCKS and refloated the water to the bridge at Emigrant, this time in a Mackenzie drift boat, the heavy double-prowed fiberglass craft often used on the big steelhead rivers of the northwest. The kayaks had proved too tippy to flail a fly line from. The Mackenzie was rowed by guide Roy Senter. Roy, who is sixty-two, is not much for white-water thrills. He goes for trout, large trout. This means fishing close to the banks. "I fish where other people stand," scoffs Roy, making fun of the well-equipped Orvis brand of fly-in fisherman, who can cast twenty yards with ease but rarely thinks to dangle his grasshopper imitation an inch from the overhang at his feet. That would be too easy.

Roy and I did some easy fishing, hitting the banks with a certain success, catching and releasing several nice browns. Roy did all the hard work, maneuvering the heavy boat close to shore and crisscrossing the Yellowstone according to the best trout water. In fishing the Yellowstone, knowing where the fish should be lurking is as important as presentation.

Roy Senter always catches trout, but I like to fish with him because he tells a good story. This time, he told me of floating the month before with a plucky eighty-two-year-old from Arizona. This old boy was mostly deaf and completely blind. But before his various infirmities had impinged, he had been a very good fisherman. So Roy would call out: "Ten o'clock!" and the man would cast two degrees to the left of midnight. "Set!" Roy would then shout, because the old man's cast had been perfect and the trout was taking the fly. The man would raise his rod then, setting the hook. When the trout was tired and close to the boat, Roy would yell, "Now!" and with his free hand the man would follow the bend in his rod to the line, and the stretch of his line to the water and the fish's head. The old man would touch the fish with one finger, and smile, and then Roy would take the trout off the barbless hook and let it go.

A beautiful story, perhaps, but what does it have to do with kayaking—that is, with thrills, and with confronting oneself with the twists of the Yellowstone River at my tender age? I only hope that when I am eighty-two, I am not both deaf and blind, because how then would I figure out the guide's commands?

"Set!"

I was beginning to notice great blue herons more and more. With my new Montana dinosaur perspective, I could see that the herons resembled pterodactyls—their snakey necks, the shoulders thrown forward, the bony head, the soaring flight.

Just above Carter's Bridge is a heron rookery. The round twig nests glued into the topmost branches of the cottonwoods stand out like basketballs that have been tossed up, never to come down. The rookery was peaceful when I floated by, but I recalled this quote from ornithologist Edward Howe Forbush (as quoted in *Watchable Birds* by Mary Tayler Gray) about a night spent with the great blues: "A nervous person might have imagined that the souls of the condemned had been thrown into purgatory and were bemoaning their fate . . . cat calls, infant screams, shrieks, yells, and croaks swelled the chorus, all intermingled with the beating of heavy wings."

I also thought about the raucous magpies that dive-bombed our kayaks from time to time. These relatives of the crows and jays, in their black-and-white tuxedo coats, with tail feathers long enough to put a cockatoo to shame, are highly controversial creatures in Montana. The state bird of Montana is the western meadowlark, a sober, brown-feathered fellow with a beautiful trilling call. It once welcomed a generation of pioneers, one of whom said the meadowlark was whistling: "METHODIST PREA-CHER! METHODIST PREA-CHER!" But state senator Bill Yellowtail, Jr., who represents the Crow reservation, downriver, took issue with the favorite bird of the state's white pioneers. The meadowlark, he said, was not a true Montanan. The meadowlark flew south for the winter. A true Montanan would stick it out. A true Montana bird would be the magpie, and the state bird should accordingly be changed.

All hell broke loose in Helena, the capital! The magpie, said those senators who represented ranching counties, was a carrion eater, a camp robber, a loudmouth son of a bitch. On the contrary, said Yellowtail, the magpie, like Montana's Indians and unlike many wealthy cattle and wheat ranchers, did not retreat to a condominium in Florida when the temperature dropped below zero, although perhaps the bird did enjoy a bite of road-kill skunk once in a while. We all have to eat.

In the West, arguments over things as silly or as serious as the state bird tell a lot about what is going on. Out in Hawaii, for instance, there is a fight over the state fish. In a referendum held by the daily newspapers, in which it seemed more people voted than did in the presidential election, the *humuhumunukunuku apua'a* fish won out over the marlin, the darling of the state's sport fishing industry. *Humuhumunukunuku apua'a* is also the longest word in the Hawaiian language, and it means, basically, "pig snout." The humu is a small denizen of underwater reefs, also known as the Picasso trigger fish. Its election was a slap in the face of the sport fishing industry just as the nomination of the magpie was a slap in the face of Montana's ranchers.

The Brazilian was not particularly interested in my fish and bird musings, at this point. In some ways, our family expedition was being derailed. I was doing the paddling, and Ines was taking care of the two boys. The river had to be covered, and neither of us was confident of our nanny, Geraldine. At the same time, Ines lacked confidence in her own ability to kayak these waters. She was reluctant to float on her own while I took care of the boys. I often thought of single friends and adventurers who had run the Amazon or raced across the Transamerica Highway. Yet perhaps our journey was something new.

Things were fine when Aunt Persis was along, but she, having proved something to herself after Yankee Jim, had taken the first plane back to California. It was a rushed parting. We drove seventy-five miles to Gallatin Field, in Bozeman, in fifty minutes. As we drove, I related to my sister the story of the day I had obtained my first Montana driver's license. I was fifteen. I asked my father for the keys to the car. He gave me a long look along with the keys. He knew what I was about to do with his '57 Chevrolet Impala, green and white, no whitewalls. My father always thought whitewalls were an affectation.

I took the car out on the Laurel road and brought her up to 70. It was the fastest I had ever driven. Before, my father had always been in the car with me. I brought the beast up to 80, then 85. At that time, before Richard Nixon had betrayed the voters of Montana and instituted the 55-mph national limit, there was no speed limit in the state at all. Even today, if you happen to be cruising at 85 during daylight hours, you may be pulled over by a state trooper, but the trooper will only issue a paper ticket for $5, to be paid on the spot, in cash. The demerit will never appear on your driver's record. This ensures that the flow of federal highway funds will continue.

January 4, 1964, I took the Impala up to 100. This was enough to give a good boy with a straight-A average a nice chill. These days, a quarter-century later, taking a car, a good car, up to the century mark is no big deal, though few ever do it. But a late-fifties car begins to vibrate around a hundred. I decided to see what the car could do. At 115, I was shaking more than the Chevy was. If Detroit still made cars like the 1957 Chevrolet Impala, there would be no balance of payments problem in this country. But I could not go on—I could not take her to 120. It was a cold day, the little railroad town of Laurel was flying by, and I was sweating in a T-shirt. An hour later, I handed the keys back to my father. I could not look him in the face. I would have smiled.

"Chevy's a good car," said my father.

My sister was not impressed with my story. But she made her plane.

So we were beginning to have logistical problems—namely, how to get on the river together, and also what to do about the nanny, who fought with the two-year-old like a two-year-old herself. Geraldine still had not finished *Silence of the Lambs,* or perhaps she was rereading it. But, like other adventurers, in very different circumstances, we as yet refused to acknowledge our difficulties. We had made it through Yankee Jim Canyon, and the exquisite slide of Paradise Valley, and now we had reentered civilization, such as it was: Livingston, the cowboy literary capital of southwestern Montana. Our idea was that when we got to Livingston we would put aside the kayaks for a few days and float the river with a raft, in order to take on passengers. The guests postponed the inevitable river reckoning.

SKY

Carter's Bridge

Kᴇᴠɪɴ Yᴀʀᴅʟᴇʏ ʙᴇɢᴀɴ ᴛʜᴇ ᴅᴀʏ'ѕ ꜰʟᴏᴀᴛ by leaping twenty-five feet from Carter's Bridge into the Yellowstone. "You have to be a little careful," he said afterward, "that you don't break your back."

Kevin Yardley is a handsome, impulsive, third-generation native of Park County. Tom McGuane, Jr., and I watched from the bank, at the put-in just below the bridge, with its stand of leafy cottonwoods guarding the opening to Paradise, four miles south of Livingston, where the tall granite of the Absarokas kisses the squat rock of the Gallatins. The day was cloudless, high eighties, the water was clear, if perhaps a little shallow to perform the trick Kevin had managed many times in high school.

This would be a guys' float, an introduction to the next generation of Montanans. The Brazilian was ashore, purchasing supplies.

Yardley, twenty-five, a recent graduate of Harvard, was just back from an epic road trip from Livingston to Prudhoe Bay, Alaska, with his fiancée, Chris. They would wed in Philadelphia in a few weeks, before, by way of a honeymoon, driving from Pennsylvania to Costa Rica, where Kevin would end up selling real estate and starting a tree farm and Chris, a recent Radcliffe graduate, would teach school in an outreach program.

When he was younger, Kevin used to jump off Carter's and bob through Livingston's town rapids to the Ninth Street Bridge, opposite the clinic we had taken the boys to a month before. On these outings he would wear a wet suit without a life jacket, his body submerged, his eyes skimming the top of the current like a blond otter, just cruising life. Sometimes his more timid older brother would accompany him, straddling a truck inner tube. The two became roommates at Harvard, and the older brother graduated magna cum laude, but not before almost being expelled for holding two bottle rockets in his hands and shooting them, like festive shotguns, out a window above Harvard Yard at some Yalies in the square below. This sort of thing made folks laugh back in Livingston, but Cambridge was not yet ready for Montana fun. Currently, the older brother is an arbitrager in Switzerland.

Kevin climbed onto the steel guard rail and balanced himself between the two mountain ranges.

"Whoah, I don't know about this!"

He waved, wobbled, pretended to lose his balance, swan-dived. The water came up a little too quickly, and he landed with an uncontrolled splash. He swam over and climbed into the orange Momentum raft Strobel had loaned us while he was off kayaking the Colorado.

McGuane was driving a new Mad River canoe, with the Mad River logo of the Wonderland white rabbit smoking a pipe printed on the bow. McGuane was wearing a Hawaiian shirt and baggy green pants. In the agile canoe, he was able to run circles around Kevin and me in the raft. McGuane made art knives for a living. He had exhibited at the Danforth Gallery in town and was preparing a special sticker for Kevin to take to Costa Rica. Kevin would probably be the only real estate salesman in Central America armed with a twenty-two-inch bowie knife.

Kevin and Tom said jumping off bridges was nothing. The dangerous sport indigenous to Livingston was wind surfing. Not the usual variety, performed with sails and a wet suit at Dailey Lake near Chico, but the existential variety executed from the top of a cliff during a winter storm. The winter gusts in Livingston can reach 100 mph. The slopes east of town are dotted with municipally owned windmills. Still, cliff wind surfing is a minor sport. Only two people in the world, two brothers, have done it, and one would drown a year later in a windsurfing accident off Alaska. I once saw a picture in the Patagonia clothing catalog of the brother who later died. He was aloft, holding his coat out with his arms. He was suspended by the breeze four feet above the lip of a cliff one thousand feet above what in Livingston is called Beer Can Hill, which overlooks the Crazy Mountains.

Like Kevin Yardley, McGuane was good river company. He told

funny stories and possessed physical charisma. He said he did not like to fish or hunt. Killing animals bothered him.

McGuane Jr.'s father is the novelist who had repopularized Montana in the 1980s. His mother, Becky, had gotten remarried, to the actor Peter Fonda. When we had inflated the raft at a filling station on Park Street, Peter and Becky happened by. The encounter went like this, everybody sincere and kidding at the same time:

"Mommie, dear, how are you?"

Becky Fonda smiles. Her smile is answer enough. She is short, with killer thighs, a direct descendent of Davy Crockett, wrapped in a leather miniskirt. In describing her, the words *pep, verve,* and *moxie* come to mind.

"Mommie, mommie, dear, how are you?"

"Love ya, son. Love ya son," says Peter Fonda.

"Be careful, Thomas," says his mother, kissing Tom on the cheek.

A few added words to the mechanic about their car.

Peter Fonda is wearing coal-black sunglasses, tight black leather pants, turquoise-and-silver belt, cobra-skin boots. The old people seem strongly dressed for two o'clock in the afternoon, at a Conoco station in Livingston, Montana, but two movies were being shot in town at the time, McGuane's *Keep the Change* and Robert Redford's *A River Runs Through It.* I imagined the Fondas were on their way to a party in Bozeman. I knew that we were running late, as usual. It struck me as funny that everybody in town had their 4 x 4s fixed at this station. When the Trooper needed new brakes, I had asked Kevin's mother whom she recommended, and she replied, "I always take the cars to Bill, when he's not in jail."

Bill was the best mechanic in this part of Montana, and the Livingston consensus was that only cruel fate and a crueler justice system had conspired to revoke Bill's parole whenever one's Suburban or Jeep needed an honest valve job. Months later, before we drove on to the Northern Cheyenne reservation, the Trooper required a routine tune-up. We dropped by a fancy Bozeman dealer. The dealer shocked us by saying the vehicle was leaking oil into the radiator. The head must be cracked. It would cost $1,500 to fix it. If we waited, the engine would have to be mostly replaced, minimum $4,000. The dealer made an artful pitch. He wore a tie and a clean white shirt. We took the

Trooper to Bill in Livingston for a second opinion. Bill wears glasses with one lens completely cracked, like a vein of gold running through clear white quartz. He drained the radiator and refilled it. No oil appeared. "You are," he said, a little embarrassed, "being put on." Bill charged $30 for the reappraisal, which included the cost of new antifreeze. Montana might be changing for the worse, I decided. Movie stars in cobra-skin boots were fine, but Texans (or whoever) purchasing auto dealerships in the larger college towns in order to rip off those they took to be immigrating Californians was not a good sign.

They say a lot of celebrities are moving to Montana. I myself would have liked to have met Gary Cooper. Coop was from Helena, where his father was a judge. It could be said that Cooper was part of that first wave of Montana celebrities, along with Ernest Hemingway, Mae West, and Myrna Loy, the clever star of Dashiell Hammett's *Thin Man* series. Loy was from Butte, which was also the subject of Hammett's novel *Red Harvest*. In those possibly more innocent times, Cooper, the laconic star of *High Noon*, set the tone for celebrity deportment today. Dress down. Keep your tongue in your cheek. Don't show off. Get as drunk and as loud as you want. Never, when drunk or loud, pretend you are any better than the bartender. Remember, you are in Montana, not Sun Valley (or, today, Aspen).

I know a movie star who moved to Montana recently. In bars he comported himself not like Gary Cooper but rather like an asshole. Either the mountains or the prairies interceded, or else his native intelligence told him he was not exactly in Colorado, but now you do not hear much about the man's lack of comportment. Takes a while to settle into a place like Montana, slough off urban detritus, status positioning, and sloppy drinking habits.

The media finds it a fascinating study in contrasts that someone might want to abandon Malibu or Marin to buy a ranch here. Mostly, though, these journalists wish to spend a week fly-fishing and must pump up their editor or producer to get permission to fly to Montana to do the story. There are plenty of famous people here, and there always have been—from Sir St. George Gore, to Teddy Roosevelt, to Malcolm Forbes—but the aggregate is fewer than can be found within a stone's throw of the Hotel Jerome in Aspen. It's probably just more fun here.

Montana is the Paris of our time, with spurs.

True Montanans are a little embarrassed by the whole subject. Old Montanans strive to treat these people about the way they would treat any other elk hunter or poet, which is why these folks move here in the first place. To go ga-ga would be demeaning to all concerned and undemocratic to boot.

In Billings, we would lunch with some middle-aged oil men. One entrepreneur told of eating dinner once at a ski resort in Red Lodge, when his daughter had become excited and called out, "Dad, that's Mel Gibson!" The father had examined the Australian movie actor, who keeps a ranch close to the confluence of the Stillwater and the Yellowstone. "It can't be," he replied. "He's dead." The father had confused Mel with Hoot, the country-western singing legend, but the joke was on the daughter. Celebrities come to Montana, not the other way around.

Inside Montana, the Hollywood presence has become a smoke screen for something else. Typical is the letter to the Bozeman *Chronicle* trashing the "great migration of Hollywoodites" because these people condemn "miners, oilers, ranchers, and loggers," while hypocritically building huge log estates, operating multiple vehicles, and flying around in Learjets. The letter stated:

> They are leaving southern California, that great moral and environmental cesspool, and coming here to rescue the West from its clumsy and careless inhabitants. Though we unenlightened bumpkins, who have in one way or another worked this land for years, are thankful for their expertise on environmental stewardship, we do not need or welcome these self-appointed protectors of the planet acting as our conscience.

This summer in Montana, as throughout the mountain West, a war was going on. It was not between outside eco-celebrities and Montanans, who tend to be, if anything, more environmentally conscious than most westerners, but rather between the old extractive industries, which had fueled the state for a century, and the new service and tourist businesses, which had provided the state with much of its job and income growth in recent years. Some of the old industries were ailing or in a shakedown period, and high-profile newcomers were being made the scapegoats, by folks like the letter writer. Environmentalists believed that for decades cattle ranching in the more mountainous or arid parts of the state had not been particularly profitable. Ranchers in other areas countered that cattle prices had been high since the winter of 1987. Though Americans were eating a little less beef per capita, there were more of them, and the export market, especially in Europe, was developing a fancy for American red meat, which had become leaner. Horse raising—except to sell horses to rich Californians—had not been particularly profitable since the Boer War. Logging was heavily subsidized by tax dollars and the national forest system. Increasingly, the recreational industries were worth more than all the rest, with the exception of mining and oil. An unlogged hillside had become more valuable than the logs on it. An unpolluted Yellowstone was becoming more valuable than some of the ranches alongside the river, to kayakers, fishing people, hunters, and hikers, and those who serviced them.

There was a down side to this shift, of course. Newcomers fenced off their properties—whether 120,000-acre spreads or 20-acre ranchettes—and patrolled the borders like city people, when in the old days a sack of apples and the morning paper bought permission to hunt pheasants. And these newcomers could be snotty.

Montana was changing this summer, but so was the rest of the mountain West; in fact, so was the rest of the world. America's cities had become painful experiences. Electronic communications allowed some lucky people to leave them. "Turn me loose, set me free / Somewhere in the middle of Montana," as Merle Haggard sang from Bakersfield. The new people did not like clearcut hillsides, cyanide-leaching gold mines, nor the burning of toxic wastes trucked in from New Jersey. The letter writer had forgotten that Montana was the only state to turn down, in a referendum, the use of nuclear power.

This summer, Montanans such as the letter writer would view the return of gray wolves to the Yellowstone as detrimental to sheep and cattle ranchers, while other Montanans would write that the desire to see wolves generated new tourist income in excess of ranchers' profits, certainly from the hardscrabble mountain ranches that bordered Yellowstone Park. These Montana environmentalists would speak of the eighteen-million-acre ecosystem formed roughly by the Yellowstone River on the north, the valleys of the Gallatin and Madison to the west, the Clarks Fork to the east, and the Wind, Salt, and Snake rivers to the south. In such an ecosystem, all living creatures, from lichen to grizzly, were linked in a fragile web. In order to protect the elk, the autotropic bacteria of Mammoth Hot Springs in Yellowstone Park would also have to be protected, and with equal passion. This was new thinking, and there were good people on both sides of the argument.

There was also a great deal at stake. Montana has much more coal, for instance, than any other state. Just one mine, located high in the Beartooths between Big Timber and Cooke City, held an estimated $30 billion in platinum, palladium, and other heavy metals. There are still undeveloped mineral deposits in Montana that rival anything found in South Africa or Brazil.

Protecting the greater Yellowstone ecosystem, as well as other ecosystems, such as the prairie to the east, carried with it a danger just beginning to be understood, as the letter writer seemed to think. Montana could be turned into one vast theme park, with buffalo and wolves the uncaged attractions and Montanans the zookeepers. It was an irony we would explore farther downriver, but it is enough to know now that in Montana the environment is not an exquisite side issue as it might be in California. In Montana, these days, the environment is the only issue.

In one form or another, it was all anyone talked of, this summer, from one end of the Yellowstone to the other—with the exception of the subject of children, and of sex, both of which, I believe, could be said to bear some relation to the ecosystem, too.

Back on the Yellowstone, our closed riverine system was about to drown us. We had reached the approach to the Ninth Street Bridge, in the middle of town, at Sacajawea Park, across from the Park County Clinic. There is a standing wave here, and the bridge itself is set sideways to the current. Most of the time, you must shoot through the middle pilings, or capsize. In his slick canoe, McGuane went through with a painted smile. On the raft, Kevin shouted that he wanted to take over the oars from me, but I insisted on paddling.

As the current whipped us sideways to the bridge, Kevin barked orders. It proved impossible, at least for me, to steer the raft straight through the pilings, head on. If either the front or the back of the raft hit the pilings, the raft would most likely spin out of control. I was afraid. Kevin, the bridge jumper, was not. He started laughing. He stood up on the floor of the boat, which is hard to do in a rubber raft in rough water, and whacked the piling with a paddle as we squished through. So what if we pitched and swam? After all, he had done the dangerous stretch in a wet suit.

Kevin was anxious to get information about the road from Philadelphia to Costa Rica, for his honeymoon run. He thought it would be a good idea to invite Tim Cahill along for the next segment. Cahill, the author of *Jaguars Ripped My Flesh,* lived down the street from Kevin's parents, and he had just set the land speed record for travel between Tierra del Fuego and the Arctic.

Cahill, who is a large, measured man with heaping round shoulders, a stomach, and a civilized beard, has been everywhere. He had just returned from Kuwait, where at one point, he said, he and his driver saw two corpses lying in the sand off the road. A severed head from one of the men lay on the stomach of the dead body. Cahill thought the Montana thing to do would be to bury the bodies, and he had a shovel in the back of the Land Cruiser. They looked around for a good place to dig. Then they noticed that they were in the middle of a minefield, hundreds of flat little mines all around in the sand, like camouflaged smoke detectors. They thought maybe they should just put the Iraqis in the back of their car and bury them later. Then they grew a little queasy at the idea of lifting the severed head.

"It occurred to me," laughed Cahill softly, "that probably other good Christian souls had stopped their car before us, and seen these dead Iraqis, and finally come to the same logical impasse we had. So we drove on."

The Yellowstone was passing out of its mountain fastness and becoming lined on the north bank with sandstone bluffs, the remains of an undersea river lip from the Cretaceous. We had rounded the Great Bend at Livingston, and now the river flowed more east than north. The bluffs were capped with cactus and the occasional juniper. The mountain forests of lodgepole pine and Douglas fir lay to our backs, in the Absarokas.

We would take out near the mouth of Shields River. William Clark had named the river after one of the sergeants on the Lewis and Clark expedition. Tuesday, July 15, 1806, Clark crossed over the Bozeman Pass and regained the Yellowstone, about where we were floating now. Before Clark, the Indians had called the Yellowstone Elk River. Lewis and Clark called it the Rochejhone, which was a misspelling of the

French *la Roche Jaune,* for "yellow rock." At the Shields, Clark began what he must have thought would be a smooth slide to the confluence, where he would rejoin Lewis, who was making his own way down the Missouri. The two had divided the return expedition in western Montana. From here downstream, Clark and his companions would be like ghost riders to us. They had done the Yellowstone before.

"Why did you move to Montana?" I asked Cahill. This was becoming an operative question on the river.

"There are no warrants out for my arrest in Montana," he said. "Also, one day, I looked around and I realized the tide had gone out for my kind of people in San Francisco."

Cahill had moved to Livingston from San Francisco a decade before. In San Francisco he had lived on upper Montgomery, a flower-lined block atop Telegraph Hill so steep that cars are not allowed, only pedestrians. "We called it mescaline steps," said Cahill.

"Besides, if I lived in New York I would probably be living in a studio apartment." In Livingston, Cahill owned a roomy Victorian. "And," said Cahill, lifting a hand off one oar to sweep it across the horizon, "where else can you have this?"

The sun was starting its slide behind the Bridger Mountains. A dozen shades of brown and orange were visible. The spectrum was a bit gaudier than the large Russell Chatham work hanging in Cahill's living room. Chatham, who lives in the Paradise Valley, had sold it to Cahill cheap because the colors embarrassed him. "Russell hates vibrant colors," said Cahill.

Cahill did all our rowing. He said he enjoyed it, and he was not much for fly-fishing, at least this day. One of the most interesting things he advanced on this float was his theory of metabolic par. "Some men are born two drinks short of par," the Irish Cahill quoted a Scottish proverb. "These people are in constant need of something to push them up to normal."

I thought of Kevin, the bridge jumper, of Strobel, Rowdy, and Cahill himself. The Brazilian and I, at least at this point on the journey, were far too high strung and stressed out to be in need of raising the metabolic ante.

Day Care Rapids

T ENSE FLOAT.

Ines still does not trust the nanny to take care of both boys now that sister Persis has gone back to California. For this segment, the boys are installed in the Pooh Corner Day Care Center in Bozeman, necessitating an early morning drive over the Bozeman Pass and back to the gravel road above the cliff beside Sheep Mountain, a commute of sixty-two miles.

We slip and slide bringing the big, newly arrived Aquaterra hardshell down the loose dirt embankment to the river. Then we place the second kayak, a rubber one, at the edge of the water. We jump in both cars and scoot 80 mph to the take-out, which is I-94 exit 350, and leave the rental Subaru there, keys under a rock. (The nanny does not have a driver's license.) We drive the Trooper back to the put-in at Sheep Mountain. We are rushing to get in, so quickly that we do not speak. We launch at eleven, which is early for us but actually late, given the schedule of picking up the kids over the hill in Bozeman. Consequently, a bit of a Harold Pinter scene occurred at streamside:

She, swirling into the current first, in the Rubber Duckie: Come on!
He: You want to be on the river early, you get up at six, like me!
She, approaching first set of rapids, which could not be seen from the road: It's always the same with you! It's always five miles longer, and more rapids!
He: Faster the water, the quicker we'll get back to Pooh Corner!

She: You didn't say there would be any rapids!

[He is surprised, himself. Didn't expect this much current here.]

He: Honest mistake! We've both been down the road ten times! You can't see the rapids from the road! There's no rapids in the first mile and no rapids in the last mile! Can't see the rest! It's not me! It's kayaking!

She: Shit! Shit! Shit!

She means the rapids, but it is hard to hear her now.

Within ten more minutes, we have passed over two series of minor white water. The river drops, pours over bars of small stones and solid shelves, passes through farm country, drops unexpectedly again. The Crazy Mountains are to our back, the Absarokas to our front, to the south. The play of light across the Absarokas becomes captivating. As we cover the river miles, the shadows upon the mountains open like petals on a morning flower, until one sawtooth glacier becomes a sunny backlit bowl of shimmering granite and ice. I do not note the obvious: it is snowing in the mountains. The expedition clock is ticking.

A bald eagle wafts overhead. Another. We are becoming enraptured with the raptors. A third eagle, but it is hard to tell whether it is an immature bald or a full-grown golden.

"Eagles," smiles Ines.

"Yes."

The river has cooled us out.

Ines says the escarpment of Sheep Mountain reminds her of the palisades at Chapada das Guimaraes, in Brazil's Pantanal. The Chapada das Guimaraes is the geographic center of South America and is considered by some to be one of nature's chakra points. I say, the geographical center of North America is Smith Center, Kansas, but few in Kansas use the term *chakra* to describe Smith Center.

In the open valley section of the float we encounter a large band of sheep being guarded by two llamas. The llamas are positioned at diagonally opposite ends from each other, staring out at the opposing mountain ranges over the burr heads of the band. Watch llamas, these beasts are called. People raise llamas all over Montana now—they say that they guard sheep against coyotes. Llamas run at Brother Coyote, spit upon him, and, should spitting not be discouraging enough, stomp him with their front hooves.

We come to the end with a nice swirl of the boats in a broad, turning rapid. Here at mile marker 350 on the interstate, the bluffs crowd the river. As I pull off my socks, I notice that my heels have become numb, resting as they were on the bottom of the kayak. The Yellowstone is turning cold.

Onshore, the situation was maddening, and it had gone on too long. We took unusual steps to correct it. Ines, Cody, and Jack flew back to San Francisco to find a river nanny, one who could heft kayaks and drive a car as well as change diapers. The expedition met with unexpected good luck. An ad in the San Francisco *Chronicle* elicited over sixty replies in three days. Students wanted to see America. San Franciscans wanted out. Some of these women and men had advanced degrees, or great experience. Ines chose a British woman named Stephanie, who was twenty. Stephanie was tall, about five-foot-ten, with curly hair and an ever-polite and cheerful demeanor. She also looked as if she could hold a baby in one hand and lift the end of a kayak with the other. Her father was a doctor. A knowledge of first aid might come in handy. She even seemed as if she might get along with us and our obsession to run the longest free-flowing river in the lower forty-eight—no easy task, I think, either one.

Until reinforcements arrived, I continued to set up raft floats with people who could teach me more about Montana.

Whiskey Creek to the Bucket of Blood

INES AND THE BOYS ARE STILL IN SAN FRANCISCO. I am tired of rafts. I want to jump in a kayak and feel the current again.

I am awakened by a tapping noise in my third-floor room at the Guest House Motel in downtown Livingston. It is dawn. I imagine the tapping to be birds walking across the top of the air conditioner outside. But this does not compute. I pull back the curtains. It is raining hard. I open the window and thrust my palm into the dawn. "The orb of day rose as red as blood," said John James Audubon of an earlier Montana dawn. But this dawn is more like sparrow gray. It is also cold. Yesterday at sunset it was eighty-five degrees. I turn on the Weather Channel. It is now forty and falling. Snow is predicted. I can just barely make out Mt. Delano and surrounding peaks from the window. Delano is already dusted. Montana weather. All dressed up with nowhere to go. I go back to sleep.

At one, as planned, Strobel drives in from Bozeman. He is not happy about the idea of camping along the river in the snow. We discuss the matter over beers at the Whiskey Creek Saloon across from the Guest House.

Strobel has recently returned from the west fork of the Colorado, near Moab, Utah. He talks of running Skull Rock with some friends. The Colorado turns at the base of Skull Rock with such force that a watery cave, called the Room of Doom, has been created. The current in the room forms into a whirlpool. Brush and logs become caught and circle round. Sometimes dead sheep or cows are also trapped, and kayakers must dodge them. Strobel said there was a live jackrabbit trapped in the Room of Doom when he passed through. He tried to scoop the rabbit with his paddle, but the current was too strong, and the rabbit too afraid.

War stories from other theaters. At the Whiskey Creek, we had another round. On the Rochejhone, Lewis and Clark would have kept paddling, snow or no snow. As for us, we had free rooms in the Guest House, which was then owned by Kevin Yardley's parents, Ray and Jo Ann. We could wait out the weather if we chose to, demoralized.

"We are completely prepared to hit the river, Dave," I said, "except for the snow. If it's really going to snow at this elevation. Maybe we should just do it."

"We've already had two beers, and it is only two," replied Dave.

"What do you mean?"

"We are already here, and we are more prepared for a pub crawl."

One of the reasons I like Strobel is that he is a resourceful and competent river person quite prepared to snatch victory from the jaws of defeat.

"Dave, it is a little un-dark for a pub crawl."

"We'll be able to see where we're putting our hands and knees," said Strobel, "in the light."

Out of loyalty, we began at the Guest House. The Guest House bar is a cheerful cave—no windows, but without floating sheep carcasses, either, as in the Room of Doom. Here we picked up Jo Ann Yardley, who is a sixtysomething blond of Pennsylvania Bavarian extraction. Jo Ann quickly determined that the expedition needed chaperoning. She accompanied us down the alley behind the American Bank of Livingston to the Owl Lounge.

The Owl is owned by the Latsch brothers, Dana and David. Dana used to be a switchman for the Northern Pacific, but now he is a recreational biker, oldest member of the Livingston Bros, a Harley's-only motorcycle club. Both brothers have curling ZZ Top beards that fall well below their sternums. The bar is thickly carpeted and, like the Guest House, without windows. Stuffed owls, wooden owls, and assorted owl trivia adorn the shelves and walls. The stereo system is loud and of great bass range, the CD collection extensive. Dana Latsch used to work for Bill Graham Presents in San Francisco, and he likes the sound turned up. On an earlier visit, Dana Latsch told me of his youthful wanderings in California, and he finished by saying that when he walked out of the cabin where he lived on Mill Creek, which his Norwegian grandfather had built, he sometimes asked himself what had ever possessed him to leave Montana at all. It was a question that I was asking increasingly, also.

The Owl, I thought, was the place to lick wounds and nurse cowardly indecision. The Owl is also something of a literary outpost. Books by regulars are displayed above the cash register. There are a lot of excellent Montana writers and they are all respected by the local liquor distributors.

This reminds me of a story about a bar in Jackson Hole, Wyoming, a state as far from Montana as China is from Japan, though no farther. Wyoming never had the ethnic mix that major mining, logging, and homestead farming gave to the Montana character. Long ago, however, Wyoming was not as different as it is now, and folks from Livingston would drop down through Yellowstone Park to Jackson for the weekend. This was just before World War II. The tender of the Jackson Bar lived in the basement, in a room whose walls were formed by thousands of artfully arranged tins of Japanese crab. Crab to the ceiling. When he was hungry, late at night, or for breakfast, the man reached out from his bed and opened a tin of crab. The man loved Japanese crab. December 7, 1941, around noon, mountain time, the owner rushed into the bartender's basement quarters.

"The Japanese have just bombed Pearl Harbor!"

The bartender set his breakfast tin on the night table. "My God," he said, "what does this mean for the supply of Japanese crab?"

A true story, originally related in that forgotten classic of Western literature, *The Cocktail Hour in Jackson Hole*. The cocktail hour in Jackson Hole extended in those days from first snowfall in September to ice-out in May, before they brought in the two-lane blacktop.

Literary criticism aside, Jo Ann, in the Owl, was purposely ordering exotic "girl drinks" that took many minutes for Dana to formulate. Jo Ann liked to counter the trend at the Owl for bourbon, bourbon and water, bourbon and beer, and just plain beer. She also liked to annoy Dana. One of Jo Ann Yardley's summer projects was to attempt to turn the biker and railroadman's Owl into a fern bar. Several of her hanging plants were already festooned in the corners. Jo Ann would let herself in in the morning, since the Owl is seldom locked, and do her redecorating before the Latsch brothers showed up. For his part,

Strobel was ordering Heinekens because life is too short to drink bad beer, and because I was paying.

Of course, we were teased for our lack of resolve. Fear of snow and talk of discomfort elicited only derision at the Owl.

"Paddlefish punctured the kayaks," explained Strobel, finally. This was a much better excuse, I thought.

"Freshwater sharks, all the way from the Mississippi."

"Rabid wolverines rent our tents. We are waiting for them to be resewn."

"Wild boars—"

"There are no wild boars in Montana," said Jo Ann.

"Except in bars," interrupted Dana Latsch.

"Crocodiles. You should see the teeth marks in the polyethylene!"

"I can believe that last explanation," said Jo Ann sweetly. "It's a croc."

Jo Ann had recently returned from Southeast Asia, where she claimed to have seen some real crocodiles. She also said that she took too much Lomatil, a medicine for diarrhea, and her tongue turned black as a chow dog's. She said that she had read up on Vietnam before she left Montana, and that one of the things she had most wanted to experience were the three-story tunnels of Kutchi, outside Saigon. She said she had even brought a carpenter's level from Livingston to measure the floors of the caves. To prove this strange boast, she opened her purse and took out the level. She placed it on the bar. The bubble stood to one side.

"This whole town is slanted, Jo Ann," said Dana, defending his bar and pretending to wipe up an oil spill at the same time.

Jo Ann glared at Dana for taking the last word. In revenge she switched from Fuzzy Navels to something she called a Colorado Motherfucker. This drink is made by walking down the well and pouring a shot each of rum, gin, vodka, bourbon, scotch, rye, and tequila into a mixer, adding Gulani liqueur and cream, and shaking the resulting pottage like a malted, over ice. Dana did as he was bid, and I think he gave Jo Ann an extra dose all along the line, to extract his own revenge. Strobel ordered us more Heineken.

I marveled. Jo Ann had packed a carpenter's level for a trip to Vietnam. In my experience, there are two types of Montanans, those like Jo Ann Yardley and my mother, who travel everywhere, sometimes late in life, and those such as Jo Ann's husband of many years,

Ray, who had never left Park County in his life, pretty much, and probably never would, and my own father, who never went anywhere besides Hawaii or Acapulco, and only in the winters, and only then at my mother's urging.

My mother was sixty-eight and alone before she hit Africa. There was a revolution in progress, in Ghana. The usual disorderly change of the usual pathetic power. My mother wanted to catch the bus for Kenya. She was prevented from this by the police. Few well-dressed American women of advanced age had ever thought to travel by bus through equatorial Africa in 1968, alone. My mother paid a visit to the U.S. consulate, where she was rebuffed. She decided to try the British consulate. Her family, the Massee-Davenports, was once British enough, two or three hundred years ago, and had even invented the sofa, I think, or so she sometimes claimed, and she wanted that visa.

"Is there any reason, Mrs. Chapple," asked the consul, "why I should not grant you a visa?"

"Well, yes," replied my mother, a woman who kept Alaskan crab legs in the freezer, next to an ostrich fan, though never cared much for tinned Wyoming crab. "I voted for a Communist in 1932, in Montana."

British consuls in Africa, I imagine, love this kind of thing. Daily life has been boring for the British since Jo Ann Yardley's father-in-law, and my own father, in a biplane, first helped to rescue the European Community from its early-twentieth-century tribal excesses. In fact, before this country entered World War II, Ray Yardley's aunt hosted cocktail parties at her sheep ranch along the Yellowstone near Big Timber. These galas were in support of the British war effort. They were in contradistinction to the views of much of the rest of Montana, which was isolationist at the time. Montana, it should be clear by now, has always viewed itself as a country unto itself. In fact, Clark, and later the gold miners of the 1860s, always talked of floating the Yellowstone "back to the U. States."

Back in that air-conditioned office in Ghana, the British consul asked my mother, "And who was that Communist you voted for, Mrs. Chapple?"

"Franklin Delano Roosevelt," replied my mother. Unlike all U.S. consuls, many British consuls have a sense of humor. Mother was allowed to proceed on her measured old woman's journey around the earth.

"Truth is a casualty of reality," I finished.

"We must not let that happen to us," said Strobel.

"Let's check out the Murray," said Jo Ann. The Colorado Motherfuckers seemed to be having no effect on her at all.

We sashayed out the front door and proceeded down South Second Street to the Murray Hotel. It was not a far proceed, about two hundred feet, small shoe size. The big sky was darkening. It was almost four.

The Murray used to be a run-down railroad hotel across from the Livingston depot, back when the depot still hosted passenger trains. The passengers stayed the night, then took a car to Yellowstone Park. Now the depot is an art museum, funded by the Danforths. Jo Ann Yardley is a director of the museum. The new Murray looks like the original Murray, with the intervening decades forgotten.

A few years ago, a movie director named Sam Peckinpah lived at the Murray. Peckinpah made good movies—*The Wild Bunch, Straw Dogs, A Bridge Too Far*. He was a man obsessed by sex and violence, and I think he thought the West would continue to provide.

Though sexy and violent, the West does not offer up these things on a pewter plate. The charm of the West is that it allows one to stumble into trouble. More of a Nazi than a Montanan, Peckinpah might better have settled in northern Idaho. He once gloried in his own bypass operation. Peckinpah told the media that he took the cure in Montana, out of loyalty to his adopted state, and was glad of it. "I can't imagine anyone who could afford to, suffering a major heart operation in Montana, in those days," said my mother when she heard the story.

Maybe she was right. Maybe she was wrong. Sooner or later, the director died. Either way, Jo Ann said it was possible to see Peckinpah's ghost in the old private bar with Peckinpah's name on the door, at the end of the hall on the third floor. After a couple more Dutch beers and another CM for Jo Ann, we mounted the cracked white marble stairs. The dark door was unlocked. We went inside. Peckinpah, though dead, was sitting in one of the leather wing chairs, a green one.

"Ask him about *Straw Dogs*," I said to Jo Ann.

"I hated that movie," said Jo Ann. "You ask him."

I didn't like *Straw Dogs* much either, really. (It is a macho-male-wimp rape-the-wife fantasy.) We left.

But seeing Sam Peckinpah's ghost put Strobel in the mood to talk of TV hunting.

"What did you say, Dave?" said Jo Ann.

"Jo Ann, have you ever been TV hunting?"

"No, Dave, I have not."

At some point in our pub crawl Jo Ann had enlisted us to move an enormous consul television set, and this recent memory may have triggered something in Dave, in conjunction with seeing Peckinpah's ghost.

Dave explained that he had a friend who had a ranch in the foothills of the Big Belt Mountains north of Bozeman, where they hunted televisions, for sport. The televisions, and sometimes radios, which present a smaller target, were hidden behind spruce and rock, and when the hunters spied one, they fired off with their shotguns. Dave claimed that TVs explode with great vigor when struck in the tube by slugs or bird shot. TV hunting in old Montana.

"Truth is a casualty of reality," I said.

"We must not let that happen to us," said Strobel.

"Let's check out Madam Bulldog's Bucket of Blood," said Jo Ann.

Jo Ann meant the Livingston Bar & Grill, which used to be the NP Connection, and before that the 10½. Only long before that, 1882–85, was it ever called the Bucket of Blood Saloon, frequented by Calamity Jane, who lived nearby, and owned by Mrs. Daniel Robertson, who used to be Sarah A. Robinson, after she was Kitty Leary. Robertson-Robinson-Leary was called Madam Bulldog because she stood six feet tall and weighed over two hundred pounds, "had strongly muscled arms and legs," according to one historian, as well as "the fists of a pugilist," and in sum was "built like a mastiff." Bulldog liked to run a decent place where there would be "no damn foolishment," she said, and she liked to do her own bouncing because she could do it "better than a plug-ugly hired man." She once bounced Calamity Jane because Calamity Jane slapped a man across the face and shot off her pistol into the ceiling, and also because Calamity was using "mule skinner language."

Obviously, there were a lot of ghosts in Livingston besides Sam Peckinpah's. We had to be careful. On the other hand, I figured no matter how many more Colorado Motherfuckers Jo Ann drank, there was no way, no matter what we did, that we would stand out, given the earlier competition.

Truth is a casualty of reality, but Madam Bulldog's Bucket of Blood, the room, the cherry wood back bar, and the building, at least, still stands at Park and Main, under new management. In the tunnels underneath, which I don't think Jo Ann ever measured with her level, though she had visited them, Chinese railroad workers used to smoke opium, long ago.

How did the joint acquire its name? "Two sheepherders got into a fight," reads one account, "went outside, and one came back with the other's head. He put it on the bar, saying, 'Can you set my friend up with a drink?'"

Where were we, Kuwait?

Understand that it is rare to meet a sad Montanan, at least a sad Montanan who was born here. An angry Montanan, a violently depressed Montanan, yes. A murderous farm wife who flicks match heads containing arsenic into her gross husband's soup night after night in order to do away with him. Arsenic in match heads was once banned by order of the Montana state legislature, and at one time more men, per capita, were killed by rifles held by their wives than in any other state.

But Montanans are not neurotic. They tip right over the edge to psychosis, should things get a little too weird, as they say down in Colorado.

They shoot up the Bucket of Blood.

It all has to do with the cold. You either laugh at it or you leave for the Bahamas.

Columbus: Montana Weather

INES, THE BOYS, AND THE NEW BRITISH NANNY arrived from San Francisco. It was about time.

We set up camp at the Grand Hotel in Big Timber. The Grand is an old railway hotel built in 1890 and elegantly refurbished, much like the Murray or Chico Hot Springs Lodge. Spectacular pictures of cattle roundups hang in the dining room. The Grand was more unexpected than the other places we'd stayed at, however, located in a town that used to be known mostly for the prodigious carloads of wool it once shipped east. Big Timber was the Australia of its day, once upon a time. Later they had a neighboring sheriff who received too many DUIs, even for Montana. They took his patrol car away. He pulled speeders over from his horse.

Up the Boulder River is McLeod, where my older brother used to swim, in the old hot springs plunge. Black bears and mule deer still wander through metropolitan McLeod, where the actor Michael Keaton now bucks his horses, and where there is a pretty decent bar named after dead highway animals, the Road Kill.

During our first dinner after the entourage had returned from the coast, the toddler bit the granddaughter of the Grand's owner, which put a crimp in my plans to ask for winter rates, early. That was a dicey night, for the expedition, looking back on it.

After the savages were put to bed with a double dose of *Goodnight Moon*, I wandered down the street to Armand's Madhatter Saloon. At the back, two rodeo cowboys were getting drunk with a blond woman and an Indian woman. Shot glasses lay all over their table. The group was neither calm nor raucous but quietly animated, as if drinking hot chocolates.

There was no one else in the deep, narrow bar. On the overhead television, "Saturday Night Live" was playing softly. It was the "Get Whitey" segment. A brunette movie star sat down with the Get Whitey guy. The Get Whitey guy and the brunette movie star laughed. The table at the back did not look up.

Crack of noon, as usual. We drove the Boulder north past the Road Kill Cafe to the Natural Bridge and Falls. The Boulder once cascaded under the Natural Bridge in a waterfall, but the river bed changed a few years ago, and now the arch stands dry.

When we returned to the car, Cody said, "Keys inside, I lock the door."

We were thirty-five miles from nowhere. We thought about this for a few minutes.

A man with an archery bow, a boy, and a woman walked off the mountain to the parking lot. Their name was Larsen and they had been elk hunting. Stephanie took charge.

"Pardon me, but could you help us? The child has locked the keys inside the car."

Larsen turned out to be a truck mechanic. He had worked for Mack and for Kenilworth in Casper, Wyoming. His wife was a nurse. They had always wanted to live in Montana, and had recently moved to Billings. Mr. Larsen got a coat hanger from his trailer, but the Japanese had hanger-proofed the Trooper. He went back to his truck and returned with a thick, narrow metal bar, a ball-peen hammer, and a small, five-pound anvil. He bent the bar upon the anvil, returned to his truck for a long screwdriver, opened the weather-stripping of the Trooper delicately with the screwdriver, leveraged the bar against the push latch, and we were back inside.

No point in getting upset about the little things, in Montana. Not with this kind of luck. I was also impressed with Stephanie.

The following morning, Ines and I put in at the Big Timber bridge, where State Highway 191 leads north to Twodot, a town as small as its name.

We saw two mule deer does swimming. They seemed hysterical.

Their eyes were large. The current whipped them around the bank. Five more deer picked their way up the cliff to escape us. The two swimming deer reached the bank and hopped up to join the others. I wondered if deer ever broke their legs.

We had begun the float in bathing suits and T-shirts. As soon as we were met by Stephanie at the Laubach sheep ranch, we pulled on sweaters and jeans. Stephanie had already dressed the boys in long pants and sweatshirts. We lashed the kayaks to the roof bars, and started down the interstate. Twenty minutes later, it was snowing, big wet leafy flakes.

We drove past Reed Point without saying much, to exit 300, where we took the side road, slowly in the layering snow, to the Eagle Nest Ranch, where we were to stay next. There was nobody home. We had been told over the phone we could stay in the old white bunkhouse, which had been newly remodeled. The door was unlocked. We moved in.

By midnight the temperature gauge outside the kitchen window of the bunkhouse read minus fourteen degrees. Not ideal kayaking weather. The Brazilian never paid much attention to American thermometers; translating between centigrade and Fahrenheit was too much trouble. I guessed that Stephanie might know how cold fourteen below was, but she said nothing. I lowered the blinds.

Around 2:00 A.M., I went for a walk to the river. It was very dark with the cloud cover. I sensed something moving beside me in the snow. I thought it must be several deer. It was four horses. I felt spooked, I think because of what this change in the weather meant. The horses walked, then trotted for me. I stood my ground. The horses ran right at me. I turned and ran from them, through the thick snow, stumbling a couple times, until I found myself standing inside a rusty metal construction culvert that lay on top of the ground. The moon came over the southern foothills and I could see better. The horses were staring at me inside the enormous bridge pipe. Did they expect apples, something to eat? I heard the heavy rattle of a freight train approaching on unseen tracks. The sky was clearing. Through the far end of the culvert I could make out the Big Dipper. I stepped out and walked to the Yellowstone with the four horses tagging behind, nicely now.

Chunk ice had formed on the river. The Yellowstone was freezing over before my eyes. It was beautiful, but it did not look beautiful to me. I stared at a once-swirling pool of river water. It looked like the eye of a sheep caught in a storm. The sheep was dying from the cold, and its eye was clouding over with frost. There was nothing to do but hole up in the bunkhouse and wait it out.

Though we did not know it at the time, the Finks, who owned the Eagle Nest Ranch, also owned the largest country-western bar in Montana, in Billings. I do not know why they rented their little remodeled bunkhouse to us. The ranch comprised six thousand acres along the Yellowstone and north into the hill country. But we had chatted over the phone, and here we were.

Glen Fink was a large, calm man in his late forties. He had graduated from high school, done commercial construction, always had a premonition, "You know when you want to be something or do something, and what I wanted to do was start a country-western bar."

He tried to start a Mother Murphy's Chowder House franchise, but he could not get financing. He owned a lot near the fairgrounds in Billings. In 1983 he just decided to build his bar there. I believe he believed in God. "For two years I was the last person to leave at 3:00 A.M., and the first to arrive in the morning. I slept in the afternoon."

Fink was very proud of the number of bathrooms at the Eagle Nest Lounge. He did not talk much about the music, except to say, "We tried to make it a country rock thing, a contemporary scene, not the old Hank Williams but the new Hank Williams, Jr. Hank Williams, Jr., is a pot-head, a dope-head, and that seems to fit the picture now. We keep a fun-loving orderly scene." I recalled that Hank Williams, Jr., had recently moved to western Montana. We went to the lounge one Saturday night, and everything Fink had said was true. It was a raucous sweat palace so designed that a Methodist schoolteacher could have a good time and would return each Saturday night until she was well married.

The ranch's bunkhouse was next to the main house. There were several animal heads mounted on the walls of the main house: a normal-looking moose, a trophy elk, and a buffalo that appeared angry even in death. This buffalo head came with a story.

A rancher friend of the Finks had two bull buffaloes that fought constantly. They bellowed and smashed around the pasture, goring each other, "causing kind of a ruckus." Somebody in the rancher's family was getting married. The rancher decided he would shoot one of the bulls and use the robe as a wedding gift. He needed some money for the processing, so Fink offered to buy the head, and they went out and shot the buffalo. Even at close range it took three or four shots to kill the bull. Suddenly, the other buffalo, who had been warring with his brother for a year, stood over the fallen animal, and the hunters were unable to approach for over two hours.

"They were like two brothers who fought all the time," said Fink, "but the minute someone comes in and injures the one brother, the other fights for him." I thought of the mounting rivalry between my sons, Jack and Cody.

Cody loved the ranch. There were cats, cows, dogs, horses, fowl of every description. We would bundle up and go down to the turkey pen in the morning. There was a wild pheasant that liked to steal the turkeys' grain. The pheasant was funny to watch, because you could see him sneaking out of a ditch a hundred yards away. He was a brightly plumed cock, unmistakable against the snow, and yet he slunk and slithered like a cat burglar, fooling nobody.

The turkeys were another matter. Tough and brazen, the toms with their red fleshy heads and hanging blue wattles looked like assassins from another planet. Once, Cody held out some corn in his mitten and one of these swaggering birds grabbed his thumb. He screamed. The bird pulled the mitten off. The other turkeys rushed for the spilled corn. I laughed. Cody cried. I gave him my glove, though I was more worried about his tears. It was so cold that morning that they could have frozen on his face.

The snow came down like slices of white bread. It piled up and it was bad. We drove to the overlook above the confluence of the Stillwater with the Yellowstone, between the ranch and Columbus. The river was more than half-frozen. Chunk ice and slush pushed through the open channel. Snow covered the fields beside the river and the sandstone bluffs above, and sun reflected high off the Beartooths, behind. The Beartooths, which I was beginning to acknowledge were becoming one of the loves of my life, were covered white as a polar bear's coat. Scenic. But not ideal kayaking weather.

We waited for the cold to end. If the temperature could plummet from eighty-four above to fourteen below in seventy-two hours, perhaps the reverse might be true.

We took a side trip to nearby Rosebud Lake, which lies in the heart of the Beartooths, at the end of a blind canyon road. Mountain goats white as marshmallows used to appear high on the crags above that canyon road. Mt. Inabnit rises almost ten thousand feet straight off the south side of the lake. My family had a cabin on the north shore for forty years. The road to Rosebud passes through Absarokee, in 1868 one of the centers of a much larger Crow reservation, and also through Roscoe, once a town of only four buildings, three of which were bars. The Grizzly Bar is more of a bar and grill now, catering to the summer cabin crowd, but we always called it the Place Where the Cat Drank Bourbon. The owner of the Grizzly would invite patrons to buy his special cat a drink. Customers would ante up fifty cents. Barkeep would pour a full jigger glass. Tabby would lap it up like cream. After a few months or so, the poor cat would die of a feline approximation of cirrhosis of the liver, the owner would train another victim, and so on. The owner taught these cats to drink by smearing a bit of canned tuna fish on the rim of the glass.

No animal lovers protested in those days, the middle fifties. Those days in Montana they also had a bar near Anaconda, the slag heap smelting city to Butte, where buffalo were jumped off a fifty-foot platform into a pond. Buffalo Jump they called it. People paid even more to watch buffalo fall into water than they did to watch cats drink bourbon.

We went inside the Grizzly. It was still made of logs, most of it, but now they had cloth tablecloths, and the bartender was a massive black man about twenty-two years old. He was conversing about pro football with three ranchers in stained canvas coats and caps with fur flaps over the ears. We left the bar without having had a bourbon.

At Roscoe, Highway 78 turns toward Red Lodge, and the road to Rosebud turns to dirt or, as it was that day, to snow. The Rosebud River under the wooden bridge before the old Branger Ranch was not as frozen as the Yellowstone, though it is a much smaller stream. There were no other cars. The snow was two feet deep in spots. The Brazilian was a bit bothered whenever the Trooper skidded and slalomed down the road. Sometimes it was hard to find the track. Stephanie cackled as we slid, or when I gunned the engine. This competent woman with a sense of humor appeared to be a bit of a trooper herself.

Somehow we made it up the last ten miles of forest service track. About halfway to the lake, there is a strangely placed stretch of pavement. Decades back, the old families that owned cabins on the lake grew tired of the slow dirt road and persuaded the highway department to pave part of it. But they wanted to keep their lake a secret. The highway department was told not to pave the whole thing, only an island far enough from the turnoff that tourists would assume the road never got better.

The lake was completely frozen. Swirls of snow blew across the ice as if in a race. We stopped the car to gawk. It was a couple degrees below zero. We started again, but the tires spun. Bits of rubber powdered the snow. We slowly fishtailed into a drift. I inexpertly put the gears into four-wheel-drive low. But we were stuck. The smell of burned rubber clashed with the purity of the vista.

However, we were only a quarter mile from the Clubhouse. The Rosebud Lake Association had been started in part by an eccentric Scot, who, almost the first thing upon immigrating to Montana a hundred years ago, built himself an alpine golf course and a large log clubhouse for his friends. The caretaker was home, with his family. They were preparing to go hunting. The man hooked up a cable to the Trooper and jerked us free with his truck.

It was too cold to sightsee, though I was flooded by memories. The Brazilian asked the caretaker if he could follow us back to Roscoe, in case it began to snow and we became stuck once more. She was bothered by our encounter with the snowdrift. The caretaker was not happy about wasting the day pulling Californians from the drifts. He said he was going moose hunting.

We started back. Five miles down the road, at the start of the secret pavement, Stephanie shouted in her lilt: "My God, look, a moose!"

It was a moose, all right, a big fellow, with a trophy rack of antlers. And it was only about a hundred feet in front of the Trooper. We got out of the car and took pictures. The moose stared at us. In a minute, we heard the sound of the caretaker's truck. I wanted to return the favor. I waved my arms and shouted, "Hey! Here's a moose, right here!"

Stephanie was beside herself. "No! No! Don't *tell* them!" She ran toward the moose. "Go, moose, run! Go! Be off!"

From the caretaker's car, they could see us, but they could not see around the curve in front of us to the moose. They immediately turned off the main road, a bit too soon, and disappeared, disgusted, I suppose, that the wussy Californians had gotten themselves stuck again.

The moose tired of staring at us and ambled extremely slowly off into the trees.

"This is fun!" said Stephanie, back in the car, with the heater blasting.

We proceeded.

But the weather did not break. I put a call in to my high-school girl-friend. She recommended calling the columnist for the local newspaper in Billings, Roger Clawson, who liked to write that he jumped on the Yellowstone every month of the year, and had for twenty years. This sounded hardy. She said he called it Canoe Flying. Maybe he had a special ice pick. I called him up.

"Well, I don't think I'll be putting the canoe on the Yellowstone this week," drawled Clawson. I guessed he did not have such an ice pick.

But a few days later, he called us back. It was a Sunday morning, early. "Would you like to sweat?" he asked.

HOME

Pryor Creek: Sweat

THE "SWEAT" WAS TO BE HELD ALONG PRYOR CREEK, in a lodge built below the double-wide trailer of Fred Gone-to-War, of the Gros Ventre tribe (an offshoot of the Arapaho), and his Crow wife, Sylvia Turnsback, in the foothills of the Pryor Mountains. Pryor Creek slid in and out of view as Roger Clawson's old Volkswagen Rabbit wound higher. The Rabbit was littered with books, cross-country skis, and several Thermoses of hot coffee. Clean snow capped the Pryor Mountains beyond. Dirty snow from the week before lined Pryor Creek like stripes on a raccoon's face. Clawson, a white man raised in Custer, would be adopted by the Whistling Water clan of the Crow tribe in a year. He is a rangy loper, about six-foot-three or -four, with stooped shoulders, long arms, fat spider hands, full grizzly beard, and sad, intelligent eyes guarded by polarized glasses that darkened whenever the sun came out from behind the clouds.

A backwater newspaper columnist a bit too good and a bit too populist for the national syndicates, one of those people who always looks like someone who has seen too much and then croaks "Let's see some more," Clawson is one of those Montana print anachronisms that makes you want to take your TV out to the Big Belt Mountains and shoot it.

We stopped by a clump of chokecherry bushes to rid ourselves of some of the coffee. "I have found," said Clawson, "whether in Chicago or the Amazon, if you make the effort, people don't care whether you make a mistake in the ritual."

We continued the slow drive south, down County Road 416 from Billings. A few miles away, up the Yellowstone, July 24, 1806, Sgt. Nathaniel Pryor had been instructed by Captain Clark to take a band of horses overland to the Mandan villages for trade, while Clark and the main party proceeded downriver in canoes. But the second day out, Sergeant Pryor had grazed the horses near a dry creek. A rain storm came from nowhere. The dry creek rose to swimming level and the horses were swept downstream. Next morning Pryor and his men went to gather their mounts, only to find they had been stolen by Indians. Clark wrote (in his *Original Journals*): "The night after the horses had been stolen a Wolf bit Sergt. Pryor through his hand when asleep, and this animal was so vicious as to make an attempt to seize Windsor, when Shannon fortunately Shot him." Pryor and his companions fashioned two round "bull-boats" from buffalo skins and skittered on down the Yellowstone to join Clark at what is now Pompey's Pillar, to the east. The bull-boats, Pryor told Clark, rode the rapids well. What a journey! It would have been like floating the river in two upturned bass drums.

The Indians who had stolen Pryor's horses were most likely Crow. They may have gotten the horses, but their modern reservation, which we had just entered, bore Nathaniel Pryor's name everywhere.

Fred Gone-to-War welcomed us inside his trailer for more coffee. Above the green couch was a purplish picture of the Peyote God, as he was called, next to a print of Jesus Christ with his chest rent open to expose his heart. A counter divided the living room from the kitchen. Behind the kitchen table was a shelf of books and a small brown mask of a buck-toothed Indian. The caricature directly faced an early-sixties statuette of the Coppertone girl, her white butt exposed by a small dog pulling on her bathing suit. I thought of who the child model for Coppertone had been—Jodie Foster, the actress. Things change. People grow older.

Fred Gone-to-War joked about a recent operation on his knee. "I used to be 100 percent Gros Ventre. Now 1 percent of me is plastic and steel." His eyes twinkled. He was a big man like Clawson, almost as tall, handsome and muscled, with rounded shoulders, in his early sixties or perhaps late fifties. "Though my grandmother, you know," Gone-to-War added, "is Crow. Don't nobody tell, OK?" He laughed.

Clawson nodded.

"Roger, you're late," said Fred Gone-to-War, not laughing.

"Would you like some coffee, Fred?" said Roger. Clawson, I had noticed, had a way of defusing any situation. Besides, these were friends.

Five of us would begin the sweat—Fred, Roger, myself, William, who was a thin Cheyenne with black braids to his waist, and a quiet white man in his early thirties named Bryan. Sylvia Turnsback smiled on the scene as we grabbed towels and our things and headed down the hill to the sweat lodge. The Crow once raided a Piegan Blackfoot village and captured two boys. They raised the boys as their own. Later these Crow were attacked by Sioux. It was a bloody battle. But in the thick of it, the Piegan boys kept coming back to carry the wounded to safety. The boys and their descendants were given the name Turnsback. Turnsback was a good name to have on the Crow reservation. Everyone knew what it meant.

The sweat lodge was made of willows of thumb thickness, tied with twine about eighteen inches apart, and forced over, like two big wooden combs. This willow shell was covered with inexpensive old blankets of many colors. Over the blankets was a blue plastic tarp. Twice in the ceremony Fred stepped outside and used boards or more tarp to cover spots that were letting in a little light.

There was a fire pit in the center, about two feet deep. We seated ourselves, and then Gone-to-War brought the heated stones inside with a pitchfork. It gave me chills to sit so close to rocks that hot. Blue sparks rustled across the veins of the stones in metallic patterns. The heat was that strong. These special river rocks had been heating all morning in the coals of a bonfire that lay a dozen feet outside.

Clawson sat across the pit from me. William, the Cheyenne, sat next to him, beside the front door, which was covered with a blanket. Gone-to-War was on the far wall to my right; the white man, Bryan, was to my left. Gone-to-War carried in four "grandfather rocks." Four is an important number to the Crows. There are four directions, and there would be four main cycles to our sweat.

"Lower the door up," said Fred when he was finally seated, and William dropped the blanket as the two Indians laughed. A Cheyenne friend with a limited command of English had used the phrase once and these two thought it was funny to keep using it.

Fred took some crushed cedar from a coffee can—special cedar, not simple juniper, but mountain cedar from sanctified places in the West—and sprinkled it on the glowing stones.

The cedar needles caught fire and smoked. Fred said, "Take some," as he drew the smoke to his body with the palms of his hands. We did the same.

Then he sprinkled on sage, then sweet grass, then what is called bear root by the Crow and bitterroot by others. These were mood enhancers, I suppose. Only the bear root had a physical effect on me. It seemed to clarify the senses.

The first cycle was to the east, because that is where the sun rises. Fred Gone-to-War prayed first for his grandchildren and his children. He was very bothered that one of his grandsons did not like school. The boy lived in Billings with Fred's daughter-in-law, but the boy really enjoyed being out in the Pryors with his grandparents, learning the old ways. He would make any excuse not to return to town, even feign sickness. The mother was trying to involve the child in a Christian evangelical church. Gone-to-War fell into a nodding trance for a minute, chanting in Gros Ventre, finishing in English, saying that he respected the woman for the good care she gave the boy, that he respected all his daughters-in-law.

The rocks heated the lodge with such a dry intensity that the smell of mixed cedar, sage, and bear root rolled against us, against me at least, like punches. I began to breathe through my mouth. My breaths became shallow and quick. Gone-to-War prayed for another grandson, who had Down's Syndrome and something wrong with his heart, too. I was taken aback to hear such personal prayer. Gone-to-War broke down. He sobbed through his prayers. The sobbing rose to cries, and the cries to a keening that sang in and out of Gros Ventre and English, ending in a prayer for all Indian children. He sighed and the language became Gros Ventre once more, though English names dropped through: *Ft. Belknap, Birney, Oklahoma, Seattle,* reservation towns; and names, *Steve, Roger, William, Brian.* He was praying for us. And tribes I recognized: *Sioux, Assiniboine, Piegan, Cheyenne, Crow, Fish-Eaters* (the Shoshone—he always called them Fish-Eaters). The words became English again. He thanked the Great Spirit for the clean water we were drinking, for the good well outside the lodge. He was concerned about gold mining in the mountains, mines where cyanide would be used to leach the ore.

Suddenly, he looked up. His face slid to calm. He was done. His eyes opened. He reached for a stainless steel dipper with a twelve-inch handle. He ladled water from the galvanized steel bucket to my right onto the glowing, sparking river rocks. WHAM! The lodge filled with hot steam. WHAM! Another cloud of steam. Like the slam of a roller coaster after the ascent. WHAM! a third roll. It was wonderful. Clawson and William rocked their bodies back on their stems. I slid to the carpet as well. The old carpet was off-white and cold and smelled of the frosty ground. As I breathed, I could see that everybody was down at my level, on their elbows, except for Fred Gone-to-War. Fred was like a statue. Then he was on the carpet, too. This was part of the ritual. Upright bodies impede the flow of prayer. Slouching bodies make way, said Gone-to-War.

Gone-to-War poured on more water. The lodge filled with steam. He poured on more. There was a crescendo effect, heat and steam, until William the Cheyenne finally bolted, lowering the door up and escaping into the air with Clawson and Bryan. A person may rush out whenever he needs to, but should do so with care. There is an imaginary line that divides the grounds of the sweat. This line extends straight out from the door through the big fire pit outside. A person must not cross that line. Proper procedure is to circle around in back of the lodge. Clawson, wrapped in his thoughts, started across the imaginary line.

"Roger," said William. The Cheyenne gently touched Clawson's arm.

"Oh, yeah," said Clawson, and he started back around the lodge. Clawson sweats every month. He calls himself a sweat hobo. His thoughts must have been serious.

Inside, I glanced at Fred. His eyes were closed. His head was on his chest. The heat remained intense. Then a swirl of cold air entered through the open doorway. It was just below freezing outside, about thirty degrees on this Montana Sunday summer afternoon. I caught up to Clawson, who was ambling down to the stream, his body pink as a cooked shrimp, steam rising from his shoulders. The pathway was covered with green recreation carpet. The bushes were tied with yellow ribbons that encircled little plugs of tobacco, totemic offerings.

Clawson marched thigh deep into Pryor Creek. Remember, now, it is thirty degrees, all joking about Montana summers aside, and Clawson is in a bathing suit. Roger pinched his nose and submerged himself in the freezing water. I did the same. It was very cold, snow on the banks, but I did not feel a thing except for a warm tingling. It reminded me of a time in a hospital when the pain was unbearable but morphine had been administered intravenously so that I was fully aware of hurt and yet felt good at the same time. Clawson stood up in that place close to where the Crow had stolen Nathaniel Pryor's horses. The current swirled through his legs. I stood up, too. We took breath. Clawson whispered, "Breathe slowly and deeply. Then you won't feel the coldness of the water."

I did and felt nothing but goodness.

"You know," said Clawson, "this is the best I will feel all week long."

I learned later that Clawson's son had been killed a few months before, when a railroad train crashed into the boy's car.

We returned for the second cycle, which was to the south. It was now about three in the afternoon. The cycle was led by William, and the language was Cheyenne. He spoke little English except to thank his host for allowing him to take part. William had been in prison recently. The sweat was a healing process for him as for all of us, in different ways.

After the cycle, Clawson and I headed for the river again. I stopped to scrape myself with snow along the way. It was a sandpaper massage. I did not feel the cold. Clawson emerged from Pryor Creek with a smile on his face.

"You know, once I walked into a river at a sweat. I heard a big slap on the water! I almost fell down. It was a beaver."

Sylvia Turnsback came down for the third cycle. She prayed completely in Crow. She did not translate. Crow seemed more guttural to me, almost Arabic. "Crow, Gros Ventre, Cheyenne, these languages will be gone by the time your children are grown," Clawson would say to me on the ride home.

The mood changed. Sylvia and Fred laughed. Sylvia Turnsback took an eagle feather, dipped it in the water, and moved it over her elbows and shoulders, across her collar bone, to the top of her head, and then held it above the fire pit.

Gone-to-War said, "All life comes from woman. She bears the pain of the people."

"I will pray," said Turnsback.

It was my turn after Sylvia Turnsback. I did not know these people. I had my problems but I did not want to air them here. I was on a mission but it was my own journey. I thought of my family. I was very lucky. The boys were healthy. I was in love. What were my worries for an older brother wandering the outback of Australia in search of more cattle ranches to buy? Rural Australia was the new Montana to him. What was my concern for my mother on the lee coast of Hawaii, raising a jigger of Glenfiddich to the setting sun as she stepped off her rubber treadmill? She was eighty-eight and strong. She could take care of herself. In Montana, she had employed Crow and Cheyenne (as well as Yugoslav, Scotch, Japanese from the internment camps in Wyoming, and anyone else in need of a buck) as maids, though she had put her small-town reputation on the line by demanding civil rights for Indians in quarters where civil rights for Indians was not some painless liberal posture. Civil rights for Indians meant a loss of grazing privileges for the descendants of white pioneers who were making not a little but a lot of money, low millions, over the years, from sweetheart leasing deals on the reservation or on Bureau of Land Management lands.

Clawson had introduced me in his prayers simply as a "Billings boy who was moving back to Montana." I thought of a picture the pioneer photographer L. A. Huffman took in 1898 of my father in a dress, age about three, beside his sister, Aunt Connie, below my Victorian grandmother, tiny John Lennon glasses covering her stern stare, beside my grandfather, who was mayor of Billings at the time. Pioneer reverie might cut it down Pryor Creek at the Petroleum Club. It would be impolite here in the sweat.

I sprinkled the elements upon the stones, cedar, sweet grass, bear root. I prayed aloud for an old man I knew who used to edit the Billings *Gazette* and was undergoing an operation this very day. I prayed silently for my children, my wife, and myself. I prayed silently for land and house and a smooth transition back to the West, white man's dreams, and I prayed for patience, a virtue I have never sat close to, and out loud I thanked my hosts. I knew, back on the Yellowstone, I had much more thinking to do.

It was dark outside now, a quarter moon so white on a clear black night that it looked punched from paper.

Except for mine, the prayers were all to save a culture that had nearly died and was being revitalized by the old ways, as Fred called them. Fred used sweats for colds, flu, arthritis. It was the religion of his ancestors. These sweats were also seen as helpful in curing alcoholism.

The fourth cycle was to the north, "where all bad things come from," meaning, in the old days, weather and Blackfeet. When Gone-to-War had mentioned AIDS in his prayers, William had interrupted, saying, "Speak only of good things in the sweat."

In the old days, a Cheyenne like William would never have sweat with a Crow like Sylvia Turnsback. The Crow raided and tortured the Blackfeet, capturing their children. The Blackfeet did the same to the Crow. All the Plains tribes were in a constant state of war and grieving.

The Crow were a small nation, perhaps a quarter the size of the Blackfeet. Yet the Crow controlled the prime buffalo hunting grounds on the continent, a strategic triangle or corridor that ran, very roughly, from Flathead Lake in northwestern Montana, to the confluence of the Yellowstone with the Missouri at Ft. Union, and south to northern Wyoming.

The beautiful heart of Crow country was smaller. This is how Chief Arapooish described it:

> The Crow country is a good country. The Great Spirit has put it exactly in the right place; when you are in it you fare well; whenever you go out of it, whichever way you travel, you fare worse. If you go to the south, you have to wander over great barren plains; the water is warm and bad, and you meet fever and ague. To the north it is cold; the winters are long and bitter, with no grass; you cannot keep horses there, but must travel with dogs. What is a country without horses?
>
> On the Columbia they are poor and dirty, paddle about in canoes, and eat fish. Their teeth are worn out; they are always taking fish bones out of their mouths. Fish is poor food.
>
> To the east they dwell in villages; they live well; but they drink the muddy waters of the Missouri—that is bad. A Crow's dog would not drink such water. About the forks of the Missouri is a fine country; good water, good grass, plenty of buffalo. In the summer it is almost as good as the Crow country; but in the winter it is cold; the grass is gone; and there is no salt weed for the horses.
>
> The Crow country is exactly in the right place. It has snowy mountains and sunny plains; all kinds of climates, and good things for every season. When the summer heats scorch the prairies, you can draw up under the mountains, where the air is sweet and cool, the grass fresh, and the bright streams come tumbling out of the snow banks. There you can hunt the elk, the deer, and the antelope, when their skins are fit for dressing; there you will find plenty of white bears and mountain sheep.
>
> In the autumn when your horses are fat and strong from the

mountain pastures, you can go down into the plains and hunt the buffalo, or trap beaver on the streams. And when the winter comes on, you can take shelter in the woody bottoms along the rivers; there you will find buffalo meat for yourselves, and cottonwood bark for your horses; or you may winter in the Wind River Valley, where there is salt weed in abundance.

The Crow Country is exactly in the right place. Everything good is to be found there. There is no country like the Crow Country.

In the nineteenth century, the Sioux were driven farther and farther west, out of Minnesota and the Dakotas. The Cheyenne, who were allies of the Sioux, were pushed west and also north. This pressured the Crow even more.

As early as 1856, Edwin Denig, the bourgeois or commander of the Ft. Union fur trading post, wrote:

Situated as they are now, the Crows cannot exist long as a nation. Without adequate supplies of arms and ammunition, warred against by the Blackfeet on one side and most bands of the Sioux on the other, straying along the Platte trail where they contracted rapid and deadly diseases, together with the unnatural customs of destroying their offspring [infanticide], will soon lead to their entire extinction.

When the whites moved into the Montana region, the Crow saw a chance to save themselves from their traditional Indian enemies, which they did, by scouting and fighting for the U.S. Army.

Miles City: Pregnancy Testing

WE RETURNED TO THE BUNKHOUSE at the Eagle Nest Ranch. We drank brandy and read books. We fed the turkeys. Like many Montanan adventurers caught in similar circumstances before us, we prayed for a Chinook, which was not forthcoming.

We decided to jump 180 miles downriver to Miles City, a place as Montana as Montana gets. I wanted to visit a seventy-six-year-old cousin of mine whom I had never met. In the family, he was always called Doc Balsam. I had phoned him from San Francisco to introduce myself when I was setting up the float.

I had written something about my father dying alone at the Mayo Clinic, and somebody had sent Doc Balsam a copy. The first thing he said to me when I called was, "You have your father's voice. If I had known your father was alone at the Mayo, I would have flown over that day." He meant in his own plane. So I wanted to meet this Doc Balsam.

Balsam had continued: "When I was a kid, I was a slave for your father and my mother in Billings. I did what they told me to do, and then I stayed up all night listening to them. They liked to talk."

I laughed at that.

"You have your father's laugh. He was just about my favorite guy," said Doc Balsam. "Come talk to me when you get home. I've got to run down to Phoenix to pick up a new car. Then I'll be back."

When you get home. I had lingered on that line after I put down the phone.

I knew Doc Balsam had made a little money in his time. He owned what people said was the largest ranch in that part of the state, the old King spread. He had a fleet of tanker trucks. He hauled a lot of oil between the refineries in Billings and North Dakota. When he was starting out, he had driven truckloads of nitroglycerin for the construction crews building the Ft. Peck dam on the Missouri. I knew my aunt, his mother, tried to stop him. The roads were a little bumpy then. My father had been his lawyer for a time, but when the big money came, he needed a more political lawyer, and my father was not the most political attorney. My father had headed up Herbert Hoover's reelection campaign in Yellowstone County, and after the New Deal dawned, he had retired from further guesswork.

Just as we were leaving the Eagle Nest for Miles City, making our good-byes, all packed, Linda Fink told me she was from Miles City herself. "Are you going to visit anybody?"

I said there was this cousin I had never met, Elmer "Doc" Balsam. She stared at me, turned in the door to the main house, and returned with the day's Billings *Gazette*. She handed me the obituaries. Doc Balsam had died at the Mayo Clinic, the day before. I could not believe it.

We were packed. We drove to Miles City.

It was a big funeral. There was a picture of Doc Balsam at the entrance to the church. He was tall, six-foot-five, wearing an open shirt and cowboy boots. We knew nobody at the funeral, except Doc's brothers from Billings and their wives. One of the brothers was a friendly oil man, who was terribly broken up, the other a contractor who could not believe an era was coming to an end. Everybody thought we had come for the funeral, when I had only wanted to drink scotch and talk to the dead man about what my father was really like.

"Doc has a perfect memory, a remarkable memory," the oil man had said in Billings. "He's never forgotten a thing. He'll tell you what you want to know."

The first time I was ever in Miles City, I had won some high school tennis tournament. I remember the courts were heaved from the winter freezes and cracked. More of a challenge that way. The second time I had been to Miles City, which was the last time I had been to Miles City before my cousin's funeral, I had spent the night in jail.

I was hitchhiking home from Yale. It was the middle of the night, middle of the summer. There were no cars, and there were a lot of mosquitoes. I walked to the town jail and asked the jailer if I could spend the night. I said there were too many mosquitoes along the river, and nobody was driving west this late. The jailer had me sign in, and I am sure he thought, Here's a boy hitchhiking home to Billings, and he doesn't want to spend the money to stay in a motel. What boy does? Which was about right.

There was a large and sad reception at the Miles City Club after the services. I had once written an article that I don't think my cousin had seen, though who knows? Several paragraphs read like this:

> Democracy has always been very big in Montana, and to Montanans the root of democracy is simple egalitarianism. Everyone is equal. This is a peculiarly retro concept in a nation now stuffed with tycoon worshipers, but a good citizen of Old Montana, my mother, often told us a story about how some British lord once came out to eastern Montana on safari and got very upset when the cowboy drovers sat down around the campfire at night for coffee with him. To the stiff lord, classes did not mix. To Montanans, what could be more natural? One campfire for all.
>
> If you had money and, of course, some people did, you didn't show it. Because you all drank in the same bar, The Stockman or The Mint. You wore the same clothes, although subtly more expensive, sheepskin instead of denim, and whenever anybody asked how crops were, you always lied, "Could be better." This didn't mean after everybody drank too much, that you couldn't drive home in the longest, softest Cadillac. It just meant that nobody would respect you unless the boots that pressed down the gas pedal in that Cadillac were carefully covered in sheep shit.
>
> Always a Cadillac, by the way, never a Mercedes. The Germans fought us in two world wars and that was two too many. Besides which, only LA-NY types would buy foreign. In Montana you never want to be mistaken for a Texan.

Doc Balsam was no Texan, but he proved me wrong about the Mercedes business. Outside the reception at the Miles City Club were six new Mercedes-Benzes, gifts to his children. These were the only Mercedes I would see anywhere in Montana. He had gone down to Phoenix to pick up a seventh Mercedes, the best sedan then available, which he did every couple years or so. The man rarely wore a suit, but he liked a car that worked.

A part of Montana died when Doc Balsam died, and I knew I would never really understand that part of Montana now. Nobody who had made this part of the state what it was would say they were the slave for my father and my aunt and then, when I laughed at that obvious joke, would add, "You have your father's laugh. Come talk to me when you get home."

We holed up at the old Olive Hotel in Miles City for a few days.

Snow continued to layer the kayaks, and we continued to postpone direct confrontation with the river, which lay two blocks from the front entrance to the hotel and about a mile from old Ft. Keogh, where the army of the United States established itself in 1877, in a ruthless, methodical, and completely successful campaign to revenge itself after the debacle at the Little Bighorn, sixty miles to the south and west. Our room at the Olive was a few doors from the room Gus McRae, the original lonesome dove, called home in 1881. McRae had helped to drive the cattle herds north from Texas to Montana. The grasslands surrounding Miles City fattened cattle much better than did Texas sage, and with the buffalo mostly gone and the Plains Indians on the run, the new range was conveniently available.

McRae's room is preserved pretty much as he left it. It is small and tidy. A tall, wide bed occupies most of the space. The foot of the iron bed almost touches the bathroom door, and one can easily imagine a man, dressed for dinner, perhaps, lying on that spit-and-muster bed, his boots perched on the end piping, as he idly watches and smokes while a lady readies herself in the oak-framed mirror of the little bathroom. In such a room, any shouting, shooting, or general scuffling would easily reverberate. Shenanigans would of necessity be sotto voce. I imagine.

There was no need to do research at the Olive. Living at the Olive was research.

In a truly good drinking establishment, certainly one in Montana, there should be no discernible difference between night and day, past and present, summer and winter. Especially summer and winter. At the Olive Hotel Lounge, located in the basement, the outside world has been carefully blotted out for ninety-seven years.

One night in the lounge, which is a twist off the lobby and down a flight of cracked marble stairs, a thin, middle-aged man with a bashed nose and intelligent black eyes was interested in Stephanie. His name was Wayne Edwards. He wore a gray cutaway suit. Edwards was careful about his attentions, gentlemanly in his approach, but determined.

Wayne Edwards is a white man who had grown up as a minority on the Cheyenne Eagle Butte reservation in South Dakota. These days, with his brother, he owns a large spread upriver where the Stillwater joins the Yellowstone. Mel Gibson, the Australian actor, keeps a working ranch close by. Unlike most rich Montanans, Edwards does not disdain celebrity. He believes Hollywood people possess some unusual lightning that jostles life the way good bourbon or a poisonous snake might jostle him.

Edwards enjoyed jostle. Jostle and sparkle lit up a dark lounge like the Olive. Sparkle and jostle were life-saving in a prairie town with some of the worst weather in America. Whatever got a jostle man through the long night of a Miles City winter was OK by Wayne.

Stephanie was intrigued, except that Edwards was a good thirty years older than she was. This small gap in ages seemed to bother Stephanie more than Wayne, who was bolstered by it.

Stephanie was off duty this night, refusing and accepting drinks, imagining, perhaps, what it might be like to be the Lady of the Manor where the Stillwater meets the Yellowstone, and then quickly rejecting the necessary corollary of Wayne as Lord of that Manor.

Edwards had interests in eastern Montana, too. He was in Miles City to pick up some cattle from his partner Dave.

Round midnight, Wayne asked me, "How'd you like to preg test some cattle?"

"What's that?"

"Gotta check 'em out, see if they's gonna have calves."

"What time?"

"Five, maybe six A.M."

"OK."

Wayne nodded to me. Lifted his bourbon. Swallowed. The ice rattled in the glass. He set the glass down on the bar and reached into his double-breasted cutaway to pull out a flip-top cellular phone. It was not what I would have expected in the Olive Lounge. I chuckled, and Wayne chuckled, too, turkey-necking his head a little. He was in on the joke. It was his joke. He held up the flip-top with one hand and punched some numbers on it with the other. Nobody bothered to look up.

"Dave. Wayne. Fellow here from California, wants to watch you preg test some cows. Might learn something."

Wayne listened for a few seconds. Then he nodded and folded the phone.

"Dave was still awake," Wayne laughed. Wayne looked disappointed that he hadn't caught his partner already in bed. "He'll meet you outside the 600 Cafe at 5:30," he said.

It would be the earliest anyone in our little party had gotten up in a week, that was for sure. "Sounds good," I said.

Wayne returned his attention to Stephanie, who smiled that delicate Sarah Miles smile she has. Stephanie refused the offer of yet another drink.

At 6:00 A.M. the 600 Cafe was like a nightclub, packed with people who were talking and laughing, high on coffee, and high on the joy of work, too.

Dave Clauson is a let's-do-business, always-in-a-hurry, cordial guy in his thirties, with a close-trimmed blond beard and rimless eyeglasses under a black cowboy hat with a broad Texas brim. His big shoulders slope to a muscled paunch. He's a bit shy of six feet.

Dave quickly sipped down two cups of coffee and ate two donuts. He wanted to get going.

The man who would do the actual pregnancy tests, however, was somewhat more lackadaisical, or seemed to be. This was Dallas Davidson. Dallas was older than Dave, late forties, with a full head of brown hair, cropped short and greying on the sides. His hands were so weathered they looked like autumn soil. Dallas wore a faded red flannel shirt, with a red kerchief around his sunburned neck. His light-blue eyes were very fresh. Dallas and several ranchers sat in one booth. Dave and I sat in the neighboring booth. Dallas positively nursed his coffees and donuts, dunking the donuts with such care, he could have been washing babies. He ate a full breakfast, too, in the manner of a man who enjoys his eggs. There would be time.

"Dallas," said a short rancher across the table, "when you gonna four-wheel it?"

Dallas did not look up from his coffee. "Ain't the real thing," he said.

"Yeah, but a four-wheeler don't eat no hay."

"What's the world comin' to?" asked Dallas of his donuts, smiling broadly, but only to his donuts. "Used to be you got on a horse. Now you mount a machine."

A waitress refilled the coffee cups at the table.

"What you squigglin' so much for?" she asked the man who was needling Dallas for still using a horse to round up cows, instead of an off-the-road vehicle. Positioned as he was across the table, it was necessary for the man to squiggle in order to get Dallas's attention.

"When I see you," said the man to the waitress, "I gots to squiggle."

The waitress laughed at that. Then she refilled everybody's coffee cup but his.

"Hey! What about my coffee?"

"Ain't talkin' to you. You don't treat me right," said the waitress, smiling.

The rancher looked down at his empty cup and laughed. Everybody laughed.

Before we left the cafe, I asked Dallas if he was a veterinarian.

"No, I'm a quack," said Dallas. Dallas blew on his hands. It was cold. Sun hadn't come up yet. Twenty-eight degrees, and still September.

Dave Clauson needed to pick up some cattle at the auction yard at the east end of town, across the Yellowstone, adjacent to old Ft. Keogh. This auction yard had been selling sheep, hogs, horses, and cattle every morning but Sunday for eighty odd years. At one time Miles City was the largest horse market in the world. Before feedlots came in vogue, the grasslands surrounding the town were considered the finest "finishing grounds" for cattle stock "on the continent," perhaps an exaggeration, perhaps not. The yard is still the largest wool shipping point in the state. We were to meet up with Dallas later on the ranch, which lay a few miles up the Tongue River.

Dallas's cattle prod was a long yellow rod with two antenna prongs poking out the business end. With its short handle and trigger, the prod looked like a spear gun. I had never seen one before. I had never seen anyone load a cattle truck, either. It was still before dawn, and still dark. The cows were scared. Each weighed about eleven hundred pounds. They staggered down a loading ramp above the truck, released by a worker we could not see. Clauson then touched their rumps or backs with the prongs to induce them into the front of the truck trailer. The cows jumped and bellowed obscenely. They crashed against the metal walls of the truck, trampling the floor with frightening noise and power. Clauson treated them with extreme respect. He was as wary of them as they were of him. With a touch of his electric whip, he could make them jump easily enough. But if they jumped the wrong way, they could crush his foot or break his back against the wall of the trailer truck.

"SONS OF BITCHES! SONS OF BITCHES! YOU COCKSUCKERS! COCKSUCKERS! YOU COCKSUCKERS! GET IN THERE! GODDAMN YE!"

In ten minutes, the cows were loaded and quiet.

"I don't believe this thing has enough juice," Clauson said of his prod, then jammed it against one of the circular metal windows cut into the side of the truck.

"Ooohee! Yes, it does," he said.

The ranch on the Tongue was owned by Dave Clauson's father-in-law, Clive McFarland, who was seventy-three. Clive was a short, soft-spoken man who had owned and operated the Bison Bar in Miles City for three decades. He wore a blue cloth cap with a pom on top, yellow chamois gloves, a couple of old down coats one on top of the other, rubber overshoes over his cowboy boots, stained canvas coveralls, and a little pixie smile that was more wise than sad.

Dave, Dallas, and Clive wasted little time. They drove the cows—black and black baldie crossbreds—from a line of leafless cottonwoods that lined the river, across a yellow stubble field, to the corrals near the house.

I rode with Dave in his new pickup. Every hundred yards or so, he stopped to spread pellets of barley feed, called cake, from the back of the truck. Once, while Dave was tossing cake to the eager cows, the cellular beeped in the cab. It was some hauler in South Dakota who was having a problem with a delivery of cattle. Still handing out cake to the cows in Montana, the phone tucked under his chin, Clauson instructed the driver where to go in South Dakota.

At the south end of the field, old Clive herded his cows before a four-wheel Suzuki. Like his son-in-law, he never slowed. He bumped across the level yellow field at twenty miles per hour. He bounced up and down on the pneumatic seat. At the north end of the field, Dallas rode his small, quick pony. The man's legs were long, and the stirrups were let long. Dallas looked like a frog riding a hobby horse. He had hauled this horse in a trailer behind his pickup. He waved his hat and shouted. His shouts grew louder as he rode up.

Soon, about a hundred cows were penned inside an iron fence. This looked to be serious work, I thought.

Clive shooed the cattle through the last corral into a wooden chute that funneled to a red metal cage designed to hold and restrain the cows while they were tested. As the big animals bolted into the cage, Dave expertly pulled two levers, which caught their necks in a pinching metal yoke. Unable to move forward, the cows reared and jumped. The heavy cage shuddered as the cows smashed against the bars, bellowing.

Immediately, Dallas plunged his arm inside the cow's anus, up to his shoulder. Green junk spilled out. Dallas was dressed in what he called his monkey suit, heavy-gauge yellow rubber rain clothes and a Playtex glove that covered his arm. Far inside the cow's intestines, Dallas fluttered his hand to test the ripeness of the ovaries just below, near the vaginal cavity. Thickened ovaries indicated pregnancy. It was a rough, delicate, cold business, painful to the animals and dangerous to the handlers.

At the other end of the cow, at the same time, Clauson would pry open the mouth with his hands and quickly feel for teeth, in order to estimate the cow's age. The teeth of older cows are worn down to "nubbins."

"This son of a bitch is older than I am," grunts Dallas, his Playtex arm deep within the bowels of a black baldie.

"She ain't got no nubbins, neither!" grunts Dave.

"Jesus, hold her," says Dallas, not quite shouting.

This animal tries to back out of the iron cage, and so Clive pokes her judiciously with a crowbar. The cow bucks.

"Jesus, release the beast!" shouts Dave.

Unlike the last twenty head, this cow does not shoot smoothly in fear from the red iron cage. She shakes her head like a grand bull and stands her ground. Her snout smacks the bars, one side, the other, maddening her further. Clauson cannot move aside in time. The cow's head pitches against his ribs, lifting him clean off the ground.

"God damn!" moans Dave.

"You OK?" asks Clive, lowering his crowbar.

Dave staggers back to his pickup, and leans against the door.

"Oh, she wounded me a bit."

He clutches his chest. Dallas and Clive look him over carefully. Then they stare down at the ground. Dave is in some kind of pain.

"She wounded me," sighs Dave again, trying to suck down a breath. He finally swallows. "She did." He tries to smile and does.

He walks back to the cage to try to get this cow released again. He still clutches his ribs under his stained gray goose down coat. He grabs at the red lever, but he lacks the strength. Clive looks up, looks down again. Dallas steps around from the back of the cage, the Playtex shoulder glove green and wet with grassy manure, and releases the lever. The cow explodes into the paddock.

"Was she bred?" asks Dave. Dave wants to get on with it.

Clive shakes his head.

"Her mouth was broken," agrees Dave, which means the cow was too old.

Eight or nine years is too old. A pregnant, or bred, cow is worth $500–1,000. A dry, or unbred, cow is worth $400–500 this year.

Pregnancy testing.

"Kind of a good idea," says Dallas, "to know what you got. Then when they's born, you got the vet at the same time. Then when it's time to brand 'em, you can brand 'em all at the same time. Time to sell 'em, they's all ready to be sold."

Another thing Dave Clauson did after he felt the teeth to see how old the cows were was to take a stainless steel dipper and pour an all-purpose insecticide down the ridge of the cows' backs. This smelly stuff was called Warbex Famphur. Dave called it "pour on." The label on the green-and-white can said Warbex was "For vaccination of health, Against Canpylopacter fetus, Leptospira pomona, Hardjo, Grippotyphosa, Canicola, and Icterohaemorrhagiae infections."

"Grubs and ticks," said Dallas.

After the cows were preg tested, aged, and poured upon, Dave marked a red X on their foreheads with a grease pencil. Bulls were allowed to pass through the cage unmolested.

There was a break as Dave and Dallas went to gather the last cows, who had discreetly backed themselves into a corner of the paddock.

Clive told me about his house then.

As he talked, two lines of Canadian geese rose wondrously off the

Tongue and flew slowly over the frozen field in the direction of Miles City, honking all the while, like cars in a traffic jam.

Behind us a hundred yards, the house appeared much like any other ranch house from Modoc, California, to Platte, Nebraska. Clive's house had been painted yellow, once. But that was not what made it unique. His place had been constructed around an old, intact cabin. This log cabin had been hauled out from Miles City in 1900, when Clive's older brother had been born, and placed on the McFarland homestead. Later, when Clive's parents were gone and it came time to build a more modern place, Clive's wife had said, "Let's build it around the old cabin."

"What do you mean?" Clive had asked.

"Clive," said his wife, "you've lived in this place all your life and I've lived in it twenty years of mine."

"She was twenty and I was twenty when we married," explained Clive. "I said, 'The cabin'll be all covered over.' She said, 'I don't care.' So we built the new place around the old. We had to throw most of the old out the window of the new. We took the roof off the cabin and tossed it through the front window before we put the glass in. But there it is," he pointed up the hill. "You can't see it, but the new house contains the old cabin."

He paused, and kind of looked down, the way he had when his son-in-law had taken the hit in the ribs from the cow.

"Why did she want to do it?" I asked. "For sentimental reasons?"

Clive sighed deep. "Yeah, guess so."

Clive said he was sorry he'd missed my cousin's funeral. "He was a pretty smart man, I guess. Made most of his money in trucking."

"Is his ranch near here?" I asked.

"'Bout thirty-five miles that way." He pointed east. "And about thirty-five miles long, too."

Miles City: Foster Walker

BACK AT THE OLIVE LOUNGE, the next night, same time, round midnight, we talked with Foster Walker, a forty-seven-year-old Oglala Sioux who said he was a professor of mathematics.

Foster Walker was drinking vodkas over ice below the J. K. Ralston mural "After the Battle." This mural of "Custer's Last Stand" used to grace countless bars in Montana. Now it is a rarity. The original hangs in the Whitney Museum of Western Art in Cody, Wyoming. In the mural, happy Indians and giddy squaws strip the uniforms from dead soldiers. At the top of the hill, prominent in the picture, a goofy brave blows a brass bugle. People used to think this painting possessed nobility.

A spry old waitress kept refilling our drinks. Her legs were bowed. She had horse-riding thighs. She was about sixty-five. Tight pants, rodeo smile. She smiled a lot. Sometimes she even danced a jig for a few feet down the slot between the bottles and the old cherry wood bar, a cigarette bobbing at the edge of her mouth like the flag of her youth.

"Would you like more?" she asked Foster Walker.

"More ice?"

"More liquid. That's all I take care of."

"Sure," said Foster Walker, "and another for my friend there, too." With a tilt of his thumb he indicated a white guy with a bullet-head haircut. "Drink goes to Randy," Walker chuckled. This was a play on what people thought about Indians drinking. Twenty feet down the big horseshoe bar, Randy acknowledged the round. "Let's dance," Walker tossed out to Randy, and they both laughed.

Foster Walker told me that his mother had been a deaf mute. She communicated with her children in sign language.

"Deaf mute sign language?"

"No, Sioux sign language," said Walker. He believed his mother's way of communicating had preserved the old ways for him.

Foster Walker said he now owned three sections over on the Pine Ridge reservation. A section is one square mile. He told me he had once lived near San Francisco for three years—he paused and his eyes twinkled as the punch line formed on his lips—"on Alcatraz." He laughed a little harder. "I was part of the AIM [American Indian Movement] occupation."

Foster Walker liked to talk.

"Neither of my parents drank," he said. "My father would ask me, 'What did I do wrong?' 'Nothing,' I'd tell him. 'Just time passes and things change.' I like to drink. Nothing ever changes on Pine Ridge, nothing whatsoever!—'cept time."

One morning on the "res" (Foster Walker smiled when he used that word), when he was still in his early twenties, he and his best friend, Eldron Bad Wound, woke up in a ditch. They still had half a bottle of wine, so they drank it together.

"Then," said Walker, "it was time to do it. To go out. We threw our arms around each other and said our good-byes." Bad Wound got his Ph.D. at the University of Colorado and became dean "of some college." Foster Walker went to Washington University, in St. Louis.

Years later they ran into each other. They had their wives along. Eldron Bad Wound married a "skin," said Foster Walker. "My wife was Irish, a white woman."

They had gone to a good restaurant. Eldron Bad Wound said to the mâitre d', "I'd like a bottle of your best chardonnay, please," and the three Native Americans cracked up, laughing. Foster Walker's wife did not share the joke.

"You boys grew up on Ripple and Morgan David 20-20," crowed Bad Wound's wife. "Now lookatchyu. Now lookatchu."

"My drinking greatly bothered my father," repeated Foster Walker. "But I like to drink."

In the middle of the night, one night when the three boys and the girl were teenagers, Foster Walker and his Irish-American wife woke up and discussed what to do with the children. There was no fighting, no arguing, Foster Walker explained. The next day they began the divorce.

Walker watched Cody dance with Stephanie as Danny, a Mexican musician from San Diego, played "I Left My Heart in San Francisco" for our benefit on his music machine, which consisted of himself, live on guitar and voice microphone, with recorded drums, rhythm guitar, and organ.

I told Walker of my sweat on the Crow reservation. This was the wrong thing to say.

"Crows were traitors," he said.

Foster Walker said he had once drunk with two Crows and their wives here at the Olive, and the Crows finally said, "It's good that we can talk." Foster Walker replied, "Yes, it is good that we can acknowledge that we are all Indians."

"But," Walker said to me, "they're still fucking traitors," and he did not laugh.

The Crow had scouted for Custer against Foster Walker's Sioux and allied tribes, such as the Cheyenne. "Fuckin' traitors," said Walker one hundred and fifteen years later, and he was not drunk.

Lame Deer

WE DROVE BACK TO BILLINGS through the Northern Cheyenne reservation. I wanted to visit with Johnny Woodenlegs, a boy I had once played basketball with at Lincoln Junior High.

I remember Johnny as alienated at the beginning of high school. Once, the entire class took one of those comprehensive national tests. Our teacher stressed how important the results would be both for our personal development and to the financial fortunes of the school district. A good little student, I took the teacher seriously. Woodenlegs was sitting next to me. The test was to last two hours. But Johnny was done in five minutes. As I watched, stunned, he took his special testing pencil, and simply drew a line through all the "A" boxes, page after page after page. Then he stood up, turned the test in with a smile, and left the room.

Woodenlegs was highly charismatic. Intelligent, a star athlete, handsome if stocky, with a cowlick of obsidian black hair, he was one of the few Indians who had many white friends.

I had not seen him since June 1967, when I had left Billings to hitchhike around the country during the Summer of Love and he had shipped out to Vietnam on the first of several voluntary tours.

We took the long way round, through the Crow reservation. That day, the Custer National Battlefield, which lies exactly between the two reservations, was officially renamed the Little Bighorn Battlefield National Monument.

The first thing you notice about the Little Bighorn Battlefield is that it is a beautiful place to die. The next thing you notice is that they had to have seen it coming. The ridge line where Custer and his men clustered looks out over Little Bighorn Creek to endless undulating prairie, white, snow-covered, and pillowed today, rising to the Pryors, where we took our sweat, on to the Beartooths, and beyond, forever, in all directions. It would have been like dying at the entrance to heaven, though perhaps much less pleasant.

Below the ridge line and for miles, as many as fifteen thousand Sioux, Cheyenne, and allied tribes, with three thousand to four thousand warriors, were camped alongside the creek with perhaps fifty thousand horses, the largest encampment of Native Americans that we know about, certainly. What must the youngest general and the most effective cavalry officer in the war to end slavery have thought, along with his brother, his brother-in-law, and his nephew, that second when they crested the ridge to overlook one of the most beautiful vistas in Montana? Perhaps Custer, because he was Custer, thought he would win, with his 225 troopers. But Custer was not Cortés, and the Sioux and Cheyenne were not Aztec.

Cody chased a rabbit through the snow among the weathered white markers, farther and farther down the hill, as I called after him. Magpies hopped about on the gravestones and called to Cody, or to the rabbit, or among themselves.

Inside the visitors' center there is a plaque that leaves a lot of questions unanswered but tells more about what happened than most white, black, or Asian Americans probably know:

> In 1874, George A. Custer led an exploratory expedition into the Black Hills because accompanying geologists confirmed earlier rumors of the presence of gold. A horde of miners invaded the great Sioux reservation. The Army sent General Crook to uphold the treaty of Fort Laramie by expelling the gold seekers. The miners refused to leave and public opinion supported them. The government yielded and attempted to buy the land. The Sioux chiefs signed an agreement to accept the treaty of Fort Laramie. Ordered to return, they were threatened with military action.

Things left unsaid by the plaque include the following: (1) Custer and his mentor, Gen. Phil Sheridan, once credited with the statement, "The only good Indian is a dead Indian," secretly added the geologists to the Black Hills expedition, knowing the discovery of gold would drive the Sioux and Cheyenne farther west; (2) the Sioux chiefs who signed were not the war chiefs of their tribes and were not representative; (3) Indians such as Sitting Bull, Crazy Horse, and Dull Knife never received the order to return to any reservation, and most likely the War Department designed the timing of the orders, which were issued in the dead of winter, knowing that the leaders would not be able to respond.

There is no reason to overstate this. Killing American Indians was not a moral offense 120 years ago. In fact, killing Indians might have helped you to be elected to the presidency ("*Tippecanoe and Tyler, too!*") should you leave the military and make a career leap, as many thought Custer was angling for in his joyous, still youthful Indian massacres across the Plains states after he helped to massacre the proponents of slavery, more than any other soldier of his age, and more than most officers who were far older. The tactics of impetuosity worked well at Yellow Tavern and Waynesboro, not so well in Montana.

When the chiefs of the Cheyenne and Sioux did respond to Washington's request that they return to the reservations set aside by previously broken treaties, they responded with more force than Washington had reckoned on.

For the Cheyenne, the Battle of the Little Bighorn could be seen as just revenge. Custer had massacred Cheyenne women and children at Washita in 1868. Earlier, Col. John K. Chivington had massacred the Cheyenne at Sand Creek, after advocating the scalping of all Indians, even infants. "Nits become lice," he had said in Denver. When Chivington's Colorado volunteers, who mostly joined up to avoid having to fight the Confederate Army, massacred Black Kettle's people at Sand Creek, the warriors were mostly absent, hunting. The soldiers cut off the children's genitals and wore the thin rims of the women's vaginas as hat bands.

So Custer lost the big battle, but within a year or two, Miles, Crook, Sherman, and Sheridan had won the war against the Plains Indians, and the reservations that dot Montana and South Dakota tell that later story.

The Northern Cheyenne reservation is only twenty-four miles from the Battle of the Little Bighorn Battlefield. It seems a peaceful, other-worldly place, almost magical, in a hard way. The Tongue meanders down an empty grass valley below sandstone bluffs that have the air of medieval ramparts. The reservation is far enough from any major highway that there are no tourists and few white people, except for the occasional semitrucker recklessly blasting through to avoid the weigh stations on the interstate. It is like coming to another world, arriving here, as if gravity were somehow stronger and breathing slower. In Lame Deer, an old man knocked on Stephanie's door while Ines and I were inside the Cheyenne Depot. She was startled. He had noticed the out-of-state license plates and simply wanted to talk to outsiders.

Lame Deer looks more prosperous than the shantytowns of abandoned cars and angry children seen elsewhere on western reservations. The Cheyenne seem cohesive and yet apart. Lame Deer is the town that the chief, Dull Knife, or Morning Star, eventually returned to after leading an escape from Oklahoma, where the Cheyenne did not like the weather, the malaria, nor the way they were being starved. In an exodus to rival that of Chief Joseph and the Nez Percé, they walked and rode by night for weeks through snow to the Black Hills. Soldiers shot the stragglers, but some lived to see the buffalo country once more, what was left of it. Their descendants make up the bulk of the tribe. We drove past Dull Knife College and the Dull Knife Cafe (that is a name).

It took us most of the evening to find Johnny Woodenlegs, who lived a little ways down the Birney road. He did not have a telephone.

We pulled up to his green ranch house around ten at night. Pinto ponies stood in back. Several white puppies tumbled over our feet before the front door. Across the road, behind, stood a large and sagging log cabin from different times. There was patchy snow everywhere.

Woodenlegs was taller, thinner, less angry than I had remembered him. We were invited in.

The inside of the house was being redecorated with new blue carpets and new Sheetrock. There had been a terrible electrical fire a few months before. The fire had started in the middle of the night. As Woodenlegs was carrying his six-year-old daughter from her basement bedroom, he had slipped and injured his back. He could no longer work as hard as he used to at a construction company he owned. The war bonnet of his great-grandfather Wooden Leg had also been burned in the fire. The year before, Johnny Woodenlegs had worn this eagle-feathered bonnet above his Vietnam staff sergeant's uniform, covered with medals, when he had shaken then-president Bush's hand on the steps of the capitol in Helena. Outside the house, I noticed, his car still carried a decayed Desert Storm bumper sticker.

At first, the conversation had an easy way of working itself back to Vietnam or to the Battle of the Little Bighorn. The two were connected in Woodenlegs's mind, but not with the many ironies with which I might have linked them. To him, they were both big fights in which the Cheyenne had acquitted themselves well—Johnny in Southeast Asia and Wooden Leg a few miles over on the Little Bighorn. Old Wooden Leg had been eighteen in that early battle, about the same age as his great-grandson when he went to 'Nam.

Johnny said that most of Custer's troopers had committed suicide once they understood what that view across the ridge to heaven meant.

"The soldiers went crazy. They drank whiskey. The plates of my great-grandfather's book were broken by the government," he said, "and what you read is a small portion of the truth."

Johnny said his copy of the original manuscript had been burned in the electrical fire, though there were several other copies on the reservation. It is no exaggeration to say that most successive accounts of the battle are actually based on Wooden Leg's version of what happened, first published in 1931 as *Wooden Leg: A Warrior Who Fought Custer.* The book, in fact, does briefly advance the suicide explanation and also talks of whiskey drinking by Custer's men.

"Scouts followed Custer from what is now Miles City," said Woodenlegs. "They knew he was coming. The medicine people wanted to know what sort of horse he was riding because there had been a prediction: If he rode a white horse it meant he came with peace in his heart, and if was a sorrel or black it meant he was going to attack. The scouts reported that Custer was riding a sorrel horse. So the Cheyenne were able to use two or three days to get their medicine together." This somewhat contradicted the published version in his great-grandfather's book. Old Wooden Leg said Custer took them by surprise that day.

After the government of the United States had avenged its momentary defeat, rounding up and killing the Sioux and Cheyenne, Wooden Leg and his brothers scouted for the army out of Miles City. They ran the Nez Percé to the ground just south of the Canadian border in 1877 after Chief Joseph made his retreat across the breadth of

Montana. "The Cheyenne scouts thought the Nez Percé were already in Canada," said Woodenlegs. "It was a mistake," he laughed, a bit embarrassed. "The Nez Percé don't like us so much now."

At the request of his father, who was then tribal chief of the Cheyenne, Johnny Woodenlegs moved to Billings to attend school. He lived with an anthropologist at the state college, because his father believed he would receive a better education there than on the reservation or at the St. Labre school, where, said Johnny's wife, Judy, the teachers physically disciplined the Cheyenne children. When I met Johnny, he was the best player on the junior high basketball team, a concentrated and charging guard, a natural athlete.

I was also on the team, an unnatural forward warming the far end of the bench. I think I made the Lincoln team because the coach thought I would be elected president of the student council. Once, coach actually put me in the game, after it was clear there was no way we could lose. Soon, I was given the right to shoot two free-throws because somebody from Missoula tripped over my large feet. The cheerleaders twirled their short white skirts and shouted in unison, "GO STEVE! GO!" I looked around for this Steve. They meant me. I missed both shots. I was, truth be told, much more interested in the wondrous white buffalo humps under those twirling cheerleaders' skirts than I could ever be in making those free-throws. Make love. Not war.

But Woodenlegs made war, and very well, as his great-grandfather had before him. He served in intelligence. Woodenlegs pointed out that more Indians had volunteered for Vietnam from the Cheyenne than from any other tribe in Montana, and he claimed that Montanans had volunteered more for that war, per capita, than other Americans.

"Why?"

"Well," he said, "this is what the Cheyenne are good at. There has been a history of this."

There is a very good book about Vietnam and about coming home, by a non-Montanan author, Robert Stone. The book is called *Dog Soldiers*. I believe the leader of the real Dog Soldiers, which is the name of an ancient Cheyenne war society, is now Johnny Woodenlegs. On that basketball team of long ago, the center, a tall, wild boy named Jeff Uhren, did not come back from Vietnam. Another starter tried to cut off a segment of his trigger finger to avoid going. I heard later he made a drunken mistake and sawed off the tip of the wrong finger.

One of the forwards on the team went to West Point. The rest of us fought against the war in the streets.

When Johnny Woodenlegs came home from Asia, he could not sit still, he said. He wandered America as a hitchhiker and a truck driver. He drank a lot, and found himself knifed in a bar on Minnesota Avenue near the old Casey's Golden Pheasant in Billings, so I was told. He spent time in hospitals. He was judged to have post-traumatic stress disorder. "I would be in the line at the market, and suddenly my mind would be in Oregon," he laughed, softly. He married three women and fathered eight children.

Woodenlegs said returning from Vietnam had been easier for the Cheyenne because war had been part of their culture for hundreds of years. The tribe held powwows for its Vietnam veterans and welcomed them home. He talked of yet another player on the Lincoln Colts. Long after the war, this white soldier had stayed for weeks in the log cabin across the road, seeking true company and advice, sharing strong stories. The cabin had belonged to Old Wooden Leg.

After Johnny's father died, Johnny began to calm down. He showed us a picture of himself and his father coming out of a sweat. The father is much older than the son. The father looks peaceful; the son, tough. Both have faraway eyes. "You never know when you're young that your father's going to die," I said. Woodenlegs was sad his father could not pass on the "old ways" to him, he said.

Johnny Woodenlegs was on a quest for the old ways.

Each morning, he burned cedar in the corners of the house and prayed for his children and for the day. Judy said she was more Christian, but they respected each other's religion. They both took part in the peyote festivals of the Native American Church. Peyote is a spineless cactus. The crowns, or buttons, contain mescaline and produce visions, or at least changes in perception. The festivals were very important to the tribe, they said, and Johnny showed us the federal license that allowed him to be in possession of peyote "as a sacrament for religious ceremony." It looked like a laminated driver's license.

Johnny put on a cassette tape of the drums in a peyote ceremony to demonstrate how different they sounded from the big drum at a powwow. He brought out a carved cedar box. Inside were a dozen green lumps, cactus pieces, each about as thick as a large thumb. This was peyote. He had more buttons growing in a pot. He said he had taken a "grandfather button" to Vietnam, as had other fighting Cheyenne, but these were usually confiscated when the soldiers returned to the States. The cedar box also contained bead work, which he did himself. I think the beads were holsters and covers for peyote cutting knives. The bead work was mostly in red-white-and-blue. "Because I'm a vet," he repeated.

Each year he drives to Laredo, Texas, to pick up fresh peyote. He hangs his staff sergeant's uniform in the back. "The cops don't like people picking up peyote," he said. "They run sort of a sting operation. They know about the source, which is legal, but not everybody is official, you know, who wants the peyote." But the police take a look at the hanging uniform, and they shake his hand, and sometimes they provide him with an escort to the house where the peyote is.

"The Cheyenne are in transition," he laughed, softly. I think he laughed because he included himself in this transformation. "The old ways are giving the young people back their roots, making them understand who they are, how valuable the Cheyenne were in the history of the Indian people."

The tribe still keeps the hat. The Sacred Medicine Hat is a buffalo-head hat that has the miraculous ability to fix itself. If the tribe is warring among itself, and leadership is weak or corrupt, then the hat looks bad, broken, and dusty. If the tribe is doing well, and the leaders are good, then the hat looks shiny and perfect. Woodenlegs said the hat has been with the Cheyenne forever. The keeper of the hat lives just down the road. He was reluctant to become the keeper, however, because keepers tend to die young. Yet he finally agreed.

The next day, we drove slowly by the keeper of the hat's house. The hat is in a teepee in the backyard. It is inside a bag that hangs suspended from the junction of the poles at the top.

The Northern Cheyenne reservation sits on top of major coal deposits, perhaps a billion dollars' worth. Woodenlegs believes the tribe needs to recover from decades of aimlessness, and then they would be able to make respectful use of the coal. He said relearning the old ways would make people proud, and then they would do right.

The huge Colstrip power plant lies only a few miles north of the reservation. Its siting was once a major environmental battle in Montana, but Woodenlegs seemed more concerned with holding the tribe together, providing jobs based on the coal so that members did not have to move off to Denver, Seattle, or Houston.

Woodenlegs sat on the tribal council, as did his sister. He was thinking of running for vice chairman, and then chairman, as his father had before him. Old Wooden Leg had been tribal judge. What Johnny had to say had import.

River's Edge

WE SET UP CAMP ON THE SIXTH FLOOR of the new Northern Hotel, in Billings. It is a Radisson now, and the lobby looks more Santa Fe than eastern Montana, but the place retains its charm. I asked the desk clerk if he knew Bill Trask, the old cattle buyer who had once ridden his horse through the lobby of the Northern after he felt he was cheated at poker (or was it just Western Days?). The clerk looked at me. I believe he was thinking what a careening horse would do to the new wool carpets. I said, "I think the lobby was bigger in the old Northern."

The Northern was hosting the convention of the twentieth anniversary of the founding of the Northern Plains Resource Council, which is why we had chosen to stay there—besides the fact that Bill Trask had ridden his horse through the lobby. The NPRC is an unusual mix of ranchers and environmentalists who had originally come together in the early seventies to save, in their view, Montana and their ranches from the construction of as many as thirty-six coal-fired generating and synthetic fuel plants, such as the one that was built at Colstrip, north of the Cheyenne reservation.

I picked up a press release written by a staffer named Dennis Olson: "I have enclosed an article, 'The Last of the West: Hell, Strip It,' that gives a good historical perspective on the genesis of the NPRC. This article contains the well-known quote of one of NPRC's founders, Boyd Charter (page 103). . . . "

I had not heard of this well-known quote. I turned to page 103. It was from an old *Atlantic Monthly*:

> Some people can't understand that money's not everything. I told that man that I knew he represented one of the biggest coal companies and that he was backed by one of the richest industries in the world but no matter how much money they came up with, they would always be $4.60 short of the price of my ranch.

The Northern Plains Council, as it is usually called, had begun by stopping coal companies from strip-mining deposits in the Powder River Basin, but now they were also allied with groups trying to stop, or regulate, the gold and palladium mines in the Beartooths, which might eventually leach into the Yellowstone's feeder streams.

The convention was mostly a congratulatory gathering of new Montanans from old families. I wandered into an award ceremony. One organizer was given the award for Most Frank Thing Ever Said to a Politician. He had introduced his children to a former governor of Montana with this line: "I want my children to say they met the chickenshit son of a bitch who let Colstrip in."

I saw a woman who used to be on the Billings Senior High *Kyote,* when I was the editor. I thought she had become the editor a couple of years after I left. She was smart. I had appointed some long-haired kid who went on to Yale and these days runs a national business magazine. But the woman said that when her turn came, the kid did not think she would be able to stand up to the principal, being a girl and all, and had appointed someone else.

We laughed.

I asked her what she did now. She was the lawyer for a large local chemical company. She said the three big refineries purposely polluted to the limit allowed by the law, not so much to save money but to keep out any fourth refinery, or any other sulfur-dioxide–emitting industry, since the regulations allowed just so much pollution. She said that both a barley plant and a chromium processing company had been shut out of "the air shed." She said when Billings threatened to clamp down on pollution, Exxon simply had appraisals done on some two hundred houses their employees owned, to underline the point that should they up and leave, a lot of real estate might flood the market, and worse. (A spokesman for Exxon in Billings states that operations were never adjusted to the disadvantage of other industries, and denies any knowledge that employee homes were appraised.)

The lawyer said the state was a Third World country. Sure, lots of rich people were moving in from all over, but who wants to live in Jamaica?

This was a point being made all over Montana this summer. It was not that the natives disliked people with money from out of state, or movie stars, or retired Californians. Or that this new crew could be snotty or lacking in sociability, or bring in drugs or false environmental values. The real point was one that might be made only in a place like Montana: The new folks could never possess the character of the old folks. And this would water down the mash. The new folks did not know who "Dirty Mouth Lil" was over in Butte, or that Pretty Shield used to talk to the chickadees, or that cats drank bourbon in Roscoe once upon a time.

She said that the "big people"—Montana Power and Anaconda—whom nobody ever talks about, divided up the state long ago. Anaconda was the copper company that used to own the largest copper mine in the world, over in Butte. It was capitalized by William Rockefeller, who chose the name Anaconda, as in strangle the competition.

I wish I had been able to appoint this chemical company lawyer the editor of the *Kyote*. If she had been a year older, we could have changed the name of the paper together. *Kyote* was laughable, and not environmentally correct, either. Just plain *Coyote* was the way it should be. Respect the trickster in us all.

From our room we could see the Yellowstone, and the Beartooths beyond. The Pryors were out the south window. There were three or four twenty-story buildings in Billings now. A tenth of Montana's population lived within sight of the hotel.

My older brother called. He was back from Australia. He said he had had a good time shooting brumbies on his ranch. Brumbies are wild horses. He said he was thinking of shipping the horse meat to the Balkans, giving it to the UN for charity. He was joking about that last part, doing anything at all with the dead horses, which he considered nuisance grazers. I asked him if he had ever seen *The Misfits,* the last movie Marilyn Monroe and Clark Gable ever made. It was about killing wild horses in northern Nevada, for the meat. "Kind of a metaphor," I said. He knew I was trying to trap him. "Missed it," he laughed from southern California. I could hear the ice rattling in his scotch glass. I knew he was probably sitting in the hot tub, at the edge of the pool, talking on the cordless. He came back to Montana only for high school reunions; he had attended his forty-fifth at Billings Senior High five years before. He said he was converting another Australian cattle ranch into a bird-watching sanctuary. The Australian government subsidized eco-tourism in a big way. He said he liked birds more than horses. Always had. That was my older brother.

He laughed when he heard we were staying at the Northern. "You remember, mother used to say Bill Trask once rode his horse through the lobby."

I reminded him that that was the old Northern.

All along the Yellowstone are located frontier cemeteries. The living seem to find consolation in staring from tombstone to rippling water and back. One of the largest, and oldest, is the Mountview Cemetery, on the outskirts of Billings. Mountview holds personal meaning for me.

I was not at my father's bedside the day he died. I was not there when he said his last words, which make me feel terrible whenever I think of them: "Things didn't turn out the way I thought they would," he said at the Mayo Clinic to a cousin of ours who was a doctor there.

I missed the funeral in Billings, too. I just did not know what had happened. He was seventy-six. I was eighteen and puking sick in a slum hotel in Barcelona. It was the summer of '68. I was hitchhiking through Europe with my girlfriend. When she and I recovered enough from whatever it was to read the Paris *Herald-Tribune,* we came upon the notice inserted in the paper by my older brother. But by then the funeral was over.

We flew from Paris to Montana anyway. I wanted to see my father. I wanted to say good-bye. I was very distraught. I got together with a couple of other good friends, located some shovels and picks, and we drove to the graveyard. It was quarter moon. Across the river at the base of the Pryor Mountains was Sacrifice Cliff. The definition of good friends in those days was that they would do anything for you. There were four of us and nobody raised the question that this was a borderline insane thing to do. Or that we might get arrested. I did not care if we got arrested, either, though I think I knew that if we had been thrown in jail, we would have been released, and no notice would ever have appeared in the daily paper.

We got out of the '67 Impala, my father's car then, and opened the trunk to get the digging implements. I was not crying, but I paused. I was not crazy, just grief stricken. I called a halt to it. My father was dead. I had my memories. They will never be enough.

Most boys growing up never understand that their fathers are growing older at the same time they are, as I had told Woodenlegs. They don't understand, until that night beside their river's edge, when they suddenly realize it is too late.

It never really occurred to me that my father was even old. Oh, I knew he was fifty-five when I was born, and that my mother was forty-four. Mother had been nine months pregnant at the wedding of Persis, then eighteen, sister-to-be.

But I never imagined that at eighteen I would be taking a shovel out of a car trunk, ready to rob the grave of my own grief.

Now I have Cody and Jack, two little guys of my own. Cody is loping down the slope of the Mountview Cemetery toward the Yellowstone, as his mother calls after him. Jack, soon to turn six months, is bundled in a snowsuit in my arms. (What an insane expedition! What an insane thought, to start down the Yellowstone with a five-month-old baby. But then, it has probably been done before, long ago.) Two babies, Cody and Jack, sweet characters who mean the end and the beginning to me.

My reasons for coming home to Montana are inextricably linked to my longing for this lost father. This afternoon, as the sun lowers itself behind the Pryors across the river, that much is obvious.

In San Francisco, the toddler once pointed to a picture of the Old Man in his summer army uniform, standing on two horses at the same time, a foot on the back of each, holding the reins with a highly concentrated smile. If either horse should take it upon itself to move a foot or two to the outside, then the young daredevil on top splits his crotch in a fleshy rip that takes weeks in the hospital to mend. Long ago, the Old Man had laughed while explaining that picture to me, because, foolish as the act was, there he was, foolishly doing it.

Naturally, I took the picture away from Cody. Who wants to set a bad example for a two-year-old? I mean, a bee stings either one of those skittish nags, and where will the great-grandchildren come from?

Pictures on the wall.

Fathers and sons.

How did I know the Old Man was going to check out of the hotel at the ripe young age of seventy-six? I guess it is a strange accident of menopausal fate and horny old people that I'm around to write this at all. Maybe I should have noticed that the photo next to the photo of the Old Man on the two horses is inscribed "Jan. 1919—the day I soloed," and it shows the Old Man standing in front of a very ancient war plane. The Old Man was a soldier not in World War II but in World War I.

Another tipoff was that the parents of my friends always addressed him as "Sir." Wisdom is a festering sore, as they say. We sons usually do not acquire it till we become fathers ourselves.

Of course, in my defense, the Old Man exercised a curiosity that crossed generations, and that could be confusing. He loved The Doors, for instance. The summer he drove me out to Yale, a year before the pain took him over and he died alone, we spent a weekend in Manhattan. He left it up to me to select the entertainment and I chose a Doors concert in the Village. We scored some of the last tickets, the most expensive, which put us in the third row from the stage. I was a little embarrassed as the evening wore on. Women stripped to their waists on both sides of us, and on a stage covered with bras ten feet away, Jim Morrison was pretty stuffed in black leather much thinner than my dad's bomber jacket in the "Jan. 1919—the day I soloed" photograph, but it was, historically speaking, a great evening.

We took a cab back to the hotel. I summoned the courage to ask the Old Man how he had liked the concert. He had been the oldest person in attendance, by a good half-century.

"What a beat!" said the Old Man.

Turned out the Old Man was tone deaf. He preferred music that rocked him in his seat.

I wish the Old Man could have lived forever. I wish he could have lived long enough to watch his older grandson wrestle with a three-foot-long plastic alligator in the bathtub. What a battle! Water everywhere, toy boats capsized, screams, grunts, laughter! Sometimes the grandson wins. Sometimes the alligator does. The Old Man would have had to pick up his book and stand back, the way I do, to keep from getting splashed.

It was my father who always read to me in the bath, or at bedtime. I got to hear the real *Jungle Book,* which is a lot more gory than today's video version. In the Kipling original, Mowgli set the tiger on fire and the tiger screamed in pain. Real blood flowed on every page, and when the Old Man got so engrossed himself that he read on ahead silently, I would have to call him back: "Dad, dad! What happens next?"

I wish the Old Man could have lived long enough to stand on the red cement steps of the Wreford Apartments in downtown Billings, where he finished his life in a $90-a-month, two-bedroom, third-floor apartment, with sleeping porch (I should also mention that he owned the building) and welcome us back to Montana.

But this day in the Mountview Cemetery, he would have been ninety-eight years old. That is pretty old. Even by Montana standards.

One winter too full of blizzards, the old folks decided we should drive from Montana all the way to Acapulco. Each night father would read aloud another chapter of Mark Twain's autobiography. Hotel room after hotel room, in places like Lander, Wyoming; Trinidad, Colorado; and Guadalajara—always over a dish of chocolate ice cream turned so slowly with a dessert spoon that I can see it still. We never made it to the end of that two-volume autobiography.

When you know you are going to die, the one thing you have left is time. The Old Man understood that.

As a parent, the Old Man had a gentle style. My mother might scream at some beastly misdeed by her little ones, my sibling predecessors from the prewar decades. But my father never did.

Once during one of their parties (parenting and partying never seemed mutually exclusive to them) I rolled a bowling ball down the stairs. It crashed through the glass doors at the bottom, calling a dramatic halt to the festivities. But nothing happened to me. My father could not stop laughing.

Before we left San Francisco, the toddler had inserted a piece of salmon in the VCR. I love that Hitachi three-head. But all I could think of was the look on the Old Man's face as the bowling ball came to a stop. The toddler didn't know what to think as I led him gently away from the stereo console. I could not stop laughing.

I think my father took childhood and children seriously. We were little creatures to him, imaginative beings with minds of our own, a strain of diminutive humanoids that he himself could learn something from. This is probably an old person's perspective. I remember that when my sister and brother organized their urchin buddies into two vicious mud ball gangs that proceeded to terrorize the neighborhood, breaking windows and about to put out each other's eyes, the Old Man, who was an attorney, arranged a formal truce. He set up two card tables on the front lawn. The neighbors gathered around. The head combatants were handed leather legal folders. My father wore a three-piece suit and the expression of a judge. The gangs finally shook hands. It was a successful summit.

My father felt himself to be a shy man, and he did not want to pass this trait on. He hit on a cheap solution. Everytime we recited the verse of a poem at dinner, we received a dime. A public pronouncement given at school garnered a quarter. This method encouraged some cheating, as well as memorization of the world's worst singsong standards, such as "The Charge of the Light Brigade" and "The Cremation of Sam McGee," but none of us turned out particularly shy, except, of course, for your author.

As far as I can tell, my father does not belong on the current menu of dad caricatures. He was not hard, drunken, and noncommunicative. He was never absent. He did not seem too soft. He was a long way from any kind of ethnic.

My father always kissed me good-bye on the cheek when I went away for a while. The idea of a man so macho that he did not kiss his sons would be a strange construct to the Old Man. I still remember the way his cheeks smelled on those occasions, or when he put his arms around me to help knot a necktie. I have never forgotten the Old Man's own neckties, either. That pre–Good War generation of American men must have been more formal than men nowadays, or else white shirts and neckties meant something different back then. But my father would always put on a necktie before Sunday breakfast. He knotted a tie before he went down to the locker in the basement and took the shotguns out of their cases to make sure they were unloaded, before we drove off to the frozen wheat fields to murder those beautiful Chinese transplants, the pheasants.

Perhaps older dads have the time to be nicer than younger dads. That makes sense, except that my father usually put playing catch ahead of work when he was younger, too. Or perhaps all the hullabaloo about absent fathers is a generational protest against that poor, oft-attacked, much confused, middle generation of dads, the dads of the fifties, that era of Ozzie and Harriet hypocrisy in the living room and everywhere else. But here is a third perhaps, one theory that definitely does not get much ink these days: Perhaps most dads are pretty nice guys who try their best, and this is what dads have always been. It is just that the sons and daughters of nice dads do not feel the need to write about it all the time. Their memories do not make them angry. Their memories make them feel damn good.

Once, testing and overtesting, the way we unthinking sons will, I played a mean trick on the Old Man. This event could have ended in disaster. It was bedtime. I had picked up an empty pint of Jim Beam my mother had tossed in the trash and then I had filled it with water and food coloring. So armed, I intruded upon my father, who was peacefully brushing his teeth in the bathroom. My father hadn't taken a drink of liquor for thirty-four years. He quit forever after a glorious week-long bender in the cabin beside Rosebud Lake, assisted by half a dozen fishing buddies and a pickup truck full of booze.

Ten years old, I took a huge swig of my ersatz bourbon. My father smiled. He guessed I had faked the contents. He turned away just long enough to wipe the toothpaste from his mouth. But I, clever little bastard, had imagined he would do exactly that.

The Old Man reached for my bottle. Nobody's fool, except my mother's, Father understood that his ten-year-old-late-in-life-gift-from-God was playing a trick on him. But in that second when he had turned to wipe the toothpaste from his mouth, I had switched the fake bottle to a similar one filled to the top with real bourbon.

He took such a heavy swig of the good stuff, spraying the liquor across the bathroom mirror, that his eyes turned instantly unforgiving, like the eyes of a grizzly who has been pushed too far by a playful cub, and I was afraid. The Old Man stared at me. Then he started to laugh. After all, it was a pretty good joke and, also, he had turned it around. Then I laughed, relieved. We laughed a little longer, a few seconds more, the both of us, I, about to begin my second decade, he, ending his seventh. Together.

Eighteen years old, pulling a shovel from the trunk of the Old Man's car on that hill above the Mountview Cemetery in Billings, a summer night in 1968, I was crazed with questions to ask him. But by then he was gone.

This day, I have only one wish: that his two grandsons could have thrown their arms around him.

*   *   *

My father's grave sits flush to the ground next to the tall, red, polished granite tombstone of his own father:

HENRY
CHAPPLE, M.D.
BORN
OCT. 21, 1861
DIED
JAN. 10, 1900

Billings: Dr. Henry

. . . In that ward there was a rodeo rider who had come out of the chutes on Midnight on a hot dusty afternoon with the big crowd watching, and now, with a broken back, was going to learn to work in leather and to cane chairs when he got well enough to leave the hospital. There was a carpenter who had fallen with a scaffolding and broken both ankles and both wrists. He had lit like a cat but without a cat's resiliency. They could fix him up so that he could work again but it would take a long time. There was a boy from a farm, about sixteen years old, with a broken leg that had been badly set and was to be rebroken. There was Cayetano Ruiz, a small-town gambler with a paralyzed leg. Down the corridor Mr. Frazer could hear them all laughing and merry with the music made by the Mexicans who had been sent by the police.

—Ernest Hemingway, "The Gambler, the Nun, and the Radio"

Sister Dorothy and I are searching for the room in St. Vincent's where Hemingway wrote "The Gambler, the Nun, and the Radio." My grandfather, Dr. Henry Chapple, started St. Vincent's. I was born there. It is a big place now, eight or ten stories, employing fifteen hundred people in its eight operating theaters and pediatric, orthopedic, and other wings. It is part of the regional medical center that is now Billings, with the oil refineries and the sulfur plant, the colleges, the banks, and the agribusiness supply houses.

St. Vincent's got its start in 1898, on the second floor of the Rademaker Building, in one of the rooms above Chapple Drugs and the Blue Grass Billiard Hall on First Avenue North. My grandfather, an Episcopalian, and Father Francis Van Clarenbeck, rode eight hundred miles on horseback from Billings to Leavenworth, Kansas, to ask the mother superior of the Sisters of Charity for help in starting a hospital in eastern Montana.

Hemingway fell off his horse while hunting near Park City. A bad knee injury.

"He stayed on the fourth floor," says Sister Dorothy, the archivist for the hospital, as we step off the elevator. It has taken a while to reach the fourth floor. Sister Dorothy stops to chat with everybody, surgeons and janitors, young and old. She treats them all the same, with respect for their work and for their commitment to the institution. Sister Dorothy looks to be in her early sixties, but she is seventy-six, the same age my father was when he died. The secular personnel treat her with the same respect with which she treats them, but with bemusement, too, hospitals being big business these days, and Sister Dorothy Hanley acting with such calm purpose that she seems to represent a former, higher, authority. St. Vincent's is Sister Dorothy's home. Its wards are her living room, dining room, and parlor.

We reach the nursing station on the fourth floor, pediatrics. Sister Dorothy nods and smiles to one of the six or so nurses standing there.

"Do you know where Ernest Hemingway stayed when he was here?"

The nurse, who is about thirty-five, dark pageboy haircut, full of body, smart eyes, replies slowly: "No." She seems to know who Hemingway was. She certainly knows who Sister Dorothy is.

Sister Dorothy turns to the other nurses. "Any of you girls know where Hemingway stayed?"

No, none of the other nurses do. Was Hemingway an early Montana doctor? They seem puzzled.

"What's this door lead to?" Sister Dorothy asks. She starts to open it.

"That—that's the nurses' locker room," says the dark-haired nurse who reads fiction.

"Oh," says Sister Dorothy. She opens the door. The room is lined with lockers.

"Beyond it is the nurses' conference room," says the nurse. This is nurse territory.

"Hemingway stayed here," says Sister Dorothy.

We walk through the locker room to the conference room. The big room has picture windows on two sides. The windows face east and south. We can see all the way to the Yellowstone, and Sacrifice Cliff.

"He had a good view," I say.

"He couldn't have stayed here," says the dark-haired nurse. "In the fifties this was the nursery."

"Hemingway was admitted in the thirties," says Sister Dorothy.

"He was?"

"Yes, fell off a horse in Park City."

Sister Dorothy thanks the nurses. We walk down the hall, down a stairway, which comes out at the TLC Ward, a place for patients who have been so badly injured that they may need help in relearning the basics of living—how to cook for themselves, how to sleep in their own rooms.

"That day," says Sister Dorothy, "Dr. Allard came in at 6:00 A.M., and took a look inside the general ward. Dr. Allard knew who Hemingway was. He walked out to the nurses' station. He pounded his fist on the table. Dr. Allard took over a while after your grandfather. He saved many, many lives during the polio epidemic. That was a scary time. 'Do you know who that man in the general ward is?' No, the nurses did not. 'That is Ernest Hemingway. Put him in a private room.'"

No wonder Hemingway liked Montana. He could not have been so famous in the thirties that the head of every small-town hospital in America knew who he was. And I wonder if Dr. Allard would have bothered to pound his fist for Rudolph Valentino, should Valentino have fallen off his horse during a celebrity hunt. The word has always mattered more than the image, in Montana, a place of hat *and* cattle.

But what kind of a man was my grandfather? He died when my father was seven. My only knowledge of him comes from recent off-river investigations.

Sister Dorothy hands me a bound monograph. It is by Sister Mary Paul, S.C.L.: "Some Contributions to the Midland Empire by St. Vincent's Hospital, Billings, Montana":

Sister Theodore McDonald and Sister Antoinette Ireton had great misgivings after their arrival in the city, for they found critically ill the spearhead of the hospital movement. Dr. Henry Chapple had gone on a sick call some 135 or 140 miles from Billings during the spring rains and his sickness had resulted. The doctor became very agitated when he saw that the Sisters were loath to recommend the hospital and said, 'If I do not live, someone else will help you. I know the country, I believe in its future. If you build the hospital now, it will be hard for a time, but I know your strength. You do not mind hardships and in 25 years the Sisters will build in Billings a $250,000 hospital.

January 24, 1892, my grandfather made another ride, this one on a sleigh, eighteen hours into the Snowy Mountains to deliver a baby. The Billings *Gazette* made mention of the house call:

Dr. Chapple had a stormy trip to D. W. Slayton's ranch in the Snowies last week. The call was urgent or the doctor would have hesitated to set out in the face of the storm then prevailing. He lost the road several times on the return trip but made the journey there and back in about 36 hours. Mr. Slayton's family is increased by one good healthy eight-pound boy, whose arrival was the occasion of the doctor's sleigh ride.

In 1904, Martha Murdoch, Dr. Chapple's wife, my grandmother, purchased a stained-glass window for St. Luke's Episcopal Church, in Billings. I stood staring at that window the other day. "In loving memory for Henry Chapple, MD," and, under the inscription, "In As Much As Ye Have Done It Unto One of the Least of These My Brethren Ye Have Done It Unto Me." Christ leans down. A woman proffers a sick child.

What did this man's life mean? I do not know. I think he believed if you were sick, you were his patient. I think he traveled too much. I know he died young, thirty-nine. I know he left no diary. His relatives revered him, but their memories, such that can be gathered, lack all detail.

"Dr. Henry Chapple died of Addison's disease on January 10, 1900, in Flagstaff, Arizona, after a lingering illness," Sister Mary adds in her monograph.

Addison's disease. Completely curable now. "Symptoms are increasing weakness, abnormal pigmentation of the skin and mucous membranes, weight loss, low blood pressure, dehydration, and gastrointestinal upsets. Once considered inevitably fatal, Addison's disease can now be treated with injections of adrenocortical hormones that enable its victims to lead a nearly normal life."

I once asked my own father why he never became a doctor. "They always paid my father with bushel baskets of wheat or cucumbers," the Old Man had said, and he laughed at the irony of what doctors have become.

What did Dr. Henry muse upon on that sleigh ride into the Snowy Mountains? Did he curse his luck? Doubtful. Did he enjoy the subtle epiphany of light off snow under moon as the lead horse trotted across ice and the woods whispered of new life? Doubtful. But eighteen hours one way in a blizzard and eighteen hours back, he must have done some thinking. Did Dr. Henry see a running cougar, as I would one hundred years later, in my own backyard south of Bozeman? Did he like to fish German browns with a bamboo rod and a #14 Royal Coachman, as my father did, or massacre elk with a 30–30? (Nobody in the family seems to have liked to murder the ungulates.) Or did he enjoy reading Shakespeare by a kerosene lamp, out loud to his wife? Montanans used to like to do those sorts of things. Did he drink too little or too much? I doubt that Dr. Henry saw himself as a saint. I think he did what he thought had to be done, and for his troubles the Queen of Spades was laid upon his chest, dying young.

Sister Dorothy takes me up a floor or two, round many corners, down a corridor until we arrive at the exhibition hall that depicts the history of St. Vincent's. It is a thoughtful and colorful collage. There, before an account of Calamity Jane as an ad hoc nurse (in town, not connected to the hospital, Sister Dorothy hastens to add); to the left of a photocopied page from the earliest admission books ("Plenty Coos," the admitting physician had misspelled the Crow chief Plenty-coups's name, who had suffered surgery on his leg); above the story of Liver-Eating Johnson, who, many claim, ate the livers of some three hundred Crow Indians and was once deputy sheriff in Billings, is a picture of my grandfather, Dr. Henry, as he looked in 1898, when he was mayor of Billings. Here is a dapper, serious fellow in winged collar with a striped tie, under a trimmed handlebar mustache.

We continue to make stops in the labyrinth of this large hospital until it is time for Sister Dorothy to show me out. In a corner of the tall lobby is a high glass case trimmed with white oak. Inside is a picture of Mother Xavier Ross, founder of the Sisters of Charity. A century and a half ago, she looked better than Anne Bancroft. Sister

Dorothy talks of why Ross became a nun, and then I think, Why did Sister Dorothy?

The question traps me for a second. I want to ask her. Sister Dorothy Hanley grew up in my family's neighborhood. She hiked the Beartooths with her father, who hiked the Beartooths with my sister-in-law's grandfather. "Rosebud Lake in the Beartooths," says Sister Dorothy of the headwaters of the Stillwater, "is the most beautiful place on earth."

"Along with the tea fields of Sri Lanka," I say, having been to both places. "I don't know about Sri Lanka," says Sister Dorothy, polite but not wanting to put the mountains of Montana in second place. I admit it is a close call.

I look at this cheerful, precise woman, with her fine bones, rimless glasses, gray skirt. She is the sort of person who makes you feel imperfect, but with a glad heart that she is doing in life what perhaps you should have, or who knows, may, in another life. Let's not be hard on ourselves just because we have been sentenced to paddle the length of the Yellowstone and muse.

I wonder when Sister Dorothy last read "The Gambler, the Nun, and the Radio." Hemingway, if you know his work, had a thing for nuns, but how many nuns have ever read him?

"When I was a girl it seemed so simple," [said Sister Cecilia]. "I knew I would be a saint. Only I believed it took time when I found it did not happen suddenly. Now it seems almost impossible."

"I'd say you had a good chance," [replied Mr. Frazer].

"Do you really think so? No, I don't want just to be encouraged. Don't just encourage me. I want to be a saint. I want so to be a saint."

"Of course you'll be a saint."

"No, probably I won't be. But, oh, if I could only be a saint! I'd be perfectly happy."

"You're three to one to be a saint."

"No, don't encourage me. But, oh, if only I could be a saint! If I could only be a saint!"

"How's your friend Cayetano?"

"He's going to get well but he's paralyzed. One of the bullets hit the big nerve that goes down through his thigh and that leg is paralyzed. They only found it out when he got well enough so that he could move."

"Maybe the nerve will regenerate."

"I'm praying that it will," Sister Cecilia said. "You ought to see him."

"I don't feel like seeing anybody."

"You know you'd like to see him. They could wheel him in here."

"All right."

. In the lobby of St. Vincent's, Sister Dorothy says, "The founding mother did what needed to be done. She did what was in front of her. She did what people needed. She wanted to help people in the most direct way. In the same way your grandfather needed a hospital."

Hemingway, if memory serves me well, was also a fallen Episcopal, like Dr. Henry.

I did not ask Sister Dorothy why she became a nun. It was my full-moon duty to ask, but it would have embarrassed both of us, especially me.

My grandfather Henry came to Billings from Toronto in 1889. Three Montana families from Canada—the J. D. Mathesons, engaged in the newspaper business, the Pentons, who were ranchers, and the John Rixons, who were in printing—wrote to Trinity Medical College, requesting a physician. My grandfather was second in his class. It was eastern Montana's second request for an Episcopalian physician. He wanted to go to Montana. This was the way it was done.

Billings was a tent town on the Yellowstone then. I have a picture that used to hang in my father's office. It is by L. A. Huffman, dated 1882. It shows a short, single street. The south side of the street is empty and fades off to the Yellowstone and Sacrifice Cliff, the same view Hemingway would later have from a higher elevation. The north side of the dusty street is lined by white canvas saloons: the Blue Grass, the Buffalo Grass, and the Bunch Grass. It is not hard to imagine the clientele who would be attracted to drinking joints with the names of vascular plants. Texas cattlemen were driving their animals north.

"At this early state in the growth of Billings, the gambler, the dispensers of strong drink, and women of the 'red light' were numerously represented in Billings and plied their several occupations, brazenly," a Congregational minister of the time claimed. What a string of moronic clichés only a Congregational minister could come up with. Not that everything he said was not true. But in what measure? And in what mixture? And who else lived in Billings? My father was buried by a Congregational minister, but at heart both men were Unitarians, if that.

Within a year the Northern Pacific had laid tracks through town. A hundred thousand pounds of silver bullion was transhipped from the Judith Mountains. The army of the plains needed resupplying. Farmlands were opening, first to pioneers, soon to waves of immigrant sod busters. Tents were folded. Buildings were built with lumber. A pretty good basin of oil north and east of town would be discovered—but not for another forty years or so, and not enough that Montana would become another Texas.

In 1887, two years before my grandfather arrived, there was a last Indian scare. It was a strange one, since it involved the Crow, some of whom had scouted for Custer on the side of the whites against the townspeople.

A young Crow warrior named Wraps-Up-His-Tail went to the Bighorn Mountains and fasted. In his vision he saw the son of the Morning Star sweep a sword through a forest. Trees fell. Wraps-Up-His-Tail understood this to mean that if he wore a sword, soldiers would fall like trees before him. In one account, Wraps-Up-His-Tail and his followers wore red flannel and rode horses of the same color. They all carried swords. Wraps-Up-His-Tail believed he was invincible because he was following his vision. He and his band stole sixty horses from the Blackfeet, then returned to the Crow Agency. They did not like the agent. They fired on his headquarters. Gen. Alfred Terry was notified. He decided to proceed with caution. Citizens of Billings called a meeting. Troops from Bozeman took the train to Billings, but turned around. A fight was soon provoked.

Wraps-Up-His Tail, who is now called Sword Bearer, made a "bravery ride" before the white troops, perhaps with the expectation that they would die when he slashed the sky with his sword. He was fired upon. His heel was hit and so was his horse. He rode into the hills. He was taking a drink of water from a creek. An Indian policeman named Fire Bear approached and shot him through the back of his head, saying, "This is for getting all these people in trouble."

My family never talked of any of this. The railroad came. The Old West ended. Civilization began.

Dr. Henry encouraged his brother James to join him. James was also a doctor. Henry and James sent for their younger brother Charles to dispense their medicines as town pharmacist. They installed him in a tent. The tent became a red brick building. The building became a landmark. "You Can Get Anything at Chapple's." My father's first job was to discourage shoplifters and to talk with old Spanish War veterans, to discourage them from buying legal morphine. This was about 1905. My father felt sad for those old sheepherders and cowboys, addicted defenders of democracy against evil Spain. Great-Aunt Jennie came down from Canada and married a British cattleman named Graham. Lou became county attorney. Tom Chapple started the furniture store. Great-Uncle Charley invited Plenty-coups and his wives to lunch on his front lawn when they came to town. Jane Rixon, Charley's wife, did not like that much, according to their granddaughter.

Billings was prospering. The town was named for Frederick Billings, a Vermont banker and Northern Pacific railroad executive. His son Parmly and his nephew moved to the town that had offered up its name to Eastern capital in that optimistic if sluttish manner of Western towns wishing to guarantee their future. The Billingses owned a huge chunk of bottom land, as well as their interest in the railroad. "I would rather be mayor of the city of Billings than president of the USA," smiled Parmly Billings. "We intend to annex New York, and there is some talk of hitching on Boston." So these transplanted Vermonters had a Montana sense of humor, at least.

Parmly Billings died the year before my grandfather was elected mayor, a year after Judge J. R. Goss became mayor. It was Judge Goss who set up the town meeting that asked the troops to look into Sword Bearer's "rebellion," as it is called now. Judge Goss's only daughter married Uncle Lou, whose son Wreford torpedoed the first Japanese ship of World War II, the *Haro Maru*. Wreford was also sent to rescue Douglas MacArthur in the Philippines but was waylaid because his submarine, the *USS-38*, sank a Japanese attack ship near Mindanao. That much is in the *New York Times*: "WREFORD CHAPPLE, 83/SUBMARINE WAR HERO DIES."

Wreford's cousin Charley, Jr., who invented the Isolette for preemies and grew up over on Yellowstone Avenue, maintained Wreford had actually rescued MacArthur, which I do not think is true. It contradicts the *Times*. My mother's version of the story, which I do not think is true either, contains one of those difficult-to-verify details that make history, not to mention the word of one's mother, always so imprecise. "Wreford's was the second submarine to reach MacArthur's position," says my mother. "They sent more than one, for MacArthur. MacArthur's furniture was there, his household effects, as well as several American nurses who had reached the beach with the general. MacArthur told Wreford to load the rattan furniture and leave the nurses. Wreford, of course, protested. He was told he would be court-martialed if he disobeyed. He took the rattan."

Americans swoon for their heroes. I doubt that the truth about MacArthur and his furniture has probably come out any more than the truth about Sword Bearer. In an account that Judge Goss wrote, he says that the news that Sword Bearer and the Crow wanted to "kill off all the whites that were in this country" came "through an Indian girl who was staying as a servant in the family of Paul Van Cleve, . . . she being a Crow herself. . . ." One wonders why, since the Crow had allied themselves with the whites for generations, they would suddenly rise up like Sioux. The Salem witch trials were also started by a servant in a home. Hysteria serves a purpose, as often as not, and soon enough. In Massachusetts, the lands of witches were confiscated. In Montana, Indian reservations were further circumscribed.

Wreford was named for my great-grandmother, whose people took their name from Wree's Ford, in Kent. She married my great-grandfather William after he returned from the 1840s gold rush in Australia. In the 1980s the Brazilian and I visited Wreford on Coronado Island, off San Diego. Wreford's wife, Mary, went to the kitchen to fix us a couple of Mountaintops. It was past lunch. Wreford could move only one side of his body by then, from stroke. He motioned quickly with his hand and eyes. Ines drew close. He put his fingers up in a V. She took the Marlboro from her mouth and put it in his. With an eye on the pantry he sucked the forbidden cigarette as fast as he could. Then he handed it back. He lived years longer, of course, checking out of the drugstore at eighty-three. He was tough. He had seen worse things than his own body giving out.

I lived out high school in the house where Admiral Wreford grew up. It was built in 1911 by his father and mother, Uncle Lou and Aunt Marion. My mother bought the place years later, in 1965. One of my girlfriends, when she got drunk, would toss pebbles against the second-floor window Wreford's mother had installed. The window is now the atrium over a hot tub.

After I heard those pebbles, I would tiptoe downstairs, high school heart pounding. One night my girlfriend arrived with another girl, who was wearing a light-green cashmere sweater with little pom-pons at the collar. (That woman is now an Evangelical. Even the transgressions of a James Swaggart cannot faze her.) I carefully slid tight the white oak doors that divided the living room from the music room, and the three of us, sitting in the same sofa chair, listened to "Surrealistic Pillow" and "Highway 61" until the morning birds disturbed us and we went up to my bedroom, popped off the screen, and shot the noisy birds from their perches with a Daisy pump. The copper BBs did not harm them, those glistening black grackles with the tiniest of topaz eyes. They flew off into the dawn, annoyed and maybe a little bruised.

The three of us in the blue sofa chair? I don't know about the other two, but I remember the clack of those stones against the window Judge Goss's daughter built, the way Proust tasted his madeleines.

Historic Homes of Billings

I T IS A STRANGE FEELING TO VISIT A HOUSE you grew up in as a child. Everything, yet nothing, has changed.

I walked slowly up the front steps to 302 Clark Avenue in the old historical district of Billings, where I had lived before high school. I could see through the leaded windows. The bookshelves still lined the walls of the living room, from floor to ceiling. The mahogany trim had been painted over, white. The open fireplace was heat-ilatered.

A blond woman in her thirties came to the door. It was 9:00 P.M., a Tuesday, snow on the ground. I explained that I had lived in the house from the time I was born until I was six. I was writing a book. Would it be OK to look around? The woman did not find this odd, nor did she refuse. She was a corporate bankruptcy lawyer, from Missoula. Her husband was a tax lawyer, raised in Hardin, on the Crow reservation. He was working late at one of the new bank skyscrapers downtown. But he would be home in a few minutes. The two of them, she said, had a rowboat, and they liked to take it out in the spring and float the Bighorn River above Custer. The pelicans were mating then, and the beaks of the males were covered with strange small bumps. Her husband soon returned.

He was cordial. He wanted to find out who had lived in their house. What were they like? It was a question I was struggling with from a different angle. I said my family had moved there in 1931, twenty years before I was born. The home had been built by a pioneer lumberman named Swearingen for his daughter. I blurted out that the place seemed so small now. "It's very cozy," they said. They shrugged about all the oak and mahogany being painted over. They were thinking of stripping off the paint. The bankruptcy lawyer was pregnant. The baby would be born about the next time the pelicans mated on the Bighorn.

The French doors at the bottom of the stairs were still there. I told them about the time I rolled a bowling ball through the doors during a party my parents were having. The upstairs bathrooms were still adjacent to each other. The same black linoleum covered one, the same blue linoleum the other. I told them the daughter of the Presbyterian minister, when she was four or five and I was five or six, used to run up from the pool in the backyard, warm up under the hot faucet in the blue bathroom, soap ourselves down, and slide around in the tub together. I looked at the tub and thought how small we must have been to slide together down its sides and across its small bottom.

The blue bathroom was next to my room, where my nephew once locked everybody out and got into my older brother's fly-tying fishhooks, which he stored in shoe boxes on the closet shelf. My mother and sister had brought in the fire department, which cranked the hook and ladder from the street all the way to the window and extracted my nephew from the boxes of hooks and flies. He was happy at his work, my little nephew. The neighbors gathered around and talked. The firemen seemed to have had a fine time. My mother and sister were not in the least embarrassed.

Next to my room was the room where my parents slept. In front of their door was the hall landing where my mother had once told my sister and brother she was leaving my father, and to get their things together, and quickly. My brother, twelve, and my sister, ten, stepped into the third bedroom, where they polled each other, and when they stepped back to the landing, the calculus of my family was broken like the sound of a bone snapping in winter snow, in a silent forest, and forever. My sister said they were not going with her. They would stay with my father. So nobody went anywhere, though everything changed. The sound of that crack provided all context for my own coming a decade later.

Next to the landing was the third bedroom, always an exciting place. We called it the Tiger Room because tigers came out at night from a half-sized door in the wall connected to an attic crawl space.

Late at night it was risky to leave the bed in the Tiger Room and try to make it to one of the bathrooms for a glass of water.

Tigers.

I told this to the new residents and they laughed. The Tiger Room was to be their nursery. It already had a crib alongside one wall.

We went outside. The trellis was gone from the south end of the sun room. The apple tree—from which I had once broken my wrist jumping from the first limb to a chaise lounge mattress, the tree whose apples we plucked to break the little glass panes in the garage, which used to hold arcade games and, before that, a pigeon aviary, where the noisy cooing pigeons were once shot and killed by a neighbor's .22 while the family was on vacation—the wonderful old apple tree was gone. The garage-aviary-arcade was now an office.

The whole place was so small. It was disturbing and caused shivers at the same time. I was a tiny person then and the rooms were like concert halls for symphonies I had no way of understanding. Yet there was the swimming pool. The swimming pool in the backyard looked even bigger than I remembered it.

"You don't need a swimming pool in Montana," said the new woman this night. "A hot tub is enough."

I laughed. I said my mother liked to swim. She liked to swim in the morning after breakfast and at sunset, too, weather permitting. That pool was as important to me as the house, for my love of rivers, and my wanderings to Hawaii and Brazil, Polynesia and Australia.

I told them that my father won the swimming pool in a poker game.

"That must have been some game," said the man.

Perhaps it was. Though poker was an American ritual then. There are many types of poker: stud, draw, anaconda, hi-ball lo-ball. But I think there are only two kinds, really. Talk-a-lot fun games and games where you pretend your soul's riding on the next card.

I don't know which type of poker my father was playing when he won the swimming pool from a local sand, gravel, and concrete man, but I know nobody in Montana ever welshed on a bet back then. I know old ranchers and old real estate people in Montana today who say things have gone to hell in this country because a deal for a thousand acres, or whatever, can no longer be sealed with a handshake, paper to be sent over by the lawyer delivery boys and girls, later. Of course, they are right.

The pot in the game was not so big that my father won the whole pool. He won only the concrete, delivered. He had to dig the hole himself. For this he went to the hardware store and bought ten shovels, then he stopped by the unemployment office and hired ten men. It was 1933, the Depression, and they went to work on that hole right away.

New people had installed a heater and a pool cover. I could understand that. We used to have a chicken wire and piping net. Neighborhood dogs walked out on the net when they were thirsty. So did raccoons.

With no heater and no chlorine, the pool was drained once a week and refilled. All those gallons. Each week during the swim season, I and the other neighborhood children scrubbed the algae off the bottom of the emptied pool and off the walls. If you wanted to swim in the pool, then as now, one of the few private pools in the county, you had to get down on the bottom with a scrub brush and scrub.

Pool opening each May was a ritual to equal pelicans mating on the Bighorn. The neighborhood was invited over. The adults drank champagne at poolside, often wearing overcoats, since the ground might still be covered with snow. We shivering kids in our cotton bathing suits prepared to dive in. The adults threw handfuls of nickels, even quarters, into the icy water, and we beach boys and girls plunged for the money, squealing.

There is a coffee table book in Montana called *Historic Homes of Billings,* and it is not too bad, full of brown line drawings and quotes from architects on the beauty and significance of the "pioneer style." My house at 302 Clark is in the book, built in 1914, a pup by New England standards, a grizzled dog by Montana's. So is that house I camped out in during high school, at 1029 First Avenue North, now fenced across from the new Deaconess psychiatric hospital. "This stately home has seen many changes since it was built in 1911–12 by Lou W. Chapple, a Billings attorney."

But the authors of *Historic Homes* did not seem to realize that the swimming pool in the backyard of 302 Clark was won in a poker game, or that tigers lived upstairs, or that over on First Avenue North, giggly girls, fun-drunk as only proper young Western women can get, used to throw pebbles against the west window and invite themselves inside while the pioneers, mom and dad, slumbered on. Or did they.

Why Montana Does Not Need Outlaws

A FEW WEEKS AGO, at a prairie dog town above Greycliff, the fourth generation, Cody and Jack, ran laughing and screaming, so excited, among the burrows, as the prairie dogs popped up here, then there, then over there, all across the sage flat and the dirt mounds north of the river, whistling and dodging, seeming to play with the boys the way canine dogs might. Fourth-generation Montanans, finally.

First generation: Dr. Henry, Dr. James, Charles, Lou, Jennie, the others. Close-to-the-chest saints with a sense of humor. Lou once answered one of those Who's Who books like this: Present work—*Disagreeable*. Official position—*Holding the bag*.

Fourth generation: Montanan-Brazilians raised, one summer, on the Yellowstone, and who can guess the outcome?

Third generation: puzzled thrill seeker, at best.

But that second generation. To me, those people are what America was when America was true, blue, and unconfused. The country maintained an innocence of purpose then. We had forgotten what we had done to the Indians. We would not yet examine, through spot-news carnage of German shepherds biting Negroes under the spray of fire hoses, what we had been doing to Afro-Americans. Which is not to say that good people had not always tried to do what they thought was right.

That is what this second generation of Montana pioneers was all about. They attempted with unwavering moral principle, rarely fueled by any belief in God (at least within my family), to do right, keep quiet about it, find mates who saw things the same way, drink a little scotch, travel the earth, never give way in the face of evil, make enough money to wake up late, after replicating the genetic material, maintain a certain shyness, by use of wry humor, always poking the listener with a little stick to ascertain if the listener found life to be as strangely amusing as they did. This was pretty much the credo of the Western WASP, a species as little understood as the kingbird.

Once a national magazine wrote a story about Wreford. This was in the days before the out-of-state media was pumping up the Kennedy and Bush biographies. The story became the basis for a television series called "Silent Service." Run silent, run deep. *Ahh—ooh—ga! Dive! Dive!* In the blue bathroom at 302 Clark, I used to act out the part where they closed the viewfinder, pulled down the periscope, and dove deep.

The sidebar of interest is titled "Lieutenant Chapple Writes About Himself." If you really took out the first Japanese ship of World War II, like some A-tag deer in the Little Belt Mountains, this is how you talked, second generation:

> . . . I was born in Billings, Montana, in 1908, to Lew W. Chapple, an attorney and Marian Goss Chapple. . . . The other three years [at the naval academy] I managed to win a couple of letters at football and boxing. In football I played in some of the big games and some of the smaller games, and gained a reputation on the squad as being the best man the Navy ever had for keeping warm on a cold day with one blanket.
>
> In the intercollegiate boxing I had the doubtful distinction of winning a three-round decision from Steve Hamas. However, due to a slight mistake, we had to fight an extra round during which he left no doubt in my mind or anyone else's mind about who was the better boxer.
>
> In my last year, for some unaccountable reason, my classmates elected me president, at which job I did little to distinguish myself. . . . I endeavored to become a flier but my instructor said that I wouldn't make one as I would be a menace not only to myself but to anyone else who might be in the vicinity. . . .
>
> In 1935 my boy was born in Billings, but unfortunately I was not present at the launching. I received a telegram from my father on my son's birth: "Six pounds, eleven ounces and all man." He later wrote that the boy looked like me but not to worry about it, that he might outgrow it.

Wreford's cousin Dick, who separated me from my mother on the floor below the floor where Hemingway gathered local color at St. Vincent's, gave an account of what it was like to do surgery underground while being bombed, during that same Good War that made his cousin Wreford an admiral:

"Major Chapple's field hospital unit was the first to operate in the South Pacific," wrote the Billings *Gazette*, "and during all campaigns serviced eight divisions. From Guadalcanal, his unit was sent to the Russell Islands, then to Kokornohu, and from there on to Munda on to New Georgia. . . . At all times the unit was within 125 yards of the main lines, and countless lives were saved with speedy surgery on soldiers critically wounded. . . .

It was never "Doc, take a look at this"; it was always "see that Joe over there, Major, he's got it bad." Their courage was courage "born of a courageous nation," said Major Chapple. . . .

In one campaign, Major Chapple worked, performing surgical operations, for nine days, with an average of two hours sleep a day, "caught in snatches, between operations."

During the unit's service in the Pacific, Japanese planes raided his outfit 453 times. . . . Major Chapple, on hospital leave until February 10, has had five attacks of malaria, and was flown out of Palau in mid-December, from where he was sent to the United States.

Now at 134 Yellowstone Avenue with his family, he looks back on his Pacific duty, and replied to the comment "two years are a big chunk out of any man's life" with a laconic, "It's a price that had to be paid."

A price that had to be paid. Courage born of a courageous nation. We no longer talk like that in America. I wonder why?

Cousin Dick died in the arms of his brother, Cousin Charley, Jr. Cousin Charley, who stayed up late inventing incubators, figuring out ways to correct hip dislocation in infants (beginning with his own daughter), postulating original theories for why congenital illness may begin in the womb. Charley, who, back then, as a lieutenant commander, angered his own navy superiors by once stating during a dinner at the Pentagon that military medicine was inferior to Montana medicine, and was immediately exiled to the Aleutian Islands only to be rescued by Wreford, who pulled some strings. Cousin Charley, Jr., who would wed five wives, was one of the few in that second generation who had time to keep a diary, because Cousin Charley, Jr., apparently did not sleep at all:

> As things quieted down finally, Dick was invalided back to the USA with a badly enlarged liver. After a time in San Francisco at the Presidio, he was sent home to Billings where he was to stay on a high protein diet. It was still war time and meat was rationed, but so popular was he with his old friends and patients that ranchers brought in sides of beef so frequently that Dick's family ate steak twice a day during his long illness. The ranchers would explain, "Well, this calf got caught in some barbed wire and was so badly cut I had to kill it," or with some other cock-and-bull story. And Dick recovered. . . .

Well, this calf got caught in some barbed wire. . . . There is a rare sense of community in Montana.

Cousin Charley's incubator for premature babies was called the Isolette. He built a cardboard model in his basement and persuaded his friend and neighbor Philo Farnsworth, the television pioneer, to manufacture the prototypes. When he had been a resident at Children's Hospital in Philadelphia, he wrote, "I saw only one baby come out of the premature nursery alive" in two years. "You can imagine the heartbreak of the mother whose tiny premature baby survived its early birth only to succumb to infection." The device worked but it had too many bells and whistles, and only Charley could service it properly. A friend who was an investment banker smoothed out the wrinkles. Soon there were three thousand Isolettes in American hospitals. Charley and his partners turned over the patent rights, and all profits, to Children's Hospital. A Montana thing to do, at least second generation.

Were these cousins a product of Montana, or a product of the times? Why did Charley come up with so many medical inventions? Why, for that matter, did a Jack Horner come out of extreme backwoods Montana (a place so backwoods there were no woods) to change our thinking about dinosaurs? Why send one of the youngest submarine commanders in the navy to pick up MacArthur, when this kid Montanan had hardly excelled at the naval academy, at least academically?

I think Montanans are used to operating completely on their own. They do not feel lonely on mountaintops. They think better up there.

They are more likely to create a corporation than work their way up in one. If the Crow steal the horses, they shoot a couple of buffalo and skin out some boats. If they happen to be Crow themselves, these days, they become Rhodes scholars or get themselves elected to Congress.

Montanans operate on their own, outside the norm, but this does not mean they are outlaws. There is a difference. If there is one operative myth about the West, however, it is the myth of the outlaw. I would argue that the outlaw is a foreign urban concept that has nothing to do with a place like Montana, and never has.

In Montana, the ethic of that second pioneer generation takes its place. That ethic is one of freedom, willfulness, independence, cantankerousness, isolationism, and, yet, responsibility.

Of course, there have been Montana outlaws. The most famous was Sheriff Plummer, who with his gang of deputies robbed and killed the gold miners of Virginia City, as many as one hundred men, over time. Nobody has ever glorified Sheriff Plummer. The town fathers did not regard him as some existential outlaw hero. They turned themselves into vigilantes and hanged him.

There have always been outlaw rustlers, too, in Montana, a few. Some of these became legal ranchers after compiling a herd made up of unbranded calves from other people's herds. This is a time-honored tradition and the descendants of its practitioners are quiet about the method of their grandparents' acquisitions. Other rustlers, even fewer, were hanged from cottonwoods, in the manner of Sheriff Plummer. And some who were hanged from cottonwoods as rustlers were, in fact, homesteaders who chanced to fence in some of the open range claimed by the big early ranchers. Granville Stuart, great pioneer cattleman, hanged both types. Some in Montana today would put him down as a criminal, though not an outlaw. But there were only a few out-of-hand ranchers, in Montana, compared with the number of those in the range war states of Wyoming or New Mexico.

No, the Montana outlaw is a myth started by New York's dime novelists of the last century and later pursued with vigor by Hollywood. The reason why the outlaw myth plays so well is that outside of Montana, average Americans must imagine their own freedom. Freedom is not much of a possibility in their own lives. If you manufacture automobile dome lights for a living in Tennessee, or punch a computer keyboard in San Diego, it is pleasant to watch videos of Billy the Kid, of Arizona; Butch Cassidy, of Colorado; or Belle Starr, of Oklahoma.

Inside Montana, what is the point?

In the Montana of the past, the upstanding citizens—from Indians, to mountain men, to miners, to cattle ranchers and homesteaders, to frontier doctors—led lives of such personal freedom and interest that there was no earthly reason for them to turn outlaw. Jeremiah "Liver-Eating" Johnson killed Crows, but this was as blood vendetta for the scalping of his Flathead bride. Nobody would put Johnson, a Billings deputy, in the category of Sheriff Plummer, not even Crow historians. Calamity Jane had room to whoop it up in Livingston, Billings, and Miles City. She never thought to turn outlaw like Belle Starr.

Modern Montana has had even fewer populist outlaws on the order of Bonnie and Clyde. It is too easy to own land here. The silly psychopath of New York, Seattle, San Francisco, and L.A. seems blissfully rare, too.

In Montana, you want to shoot an elk, shoot an elk. It is legal. You want to whip your kayak end-over-end down the Gallatin at spring rise, you can. Nobody will stop you. Nobody calls kayakers who poach the Yellowstone River inside the park outlaws, and it is stretching it to call environmental monkey-wrenchers outlaws, too. Montanans are not as alienated as other Americans. If they cannot seem to get along with other people, at least they can fish.

The outlaw is an out-of-state fantasy because Montanans do not need it, and it is an American fantasy because non-Montanans must have it.

In Montana, makes more sense to be a doctor.

It is possible to think about those in the second generation because hard copy exists on them. The second generation made the newspapers. Very hard to imagine what my pioneer grandmother was like, however.

Except for an article in the Billings *Gazette,* dated July 14, 1933, which states that my grandmother left one of the larger wills in the history of the state, anything I know about her comes from those who loved her too much or too little and cannot be prodded further.

Mattie Murdoch was also a pioneer Montanan by way of Canada.

She married Dr. Henry the day he graduated from medical school. When Dr. Henry died, she was left with three children under the age of ten, a small, yellow Victorian house that stood on the spot that now is a parking lot for the Ford dealership, and a little insurance money. By condition of my grandfather's will, her household finances were overseen by my grandfather's brothers. I imagine she did not like that much.

She got remarried, to her dead husband's medical school classmate, Dr. Armstrong. A couple of streams in Montana are named after Dr. Armstrong. He had a problem with cocaine, though I don't think this is why they named rivers after him. Cocaine alkaloid was then being touted as a cure-all by many out-of-state physicians, such as Sigmund Freud. Dr. Armstrong argued with my grandmother, I think a lot, and when sick himself, they say, he preferred to be administered to by the prostitutes on the south side of Billings, in an establishment a block from what is now the building that houses the Western Historical Society.

One such bar and bawdy house was called Casey's Golden Pheasant. My much older brother used to crawl up the fire escape outside Casey's, flatten himself, and watch the goings on. Casey's, if that was Dr. Armstrong's place, is gone now, though the soaring pheasant tail is still in use as the neon front to a jazz and blues club in Billings. I am told that as county health officer, Dr. Armstrong received $1 for checking each of the women for venereal disease. He saved these silver dollars and gave them to my grandmother for her allowance. If asked, I think Mattie Murdoch could tell you exactly how many prostitutes there were in Yellowstone County, on any given month she received her allowance from Dr. Armstrong. I imagine she did not like that very much, either. My grandmother's marriage to Dr. Armstrong was short.

Mattie Murdoch was good at figures. She could multiply three and four numbers in her head and give you the answer instantly, as if in a parlor game: 317 times 2,009 equals 636,853. She went into real estate. A relative once visited her in Los Angeles, in the 1920s. He found her playing canasta on the roof of the Rampart Apartments downtown, at a big table surrounded by other old ladies, except that beside Mattie's chair was a small table with a black telephone on it, and beside the table was a man, standing. When the phone rang, my grandmother put down her cards. The man handed her the phone.

My grandmother did business. The Depression was a good time to do business. All you had to do was sell high.

Grandmother introduced the apartment house concept to the mountain West. Not a literary concept, though perhaps it was something better, since it made a widow with three children able to smile in the face of the bankers who were often reluctant to loan her money. "The thing to understand about bankers," one of Mattie's grandsons, a spry oil man, told me in Billings, "is that bankers are stupid people. Stupid. I never met a banker that had an original idea."

The reason the apartment house concept was a good idea was that the West was aging. Those first-generation pioneers who had made money off wool, beef, wheat, and minerals were retiring. Ranches were far from the hospitals in Billings. People wanted a place in town. Mattie named her Montana apartment houses after streets in Los Angeles, where she wintered—Normandie, Kendace, Ardmore—and sometimes after the names of her dead first husband's family.

She traveled around the world twice. I have a picture of her sitting in a gondola in Venice, wearing a broad-brimmed black hat, a big woman with a strong, round chin and soft eyes. She preferred Asia to Europe, and I think that is the mark of a true Westerner, one that travels: The farther west the better.

When my own mother, who had no love for her mother-in-law Mattie, started off by herself around the world, at age sixty-four, she spent only a few hours in France, in the airport. "Why didn't you check out Paris?" I asked her.

"What's the point of Europe?" my mother answered. "That place is over."

Murdoch is a Scotch-Irish name, and the Scotch-Irish are the backbone people of the Western WASP. In old Montana, the British Isles divided into Wales, Cornwall, Scotland, and England. People knew what it meant to be Scotch, to be Irish, to be Scotch-Irish, and what the difference was. Because of immigrant homesteaders, the coal miners, and the big copper mine at Butte, Montanans have also always known that Swedes are different from Norwegians and Icelanders are different from Finns. Only in Montana would it be considered titillating to have a blue-eyed, blond-haired Swede roosting in the family tree. Only in Montana would a relative of mine say, "We're mostly British but some frog blood may have crept in, some time back," meaning the seventeenth century, or 1066.

For being Huguenots, the Chapples were booted out of France. They landed in England, and, I am told, were soon dispatched to Ireland. Soldiers under Oliver Cromwell, a few of my relatives married the Irish temptresses whose brothers and fathers they had murdered in the name of religion. Soon, they lit out for Australia in search of gold, or journeyed up the Missouri to the Yellowstone, where they found open ground. A restless bunch, the Western WASP.

Wanton Banshees

THE YELLOWSTONE STAYED FROZEN. It was hopeless. One night after dinner, we drove past the old stockyards to the bridge that is almost in the shadow of Sacrifice Cliff. We stared down at the ice cakes slugging through what current was still flowing.

We went over to Kmart and picked up a couple of plastic sleds. Then we drove across town to Pioneer Park. It was about midnight when we got there. The sledding hill was deserted. Jack was still only six months old. We bundled him round as a cantaloupe. Cody had never sledded. Neither had the Brazilian. In fact, until the storm, she had seen snow only once before, in the Andes near Machu Picchu.

Stephanie cackled with joy. She caromed down the slope in her green army surplus greatcoat and her high-top Reeboks. Stephanie had become a friend. She did not seem to view her chores as work. She acted as if she were in Tanzania, on some great adventure. I guess that is where we all were, on an adventure. It was all coming together and all ending at the same time. Who would have imagined a little river trip could tear your author's heart apart so easily and so often. I had not sledded Suicide Hill in Pioneer Park for far too long.

We took turns sitting in the Trooper with Jack, keeping the heater running. The rest of the time we screamed down the amateur powder of Pioneer Park like wanton banshees. We fell off the sleds.

We ran over each other by mistake. We missed trees and we slammed into a couple. It was almost full moon, once again. By quarter moon next, the Yellowstone would be frozen solid as a brick, some places.

Summer in Montana, it would appear, was coming to an end.

PRAIRIE

Milliken Slough

The Moon of Shedding Ponies: May 22, 1992

STROBEL AND I SHOWED UP AT THE BACK DOOR of Darrel Laubach's ranch house on Milliken Slough east of Big Timber, kayaks in hand. The Laubach sheep ranch was as far along the river as Ines and I had made it the previous October, before the Montana summer froze the Yellowstone. Now the rest of the family was in Rio de Janeiro. The game plan was this: I would complete as much of the middle Yellowstone as I could in ten days' time, alone, then fly to Brazil myself, to report on the Earth Summit. Immediately after those shenanigans were over, we would all fly north and hit the river at Billings.

Mr. Laubach welcomed us in stocking feet. On the back porch, we stood among a dozen pairs of boots and shoes. I do not think Mr. Laubach remembered me from the year before. I gave him a box of chocolate-covered macadamia nuts from Hawaii. In the last century the mountain men used to leave gifts with the Indians, and it is said that had the American cavalry been polite enough to offer sacks of grain to the Sioux when they passed through Sioux territory, many battles might have been avoided.

Mr. Laubach was surprised, though pleased, with the macadamia nuts. He asked only that we be careful how we opened the first gate on the dirt road to the river. Wild Canadian geese, almost tamed by stealing Laubach's grain, rose off the short road. The first gate was made of green iron pipe. Four horses, including a stallion, stood behind it in a paddock. We parked the Trooper as close as we could to the gate yet still swing it open.

Immediately, the big roan stallion charged. I jumped aside. The stallion pounded through. Strobel stuck his head out the window of his Honda and sipped from a Heineken. There was nothing else to do. The stampeding quarter ton of Mr. Laubach's valuable horse flesh turned on his own and started back for the gate, his tail high and flowing in the wind. What did he have in mind? Nothing. His circle followed the barbed-wire fence. He rushed the gate again, from the outside. I thought he might jump the Trooper but the kayaks were piled pretty high. He galloped back inside. Dave gunned the car and I closed the gate at a run. There was another gate to open on the far side of the paddock, but the stallion was finished feeling his oats. The horse watched us unload the kayaks and suit up.

The Yellowstone this time around was as contradictory as I was beginning to realize I was. Dirty as a sheep's coat after a hard rain, the spring river looked as if it should be warm to the touch. Instead, the Yellowstone was near icy with snow melt. The color came from silt. The banks were breaking down in the mountain tributaries and along the main river as well. In July, too, the Yellowstone is often muddy, but by then it is warm.

In the old days May and June on the river was called the Rise. Spring rise created havoc for the settlers in their flatboats and for the shallow draft paddle-wheelers like the *Far West,* the steamboat that carried the dead and wounded from Custer's Fifth Cavalry downriver, and the *Yellowstone,* which ran aground and sank in Buffalo Rapids above the Powder River. Below the Powder near Glendive, an agate hunter would tell me he had once seen a big cottonwood rolling root-over-top like a sixty-foot Ferris wheel, in the Rise. Truth is a casualty of reality, but maybe the old river still got to howling like that once in a blue moon. I hoped I would be there for it.

Of course, Strobel said the river was a piece of cake this time of year, because high water smoothed out the rapids. But, as usual, I had my doubts. Truth be told, it had been a long winter of anticipation spent in soft places, and I was a tad nervous.

We shoved off. The current caught the boats. Almost immediately, the river swept around a tall cliff of gray conglomerate rock. The next map point, long abandoned as a town, is called Greycliff. I measured the flow. The kayaks were traveling from cottonwood to cottonwood as fast as a good marathon runner could jog. Four deer appeared out of nowhere just as other deer had when I had floated this stretch with Ines. These deer also plunged stupidly into the water. The high current slapped them back to shore. The Yellowstone was pumping.

We began to hit rapids that in two months would subside to riffles. I found myself paddling for white water wherever it presented itself, for the fun of taking the spray in the face. Strobel found himself a standing wave and began to surf backward. He was stoked, and so was I. My heart soared. We saw bald eagles on the cliff junipers. The grassy hills were cheerful spring green and the trees a deeper emerald. Spring on the Yellowstone, after a winter languishing in the tropics!

Twenty miles later, we floated into Reedpoint, an old river village of two dozen houses, a white grain elevator with fading Occidental Flour signs on the side, and a turn-of-the-century wooden gym that plays home to the Montana Class C Basketball Champions, the Fighting Pirates. Reedpoint, where newscaster David Brinkley's wry partner, the late Chet Huntley, grew up, was pioneered in the homesteading days by dreamers willing to work hard, and busted by the drought of 1919, which did not respect dreams. Mrs. A. L. Guthrie penned an account of those times. She had owned A. L. Guthrie, General Merchandise, with her husband.

> 1919 was the driest year ever known . . . there wasn't enough moisture to wet a light blanket, and in vain did we try to collect our accounts . . . soon we gave up. The people had nothing and in 1920, farmers and merchants alike folded up. The farms were worth nothing . . . families that had been prosperous and happy were in despair . . . and so went out via the drought.

Reedpoint dreamed a more fanciful dream a few years ago, a Montana spoof that finally made the town prosper. Reedpoint is sheep country, and so Reedpointers felt little glory in the Bicentennial Cattle Drive that brought media attention to the state a few years back. The huge, sanctimonious cattle drive only reinforced the image everybody outside of Montana already held of the state—namely, that it was the same as Wyoming.

But people on this part of the river do not like cattle, and they do not like cowboys. They like woollies and sheepherders, washed or unwashed. Operating from the town's pulse point, the Watering Hole

("We Ain't No City Bar"), a small number of citizens came up with the idea for the Annual Reedpoint Sheep Run. Sheep would be pushed from one end of town to the other, which is not far. It would be a small affair, local, drunken, spirited, a few sheep, and no cowboys.

The first year, that's pretty much how it turned out. Next year, word got around. Ten thousand people showed up. "What do you have against cowboys?" asked one television announcer.

"We have nothing against cowboys, we just don't like them," said someone outside the Watering Hole. "We like sheep."

The main event of the Sheep Run is the Sheep and Master contest, in which the sheep are dressed like their owners. A dance hall sheep, for instance, wears an off-the-shoulder cancan dress over petticoats, as does its master.

It is easy to know, in Reedpoint, that you are back in Montana.

There was an old fisherman on the bank opposite Reedpoint. The man was in his seventies, tall and thick as a cottonwood. He was wearing blue bib overalls. An RV was parked behind him. He did not move or talk as we lofted the boats atop Dave's Honda. We sat in the car and planned the next day. We were only ten feet from the man.

Finally, I leaned out the window and said to him, "We're not staring."

He walked up the bank to us, but acted as if he had not heard.

"Want you to show me how to do it."

"Do what?" I asked.

He didn't seem to hear me.

"Want you guys to show me how to catch some of the fish here."

He was using a heavy spinning rod more suited for steelhead in the Northwest, and nightcrawlers. We had a discussion of spring baits. It was too fast and muddy to catch anything anyway. "How come you guys got two Jap cars?"

He meant the Honda and the Isuzu Trooper.

"They're good cars," said Strobel.

The man nodded and smiled behind his sunglasses, but he wanted a frank answer. I gave him one.

"Those dumb fucks in Detroit design ugly cars that break down in three years. These cars get forty miles to the gallon."

He heard that.

"I wouldn't buy one if it got a hundred miles to the gallon," he smiled. You could almost see the twinkle in his eyes behind his sunglasses. He had a very big, very smooth face for an old man, no wrinkles, a two-day beard, but clean. "I fought them Japs," he said. "That's why I can't hear. I was behind a twenty-millimeter Howitzer too long."

The man was wearing a ROSS FOR PRESIDENT button. "What do you think of Ross?" asked Strobel. Ross Perot would receive 26 percent of the Montana vote, including Strobel's, though the state would vote Democratic for the first time in thirty years. Strobel did not mind that Perot had once said the way to solve the old growth forest issue was to have a spotted owl over for dinner.

"At least he's already bought and paid for," said the man, of Perot.

"Bush has a few bucks," I said. He did not hear me.

"Clinton's totally loony," he said.

I had been thinking of a test for this man. "What if the only hearing aid in the world that would solve your hearing problem was manufactured in Tokyo. Would you buy one?"

"'Course not! 'Course not," he said again, though more quietly.

I told him that after World War II, until the day he died, my father refused to buy anything made in Germany.

"I'd buy a Volkswagen," said the man.

"What?" said Strobel.

"That's different."

"How's it different? They weren't allies."

"Well, that was in Europe."

We all laughed at the absurdity. The old man laughed hardest. He was a pretty good fellow. He up and told us what he did for a living. "I sold hardware and paint for twenty years. I sold insurance for about three years. I sold sausage for three years. I used to stay in the same hotel in Bremerton, Washington, pretty near every month, for eleven years. They always asked me what my wife did. I always said she was a professional wrestler. One time she accompanied me. Everybody pretended to be getting coffee or asking us about the weather, but they couldn't stop looking at my wife, and she's only this big—" He held up his little finger and chuckled.

"Where's the wife today?"

"Oh, this is just a fishing trip," he said.

After the man went back to not catching fish, Dave began the seventy-two-mile drive back to Bozeman, to work the night shift at the local newspaper, which his stepfather published.

Dave's father was also known in Montana. He had discovered the cure for Dutch elm disease. The cure was actually a biological control mechanism. A bacteria that grew on Montana barley plants produced an antibiotic that discouraged the fungus that destroyed the elms. Dave's father was a plant pathologist at MSU in Bozeman.

Dave said his father had recently found "the cure" for breast cancer and cancer of the ovaries, too, using a fatty substance called taxol that occurred naturally in the yew, which was a rare tree of the old growth forests south of Glacier Park. The cure had proven to be an effective treatment for 30 to 50 percent of refractive ovarian and breast tumors. Gary Strobel had discovered how to place a chip of Montana yew bark into a beaker solution and fool the bark into thinking it was still on the tree, producing limited amounts of taxol. Then he had taken a fungus that grew on the yew, discovered that the fungus also produced taxol in an exchange of microbes with the host plant, and finally genetically tricked the fungus into growing and producing more taxol. There were revolutionary elements to the various processes, but what the elder Strobel had done was comparable to what Sir Alexander Fleming had done in regard to the penicillin mold on the common orange. Dave's father would be on the cover of *Science* the next year, and I would call him up. "I was down in the dumps about my marriage breaking up," explained Gary Strobel, "but I told myself, 'You've got to go on,' so I asked myself, 'What does the world really need?'" There is a bit of a gulf between asking that question and coming up with a real answer, I thought then.

The cure for cancer. Not many river guides could say this of their fathers, and Dave had not mentioned the fact until this day. Earlier, several times, Dave had told me that he did not get along with his dad, because the father did not agree that the son should become an artist. (What a waste of genes, when one could become a microbiologist!) And Dave had told me that his grandmother was an Indian, from Pennsylvania. The father had once tried to search out his ancestors but it had proved impossible.

Strobel would return the next afternoon.

I scouted the cottonwood grove upriver for a place to camp. I circled back to the place the man had been fishing. He was gone. I decided to take a nap before I camped. I put back the seat and fell asleep. The voices of four teenagers woke me. "Oh, it's cold," said a girl's voice. I looked up. A new blue Ford pseudo-sports car was parked next to the Trooper. Four kids were wading the river where the deaf man had been fishing. They were wearing shorts and tight T-shirts, the two girls were. It wouldn't be dark for an hour. Now it was hot again. The girls were very pretty. One was a tall redhead, the other a short brunette. I missed Ines. It had been a week, a long time for an old Montanan. "Stop that!" called the redhead. "I didn't come down here to get in a mud fight!" The boys were tossing mud at the girls. The girls hitched their T-shirts and cursed the boys. The girls were growing up. The boys were not. I thought of girls I had known down on the Yellowstone, long ago. But I was very tired. Mercifully, the crowd moved upstream. I fell back asleep. When I woke up, it was long dark, and I didn't feel like setting up a tent. I guessed it would probably rain later in the night anyway.

I checked into a motel in Columbus, close to where Clark found trees large enough to burn dugout canoes, and where in the hills above town sliced by the interstate my father had once been smacked by a deer so hard at seventy-five miles an hour that the back left passenger door was stove in clean to the center of the car, about thirty inches. He and I had stood around in the garage and looked at the car. His 1967 green-and-white Chevrolet. It was a situation so bad my father did not have to say anything. "Almost killed you, huh?" I said. "Yeah," said my father.

At the motel, a truck driver in front of me was also checking in. He wanted to buy a mint pattie.

"Twenty-five cents for a mint?" he asked

"It's for charity," said the clerk.

"What's the charity?"

"It's for AIDS."

"They got AIDS around here now?"

Living a few years in San Francisco, it was not hard for me to guess the clerk was gay. This did not occur to the truck driver.

"You don't see too many AIDS charities around here," added the trucker.

"No, you don't," agreed the clerk. "Cancer and AIDS, I hope they find the cure."

While they were talking I noticed a framed picture behind the cash register. It was of another motel, somewhere like Texas. The big neon sign on top of the motel said, IT'LL DO MOTEL.

"The owners think that's funny," said the clerk to me. "It is funny."

The truck driver put back the mint. I asked for the quietest room. When I got there, I lay down on top of the bed with all my clothes on, and pulled the nubbly bed cover over myself, and fell asleep until morning.

Reedpoint: Soul of a Goose

AT NOON, WE LAUNCHED FROM REEDPOINT. Soon the river opened to a lush valley of hay and alfalfa hemmed by sandstone bluffs. The interstate crossed over the Yellowstone and the river began to run along the southern bluffs that rise eventually to the Beartooths. We came upon the Eagle Nest Ranch where we had wintered and the turkey had snatched Cody's mitten. The enormous metal barn, big as a football field, was done. The house had doubled in size, too. It was getting hot. I suggested we pay a visit. Strobel said if there was a chance for a beer this was a good idea.

We pulled the kayaks onto the low bank, and traipsed over the pasture where long before the horses had startled me after midnight and I had taken refuge in the ditch culvert that lay on top of the ground. Now everything was green, and changed.

Linda Fink was surprised to receive visitors from the blind river side. She did not invite us in for a beer, but she gave us a ride back to the river on a John Deere three-wheeler.

"My pink paddling jacket probably shocked her," said Strobel.

"Probably did."

Suddenly, we were among a family of geese. The current was fairly swift, even close to shore. The geese were floating as fast as we were. The goose and gander honked and berated us. Strobel paddled for a closer look. The six goslings swam in circles, panicked. The mother tried to lead them to the grassy bank, and five followed her. But for some reason, the last little bird dove into the eddy and surfaced farther from shore, out in the main current. He had swum the wrong way, underwater. He was being swept along with us. We were floating as fast as a man could run. The rest of the geese were on shore now. The gander waddled quickly down the bank, honking at us. Strobel tried to scoop the little gosling to shore with his paddle, but whenever he got close, the gosling dove again. Soon the little bird was fifty yards ahead of us, afloat but too tired to swim, floating on. The gander gave up waddling and honked from the bank. His honk was like a rumbling scream.

"Probably a meal for a ten-pound rainbow," I said.

"The way of the river," said Strobel.

We felt bad. Though the day could not get more beautiful.

Konrad Lorenz, the ethologist, writes that geese "possess a veritably human capacity for grief—and I will not accept that it is inadmissible anthropomorphism to say so. Agreed, one cannot look into the soul of a goose, and the animal can hardly give us a verbal report of its feeling. But the same is true of a human child. . . ."

Lorenz believed that animals are much less intelligent than we are inclined to think, "but in their feelings and emotions they are far less different" than we assume. This, writes Lorenz, is because the basal areas of the brain, where emotions are centered, are not essentially different, goose from man, while the forebrain, where the capacity for rational intelligence is centered, is indeed different between the species.

We felt bad, but the day only got more beautiful.

Dead Nurse Rapids

IN COLUMBUS, I WAS TO MEET STROBEL at the Busy Bee Cafe on Main Street, in the early afternoon. Strobel showed up with an old friend named Cha Cha, who was a surgical intensive care nurse in Billings. Her father owned a clothing store in Bozeman, and she had gone to high school with Dave. When I asked Cha Cha what she did, she said, "Suck hematomas and try to be careful not to drop nursing manuals on the chests of double bypass patients."

It was not until Cha Cha dumped at a pretty serious riffle, which we christened Dead Nurse Rapids, that I asked her how she got her name. "Just a baby name," said Cha Cha. "My grandmother was this little itty bitty woman from Yugoslavia, and she took care of me, in Butte. I couldn't pronounce my own name, Charlotte, and neither could she. I said Cha Cha. She said Cha Cha."

The Busy Bee is small. Two red plastic booths against the left wall, three on the right. The rest rooms are in the back, and clean. You can see the cook at work. Service is ambient if not slow, but the waitress never completely disappears from view. Before Strobel and Cha Cha arrived, I was trying to get more coffee. The waitress hovered over a booth with three people—two cowboys and a cowgirl. The rancher couple stood up and left. The waitress spoke German to the remaining cowboy. I forgot my coffee.

The waitress was a tall, curly blond, thick of body, natural in movement, light-blue eyes. She could have been anyone in this part of the state.

"Your German is very good," I said.

The waitress was from Bonn, Germany, as was her boyfriend, the cowboy. He was in Sweet Grass County learning, she said, "horse training."

I said, "This is like the Columbus of eighty years ago."

"Yes," she said. "I like this place. Doesn't take long to know everybody and they are all so nice. Lot of old people here."

"It's a nice place to be old," I said.

"If you don't mind the weather," she said.

She refilled my coffee. I didn't have much more to say. I thought of how we had spent Thanksgiving, the last week before we left the state. We were in the Grantree Motel in Bozeman, in the dining room, having a turkey dinner, about 10:30. The Brazilian was talking of the tropics. It was well below zero outside. We were the only people in the dining room. Then two other diners walked in. The woman was black, about twenty-two. The man was very pale, even pinkish, with a close-cropped beard. He was in his late fifties. They began to speak Portuguese. She was from Niterói, the port city across Guanabara Bay from Rio de Janeiro. He was Scottish. He was the captain of a yacht owned by a Saudi Arabian businessman, but in his off time he ran a little sheep ranch in the plains east of Red Lodge. We all finished Thanksgiving together, in the new Montana, talking about preg testing and surfing.

Strobel and Cha Cha arrived. We drove down Main Street past the New Atlas, which has one of the strongest collections of stuffed animals of any bar in America. There are coyotes, and cougars, and two-headed calves, great horned owls, and an old picture of two men in fur coats holding twenty to thirty trout in the over-three-pound class, strung on a rope between them. The New Atlas used to be a place where farmers dropped in after they had plowed a few acres in the morning and wanted a belt before lunch. There also used to be a lending library in front of the bar. When you finished a book, you returned it for another. Now video poker machines line the walls. Many bar owners hate these zombie machines, but the profit is too good. This trip, I had asked the New Atlas bartender what he thought about video poker.

"I like to hold my own cards," he said.

We drove on to the railway crossing, made a right past the Columbus Air Bowl, which Glen Fink had told me he was thinking of buying, past a factory that turned out wood stoves, to the bridge at Itch-Kep-pe Park.

Itch-Kep-pe means "rose," the Indian name William Clark used for the Stillwater, which tumbled out of the Beartooths to join the Yellowstone a little ways above Columbus. Clark had camped on an island there, July 17, 1806. Since joining the Yellowstone near Livingston, the party had not been able to find trees large enough to make canoes with. They were still on foot and on horseback.

"Shields killed a Buffalow this evening," wrote Clark in *Original Journals,*

which caused me to halt sooner than common to save some of the flesh which was so rank and Strong that we took but very little. Gibson in attempting to mount his horse after Shooting a deer this evening fell and on a Snag and sent it nearly (two) inches into the Muskeler part of his thy.

Clark dressed Gibson's thigh with wild ginger.

There being no timber on this part of the Rochejhone sufficiently large for a Canoe and time is pracious as it is our wish to get to the U States this Season, conclude to take Gibson in a litter if he is not able to ride on down the river untill I can find a tree Sufficiently large enough for my purpose. I had the strongest and jentlest Horse Saddled and placed Skins & blankets in such a manner that when he was put on the horse he felt himself in as easy a position as when lying.

Although an accomplished botanist and a man who would, with Meriwether Lewis and Thomas Jefferson, change the destiny of a continent, Captain Clark was not a speller, even by the standards of his time.

Strobel set his little yellow white-water kayak up on the clay bank above the Itch-Kep-pe Park bridge and stretched his spray skirt over the coaming. It was his intention to scoot down the bank like an otter and crash the circling pool at the base of the bridge. Cha Cha and I intended to enter more cautiously.

Up on his bank, Strobel waited for us to paddle through the reverse eddy and into the main current. My Spectrum tossed me first left and then right, like a skittish horse. After reaching the channel, I looked back at Cha Cha, who was doing fine, though stroking like crazy, in her bigger Aquaterra. I heard a bronco buster's whoop. It was Dave, slicing across the surface of the eddy like a speedboat. He was water-born.

I thought of the old Star Plunge in Thermopolis, Wyoming. Behind the big building covering one hot pool was a hill fitted with railroad tracks. You would walk barefoot through the snow in your bathing suit up the steps made of railway ties to a platform high on the hill, and there you would mount a wooden sled. I was five or six years old. The sled had car seats and no seat belts.

A cowboy threw a lever from inside the plunge, and the sled slid down the tracks and across the long, steaming outdoor pool, skimming the surface like some singed water spider. Then the sled sunk slowly into the pool, and you swam to the edge. The cowboy came out and hooked the sled with a weighted cable and winched it back up the hill. I don't remember whooping like Dave. But I was a kid, and shy. There still is a Thermopolis, Wyoming, two hundred miles south of Billings, morning drive in those days. I doubt they still have the sizzling sled contraption, but you can never tell, about a place like Wyoming.

The land river-left was cottonwood bottoms, rising miles in the distance across broken prairie to mesas. The grass on the spring prairie was as green as the shuffling leaves on the poplars.

Clark had called the cliffs to river-right "black bluffs," but nearly two hundred years later I would call them slate gray. The bluffs curled over the river from time to time like a sneering lip. On top, the mesas became foothills, knotted with cedar and juniper. The foothills were soon covered with spruce and Douglas fir until finally sandstone rose to granite, topped by the snow-covered peaks of the Beartooths, Mt. Inabnit, Grizzly Peak, the highest mountains in the state, with Yellowstone Park spread out behind them like a wilderness picnic table.

Down on the Yellowstone, we paddled on, often floating backward. There is a line in William Nealy's book, *Kayak: The Animated Manual of Intermediate and Advanced Whitewater Technique,* that says when proceeding downriver in the absence of rapids, floating backward is neither good nor bad. The lack of distinction was probably less tricky for Nealy than it was for us. I note that the back cover picture of this Nealy shows him boarding a Learjet, alone and in sunglasses, wearing a helmet and holding a kayak above his head, grinning like a five-year-old about to shoot the rapids of the Star Plunge. Most likely, Nealy was destined for intermediate water.

Our water was getting bigger. The rolling, gray cliff was becoming undercut. In the middle of the stream, all three of us were clumped together, talking, and paddling forward except for Strobel, who was drifting backward in time, trying to spot more bald eagles. We had seen one daytime beaver and three mature bald eagles so far. Full-grown bald eagles have the famous white head. Younger bald eagles do not and are hard to distinguish from golden eagles, which lack white feathers on their heads at all ages.

In front a quarter mile, the river made a turn. "That's a bad place," said Strobel, looking downriver, over his shoulder.

By now I had learned to take Dave at face value, and pile on a pound of silver. But I was enjoying the feel of the flow. Dave hung back. I was first. I rodded for the little froth of white below the cliff. The white rose to a tongue of caps three or four feet high. The promenade of whitecaps degenerated into a slippery riptide created by the flow from around an island to our left that had appeared, a quarter mile back, to be simply the left bank. Wrong. In the middle of the soup, I whooped to calm myself.

The boat fishtailed repeatedly at the back like a stock car. Water arced over my face. The nasty undercut below Clark's black bluffs turned out to be, at this time of the year, a streaking cave. Pure spring fun. The Rochejhone tasted of the mountains above it. I paddled as fast as I could, until the current pooled. I was beginning to enjoy this sort of thing. I swirled and glanced back.

Cha Cha was down. She was ten feet from her boat. Her hands were way too far above her blue life preserver. I could not see her head. Then I saw her trying to swim upstream. The boat floated downstream. Their meeting did not take long. Cha Cha grabbed the left side of the cockpit and held on. Dave raced for her, but he could not go much faster than the current would take him.

The big river swept Cha Cha past the long cliff undercut and the confluence of the channel ripping around the hidden island, to the left where the water became more shallow and she could finally pull herself and the boat ashore.

We took a break.

"Too bad we don't have any beer," said Dave.

"I could use a beer," said Cha Cha.

I extracted a split of chardonnay from the rear compartment of my Spectrum. Cha Cha took first hit. Dave broke ranks, not being one for wine on the river, but beer being absent, any port in a storm. Cha Cha drank most of the split in two gulps. We all shared some raw peanuts I had brought along. I loaned Cha Cha some spare socks. I am one of those people who believes in packing for a twenty-mile float as if it could always snow and you could always dump, and you want to be comfortable before the rescue helicopter arrives.

We took out at Park City, which used to have this pig farm that stank up the highway for miles but is now a bedroom community for Billings. We repaired at a place called Pop's, which is, unless I am mistaken, the only place to repair in Park City. The sign outside says:

POP'S INN
(WHERE SIDEWALK ENDS AND THE WEST BEGINS)

There wasn't enough room on Pop's sign for all the *the*'s.

We had some beers. Cha Cha let it drop that today was her first time in a kayak. She did not offer this as any excuse.

"We should call that place Dead Nurse Rapids," said Dave.

"Yeah," said Cha Cha.

A year later, when I called Cha Cha from a pay phone in Savage to try to locate Dave, I asked her if she had been afraid. "Scared shitless," said Cha Cha.

Duck Creek

CLAWSON IS A BACK-CHANNEL MAN. Roger Clawson, who had been my white host for the Crow sweat in the Pryors, met me at the Duck Creek Bridge, which would be our take-out. He stepped out of his gray Econoline Van wearing his blue gas station pants and a white sweater shirt. He ran his sad eyes over the kayak. Too fancy. Too good. Not a backwater machine. He suggested we ride in his Grumman aluminum canoe. We took the canoe out of his van at the put-in at Park City. He carried the canoe jammed inside instead of roping it on top, easier that way. The boat weighed a ton. Clawson is stronger than hell. He carried the heavy stern to the end of the gravel bar at the county park, bade me get in, and shoved us off, lifting the boat in the process, without even meaning to.

When he finally clambered aboard, his cheap, blue street shoes were dripping. Whenever we ran aground, and we did many times, since he eschewed the main channel the same way others in the West try to avoid the interstate, Clawson, at the back of the boat, would grab the spare paddle and propel us through the shallows with both arms, like a bear with two broken legs. I was simply a passenger.

We are about to pass under a makeshift bridge so low to the water that Clawson rasps, "Let's get down." I take the twisted thing above our heads to be the former undercarriage of a Burlington Northern flatcar. Quicker than I would believe he could do it, Clawson is lying supine over the rear seat of the canoe.

This bridge joins a cottonwood island with the extreme right bank. The island is occupied by an old trailer home and an expensive, green steel barn. Goats are tethered here and there on the island. I whip my head to the front. The low, flat, car bridge is fast approaching. I tumble to the bottom of the canoe. The ugly little mess of rusty bolts and girders could have been touched, had I the courage to reach up.

The whole minute took a second and then the end of the island sang by. Clawson was humming the old Everly Brothers tune: "Standing by the road in Sweet Grass, Montana. . . ." The side channel tailed left around the island. I could smell the spring grass and the cottonwood leaves rotting in water.

It had taken a while to reach this southernmost point of the Yellowstone between Park City and Duck Creek. Clawson had chosen right fork after right fork after right fork. Only the Beartooth Mountains lay farther right.

"I know a lot of people who wish they could return to Montana," said Clawson in his raspy monotone. It seemed Clawson always needed a quart of coffee to reach metabolic par (in the sense that Cahill used the word). "But they don't know how." He cleared his throat, smacked a low branch with his paddle, paddled harder, though there was no reason to paddle at all, the current was racing in this narrow channel.

"It's hard to give up making forty-five thousand in Phoenix to come back to twenty-five thousand in Montana, even though they know they will lose all that crime, the silliness, and get to breathe clean air." I think Roger meant "the silliness of their lives outside of Montana."

We hit a glimmering of the main channel. Clawson steered us back to the Beartooths, which at this point end, while the Great Plains finally begin.

"We appear to be in the beginning of the buffalow Country," wrote William Clark.

The plains are butifull and leavel but the soil is but thin Stoney and in maney parts of the plains & bottoms there are great quantity of prickley pears. Saw Several herds of buffalow Since I arived at this Camp also antelops, wolves, pigions, Dovs, Hawks, ravins, crows, larks,

Sparrows, Eagles & bank martins &c. &c. The wolves which are the constant attendants of the Buffalow are in great numbers on the Scents of those large gangues which are to be Seen in every direction in those praries.

The big river was about to take on a new persona. In a few miles we would reach the Clarks Fork of the Yellowstone, which slides around the east side of the Beartooths like a silver halter. It was about here that Clark finally found cottonwoods large enough to make canoes with. On his original map, Clark notes that Indians call this river the Lodge Where All Dance.

Strange name for a river, and maybe Clark got it wrong. But I wonder what that name means. I wonder what parties they must have danced in that lodge that was a river.

I used to own some land at the headwaters of the Lodge Where All Dance, at the back of Kersey Lake. At dawn, moose would appear in the meadow below the outcropping on my land where I most liked to camp, since the top of the moraine afforded a perfect view of Pilot and Index peaks, in Wyoming, only a few miles across the state line. I would stand up naked in the chill, the coals of the fire still burning, goose down sleeping bag wrapped around my shoulders, my compadre Arctic Ed, the malamute, arching his back in a stretch, and watch those big black ungulates munch my meadow grass. Then I would fall back to sleep.

In those days, I did not go to bed until three or four in the morning, even in the mountains, especially in the mountains, and in those days I always considered the uninvited appearance of bears or Sasquatch. Young and alone around a campfire above the tree line, the heebie-jeebies can tend to become your companion. In those days, if I liked the look of a lake on a topo map, I just set out for it, across whatever mountains, often so far off any path that I used to post notes on top of rock piles before leaving the main trail. If I didn't show up, eventually the forest rangers would know where to start looking. After my father died, I spent a month hiking across the Beartooths alone. The Beartooths have always been a good place to get some thinking done. It is in a little lake in the Beartooths that Hemingway's character dumps the pistol his father used to commit suicide. Montana is a literary landscape.

At last, Clawson acquired the main channel. He quit paddling, but he still hewed to the right bank.

I have a little picture of Clawson taken with the Minolta Weathermatic. The Weathermatic seemed to withstand spray and sand better than other cameras on the river, though I went through several Weathermatics. The Minolta company never bothered to honor their warranties, though I shouted at them over the fax modem from various hotels. In the photo, Clawson stands next to the Grumman canoe. Around his neck is a pair of birding binoculars, which appear to be worth more than his canoe.

On our float Clawson never said, "That's a house wren." He said, "That bird winters in Brazil. It is called a house wren." He called cormorants "corms." He said not to worry about the gosling Strobel and I had stampeded back on the Columbus section. Goslings that separate from their parents float down the Yellowstone until another pair of adult geese spot them, take them under their wings with a honk! and raise them as their own. Clawson did not say, "That's a swallow." He said, "That's a cliff swallow," or "That's a bank swallow," or "That's a cave swallow, that—barn swallow, probably lost, shouldn't be here."

A raptor soared high above us. Clawson raised his binoculars. "What's that?" I asked. "That's a good sign," said Clawson. "To the Indians [meaning the Crow, Sioux, or Blackfeet], that would be an eagle. It is a hawk. Eagles have flat wings. Hawk wings are dihedral. Eagles are good luck, so if you want to feel lucky, a hawk is an eagle. Indians are just like anyone else. They don't know their birds that well." He called mergansers "red-headed fish ducks," as Clark had. And he had a special affection for the kingbird.

The kingbird's scientific name is *Tyrannus tyrannus,* which sounds more like a dinosaur, or perhaps a Roman emperor despoiling himself, his friends, his clothing, and history itself. The kingbird is a little gray bird with a yellowish belly and a spot of red bloodish feathers at the top of its head. "You can't see the red unless it is a road kill," said Clawson.

The little kingbird is called the kingbird because it intimidates hawks and eagles. Downriver, near Forsyth, I watched as several hundred feet above the boat, two birds bumped against each other. One, a kingbird, was a speck. The other bird was a hawk, size of a tennis ball.

Some ornithologists believe that kingbirds attack hawks to drive hawks away from the kingbird nest. Ornithologists are practical people, as well they should be.

"Why do kingbirds enjoy bedeviling big hawks?" I asked Clawson.

"Well, just because they can," said Clawson. "If you were sort of a little guy, and you could fly around and make a fool out of some big joe, maybe you would."

I thought about that. Clawson is big, though not that big. He is six-three or -four, which many shorter people might consider large, but six-four is only on the verge of hawkdom in Montana. Touch the Clouds, who ministered to Crazy Horse after he had been bayoneted, was seven feet tall. A great-uncle of mine whose nickname was High Horse stood six-seven. When I was seventeen, my father and I were in New York. Boogalooing down Broadway, a little giddy from our four days of travel, my father told me the first time he had ever been out of Montana to a big city, which was Chicago, he had hung back his head all morning staring up at the tall buildings. By noon, his neck hurt, he said. I believed him. Who would say such a thing, unless it was true? But in New York, in Times Square, August 1967, my father turned to me and said, "Do you notice anything strange about these people?" I looked around us. "No," I said. "They are all short," he said.

"Now the *Wyoming* state bird," said Clawson at one point, "is the satellite dish."

I do not think I ever saw Clawson laugh. Maybe the start of a chuckle. Nothing I would call a chortle. Once he said that he and five friends had been floating the Yellowstone between Pompey's Pillar and Custer, where he had grown up, the son of a railroad worker. The six floaters piled into the restaurant at Custer, ordered a big dinner, and ate it. After a while, one of the guys says, "I'm still hungry, how about the rest of you?" Everybody concurs. Clawson calls over the waitress. "Give everybody what they had before." They had a second round of dinner the way others might have a second round of beers. "So hungry, could eat two meals." That was the big joke.

Clawson also knew his plants. He pointed out that the Russian olive, which I was beginning to notice along the banks, cropping up here and there like some hobo from Sacramento, had been introduced as a backyard ornamental but had soon escaped to the banks of the Yellowstone. Birds enjoyed the berries and spread the seeds.

Birds! I had never thought about them much, except to eat them. Now I realized the prevailing Montana view was that they were the descendants of the dinosaurs, little bobbing heads, on little bobbing necks, helicoptering off the confluence of Clarks Fork with the Yellowstone, road-tripping their way down to Rio de Janeiro, where I was about to fly, myself. *Que vida.* I was beginning to like birds. Though perhaps I was, in fact, just plain hungry.

Fried chicken.

The Blue Cat

THE NEXT MORNING I FLEW from Bozeman to San Francisco, where I holed up for two days at the St. Francis Hotel, writing. Then I flew on to the Earth Summit in Rio de Janeiro on a 747 packed full of rain forest activists, Malaysian cabinet officials, and incongruous rock stars such as Jello Biafra. Two weeks later, the family and I traveled without stopping from Rio to Sao Paulo, to San Francisco, to the KOA campground off Twenty-seventh Street, on the river, in Billings.

I have read that "of Montana's estimated 357 species of birds, nearly 150 are classified as neotropical migrants, that is birds that breed in or migrate through Montana but spend their winters in Latin America or the Caribbean."

So there was now an official name for what sort of Montanans we were: neotropical migrants. And no matter what State Senator Yellowtail had to say against the peripatetic meadowlark in favor of the stick-it-out magpie, we neotropical migrants were true Montanans in the best bird tradition.

The KOA on Twenty-seventh Street in Billings is the flagship of America's KOAs, the Mormon Tabernacle of franchised recreation. The cottonwoods are tall and majestic. There is a swimming pool overlooking the Yellowstone, a miniature golf course, many hot showers, stalls and hookups for RVs, dozens of spaces for tents, a video game trailer, a playground, a pond teeming with turtles and more.

KOA stands for Kampgrounds of America. There are thousands

of them in the United States. Like Mattie Murdoch's apartment house concept, it was an idea whose time had come. A man named Dave Drum thought up KOA. I first met Dave when I was five and he was running a pet shop, or it may have been a fertilizer and garden store with a pet department. Mr. Drum had tried his hand at many things by the time he was middle-aged, and was still cheerful. My mother had purchased a breeding pair of hamsters from Dave's pet shop, and breed they did, in the basement of 302 Clark. Soon my mother strongly encouraged me to sell the expanded herd back to Mr. Drum. She accompanied me to the store. Mr. Drum offered me an incredible $5 for the lot, which, of course, I could not refuse. It was years later before I found out it had been my mother's $5 all along.

Mr. Drum realized America was on the move back in the 1960s. He standardized the concept of camping, making it clean, safe, and cheap. The KOA corporation was listed on the stock exchange, and Dave Drum became a wealthy man. He ran for governor on the Republican ticket, and lost. The cheerful kid at the check-in counter told us KOA was now owned by the Japanese.

Dave Drum helped to accomplish one other thing. He and the others who sat on the Montana Board of Natural Resources and Conservation in the seventies saved the Yellowstone.

In the West, water controls wealth, though in perhaps no other state has a war to preserve the natural flow and beauty of a river been so successfully waged as it has in Montana. When the energy crisis of the early 1970s obsessed the country, a plan was hatched to dam and divert the river, using up to 81 percent of the Yellowstone's water to cool several dozen coal-fired power plants. I would find that the coal deposits of eastern Montana lie so close to the surface that a kayaker can burn his bow black with the decomposed bodies of dinosaurs and the horsetails they nibbled upon. Tenneco, Shell, Utah International, major power companies, and the Bureau of Reclamation rushed to secure permits for the Yellowstone's water.

But a strange thing happened. The people of the state balked. Montanans are skeptical energy users. Montana remains the only state to vote down the use of nuclear power. Hardly a "dam environmentalist," the conservative Drum seemed to be an unlikely general in the battle against corporate diversion of the Yellowstone. On the other hand, who needs unspoiled recreational land more than the owner of a company that owns hundreds of parcels located in scenic junctions throughout the West?

It was established that the Yellowstone must have a minimum flow, which meant, given the various competing demands on the river's water, that the Yellowstone was prevented from becoming a coal slurry.

So the Billings KOA came with memories for me. It was not just a place to sling a tent, though it was that, too.

Our camping space was at the very end of the first line, fronting the river, under a cottonwood, and just back from the pond where Cody and I spent hours trying to catch painted turtles with a hand net. We finally hit upon a method. I threw pieces of toast upon the water. The turtles rose to eat the toast. I tossed the pieces closer and closer to the bank. When the turtles were pounceable, we raised the net and pounced. Unfortunately, the pond's bank was steep, and both Cody and I fell in from time to time, screaming and laughing. Now three, and a good flailer, Cody usually made it to the bank. If he did not, I extended the net. Now and then we were victorious turtle catchers. Vacationers from across America gathered to watch us extract the reptiles from our trout net. The turtles, realizing they were free, scrabbled over the bank with a plunk, and the ritual was begun anew.

In the morning, I kayaked by myself from Duck Creek, where Clawson and I had pulled out, to the KOA campground. Ines stayed with the boys. Stephanie had returned to England. Though it was hot and dry on the river, a large, dark cloud floated over the Pryor Mountains, dumping rain. The cloud was often etched with silver strikes of lightning as in an old photographic negative. Yet I never heard thunder.

I took lunch beside the turtle pond with the family, and then I launched again. The surprising thing about the KOA location was that it seemed isolated and pristine, even in the heart of Billings. We saw only the trees and the river. There was even an exciting riffle as the Yellowstone dropped and swung south around a bend against the bank opposite our tent. This bank rose over the length of a mile to a towering bluff of soft, dark shale topped by lighter sedimentary earth. This was Sacrifice Cliff.

In 1837 a smallpox epidemic ravaged the Crow. Smallpox had

come up the Missouri carried by several infected passengers on a small steamboat destined for fur company forts. The legend of Sacrifice Cliff says that hundreds of Crow rode their horses off the top rather than go on living, and possibly to appease whatever supernatural forces had visited the disease upon them.

But Crow sources told me that only two men killed themselves. One returned from a hunting expedition to find his village and his fiancée dying. He was filled with grief. He proposed to ride his pony off a smaller, sixty-foot jump, and his best friend offered to go with him. Either they rode separate ponies to their deaths, or they both mounted the same white horse. The site is called Where-the-White-Horse-Went-Down.

The 1837 smallpox epidemic changed forever the configuration of the Plains tribes. The Crow learned of the outbreak and avoided the besieged forts. But the Mandans were wiped out. In the upper Missouri region perhaps half the Blackfoot nation died. Alexander Culbertson, the American Fur Company representative who dominated trade along the Missouri and Yellowstone, tried to warn the Blackfeet away from Ft. Mackenzie, but, curious and suspicious, they stopped in anyway. Months later Culbertson went in search of the tribe. He found a large camp near Three Forks, west of Bozeman. "Hundreds of decaying forms of human beings, horses, and dogs, lay scattered everywhere among the lodges."

Ironically, the smallpox epidemic may have saved the Crow from their much more numerous Blackfoot enemies to the north. Edwin Denig believed that of all Indians who came in contact with the disease, "about only one in six or seven survived." Denig wrote that after this epidemic, or perhaps a slightly earlier one, Crow chief Rotten Belly, "by unremitting exertions, forced marriages, and equal distribution of arms, horses, and other property, . . . succeeded in restoring the nation to something like order."

John James Audubon wrote that the original contagion—that is, before it reached the Crow—was in part spread by a pilfered blanket. "An Indian stole the blanket of one of the steamboat's watchmen (who lay at the point of death, if not already dead), wrapped himself in it, and carried it off, unaware of the disease that was to cost him his life, and that of many of his tribe. . . ." A reward was offered for the immediate "return of the blanket, as well as a new one in its stead, and promised that no punishment should be inflicted. But the robber was a great chief; through shame, or some other motive, he never came forward, and, before many days, was a corpse."

Just past Sacrifice Cliff the time frame jumps a century and a half. The single smokestack of the coal-fired Montana Power plant at Billings becomes visible, and very soon behind it the white beehive domes of a petroleum tank farm. The river straightens and plunges north toward the rim rocks, flowing under two railroad bridges and the interstate.

The cacophony of plague history, possible pollution, a rattling freight train heading east, and the groan and whine of three-trailer semitrucks shooting over the highway bridge had me a little discombobulated. I was also floating fast, and trying to cast a lure into the clay-lined shallows, to test whether there were any shad or bass in this industrial stretch. The green-and-black flatfish lure was supposed to imitate a swimming frog. I soon gave up, and gawked. The frog imitation trailed behind.

In a few seconds, I smelled sweet detergent. A four-foot-wide stream of whitish effluent dropped off the left bank from a sewage treatment plant. I fumbled for my camera, which I kept in a case around my waist. I leaned downstream, then upstream, snapped the picture, and fell overboard. Underwater, I was almost laughing. Of all the places on the entire Yellowstone to dump, this was the most unexpected, and the most disgusting. I stood on the bottom in the placid muck and watched the sludge sweep toward me.

Later, a Fish, Wildlife, and Parks supervisor told me that pollution on the lower Yellowstone most likely came from pesticide and fertilizer runoff from farms and ranches. Forty years ago the river towns dumped untreated sewage into the Yellowstone; these days the gook was well enough treated, believed the supervisor. One can still see rare patches of almond-colored foam. I saw foam even in the Paradise Valley. This is from phosphate detergents finding their way into the water. It was the opinion of the FWP executive that the lower Yellowstone was fine for swimming, not for drinking. A more controversial source of pollution is cattle manure. Cattle like to drink and wallow on the river's banks, and their manure is not always absorbed by the ground. This type of pollution is only now beginning to be measured.

I passed another tank farm that took in water from the Yellowstone and discharged it a little farther on. I kept paddling, and very quickly I was alone again. The river dropped in a long run of rapids beside a bank shored by riprapped sandstone boulders. I paddled on. Three mule deer appeared on a sandbar at the head of the rapids. Instead of retreating, or standing still until I shot by, these deer, like the deer below Big Timber, plunged into the water and were swept by the rapids toward the sandstone boulders. Only their eyes, ears, and nostrils were above water. I thought they might drown, but the current smacked them against the bank and they managed to clamber out. The deer bounded through the jagged boulders, and ran off.

I hardly noticed the sun was setting, and I had yet to reach the Huntley Diversion Dam. Clawson had said not to worry, that there would be two cables across the river holding a sign that said ABANDON ALL HOPE YE WHO ENTER HERE. I thought some hydraulic engineer with a Montana sense of humor had really erected such a warning. When I heard the rush of falling water, I realized I had fallen victim to Clawson's dead-pan humor.

There were two small white billboards on each side of the river, but in the fading light I almost missed them. The signs said WARNING BOATERS, HUNTLEY DIVERSION DAM, PREPARE TO TAKE OUT BOATS 2000 FEET AHEAD.

Paddling over the Huntley Diversion Dam is probably not a wise idea. The dam is not an impoundment but a curtain of concrete, like a spillway. The river proceeds apace over the spillway, while some water is diverted out a side channel, into a broad ditch. The Huntley was one of America's first federal irrigation projects. It might be a thrill to rush over the spillway during spring rise, but at this time of the year the drop was six to eight feet onto the bottom line of the spillway's boulders.

Earlier in the summer a madman (or what I took to be one) in a strange homemade plywood boat, using shovels for paddles, had gone over the diversion dam, and lived, though his boat had broken up at the bottom of the drop. I thought about this navigator as I climbed onto the bank and pulled the kayak over the dam by the bow loop.

It was almost dark now. The swimming deer, the sewage capsize, the portage, musing about what Billings had become since I left—had conspired to slow me down. I was lollygagging, and I did not know how far I had to go, in river miles. A family was setting up gas lanterns to fish for spawning northern pike. These big pike are unable to swim above the diversion. A man with a bottle of Rainier in each hand told me I had only ten minutes "at the most" before I reached the bridge at Huntley. After twenty minutes I wondered. After forty minutes of serious paddling, I relaxed.

What was the point? It was now 9:00, and I was caught on the river. I tried to keep to the eddy line off the left bank. Several times I was startled by the loud crack of beavers slapping their tails against the surface in warning. I heard choruses of slurping noises. The next day I discovered the sucking sounds were large carp rooting around in water so shallow their backs and dorsal fins thrashed and undulated in the slow current like big eels. These carp feed with their pink mouths open, and the sight is either strangely charming or a bit disgusting, depending on your point of view.

Finally, I heard the sounds of cars. Just as I could make out the Huntley Bridge, I saw Ines in the Trooper. She was crossing the bridge, and leaving. I shouted but I was too far away. As I floated closer, I could hear the sound of heavy-metal music blasting from the cottonwoods. I pulled the boat out, dragged it up the bank, and stashed it under the bridge. There was a new red pickup truck parked a hundred yards away in a clearing. Serious partying was going on inside the truck.

I was starving. I walked two miles to the little crossroads of Huntley. I was in luck. It was steak night at a bar called the Blue Cat.

Years before, I had stood inside the burned-out shell of another riverfront tavern named the Blue Cat. That joint was near Natchez across the Mississippi from Ferriday, Louisiana, where I had been interviewing the salacious evangelical Rev. Jimmy Swaggart. Reverend Swaggart's first cousin Jerry Lee Lewis used to rock out the Blue Cat before he went on to larger things.

I could not help but reflect that America had become as screwy as a sow's tail, as Tex Ritter used to say. The leading evangelicals somehow always seemed to end up disgracing themselves with fallen angels in low-rent locations. Liberals in the media had become our unofficial censors. Conservative and independence-loving ranchers and farmers were making much of their money off government subsidies, crop support payments, and systems that paid to take arid land out of tillage. Nobody cared about any of it. The sequiturs flow when you are hungry.

There was no live music at the Montana Blue Cat, but the place was still jamming. Everybody stared as I passed by the pool table, since I was in water shoes, wearing a bathing suit, with a neoprene spray shirt around my waist, and carrying an eight-foot-long, black graphite paddle through the bar. Nobody cared, though, and after I ate one dinner, I called the waitress back and asked for the same, one more time.

As I was finishing my second piece of apple pie, I noticed Ines standing in the open doorway, past the pool tables. I went to her and we embraced.

Back under the Huntley Bridge, we hoisted the boat onto the Trooper. A big man with a cherubic mass of curls pulled his pickup truck beside us. This man, it turned out, had helped Ines search for me. She had been in Huntley's other bar, the Pryor Cafe, worried that I might have tumbled over the diversion dam in the dark, like the madman with the shovel paddles. She liked the bartender, who was a nice old man. She asked him if someone could take her down to the diversion. He called over the big cherubic guy. Ines set off with him in his truck. It was a bit of a chance to take.

But now the man was here, again, still worried about us.

He also wanted to talk.

"I used to fill the underground tanks at gas stations," he almost shouted in the dark, "but I banged my ear, and some kind a catalyst got in my eye"—I could see in the light from his headlights that there was something glassy about one of his eyes—"so then I worked with retarded kids, but that was too stressful. I got disability and now I'm in college!"

I thanked him for searching for me.

Huntley

THE YELLOWSTONE IS PARALLELED BY HIGHWAY for much of its 671-mile length. Most of the time the highway cannot be seen, but it lies within one to five miles of the river. However, from Huntley to Pompey's Pillar, the river makes a looping jog north, while Interstate 94, the road to Minnesota, cuts straight east. Though Huntley is only fourteen miles from Billings and its oil refineries, this section is as lost and lush as any on the entire river. From here downstream, the Yellowstone begins to braid, splitting around islands, and splitting again.

It takes some practice to pick the channel with the most water and strongest flow. Later, I would learn to paddle for the point of an island, and make my decision at the last possible moment, when I could look down both sides of the island, as far as possible.

Immediately after launching under the Huntley Bridge, I chose the channel to the right. This proved to be wrong. Soon I was in such slow water, what is called an abandoned meander, that I was becalmed. The depth was about two feet, at the deepest. There was little flow. The banks were brushy, and I could not see above them. This was a Montana version of a southern swamp. I was reminded of Faulkner's short novel *The Bear.*

There was nothing to do but paddle. In effect, I was passing through a series of shallow lakes. What was wonderful about this watery appendix were the birds. Right off the first sandbar, eighty-one American white pelicans jumped pendulously into flight.

Pelicans are enormous birds. Their wings can stretch to seven feet.

Because they have light and hollow bones and an air sac under the skin, they float with great buoyancy. But it takes them a moment of hard flapping to become airborne. It is as if they throw themselves into flight. They seem to sling their shoulders in front of their heads like someone trying to hunch out of a sport coat without unbuttoning it. Once airborne, these pelicans looked like flying laundry, starched French shirts with black cuffs. The birds stretched across the entire river in a low-slung *V*, wing tip to wing tip.

I had taken to counting the cormorants, geese, and pelicans, and eighty-one was the largest flock of birds I had yet seen.

At the end of the first lake stood a solitary great blue heron. I saw more great blue herons on this stretch than at any place before. Sometimes it was possible to paddle within a hundred feet of pelicans, but herons always spied me a long way off and took flight.

I never saw pelicans nor herons feeding, though there must have been plenty of minnows, suckers, frogs, carp, and sauger for them to catch. Pelicans are social birds. By ganging up, they herd fish into the gular pouches under their bills, which work as scoop nets. Pelicans prefer fish. Great blue herons are less particular. Audubon, in 1840, talked of finding lizards, snakes, birds, shrews, meadow mice, young rats, moths, butterflies, marsh hens, rails, and other birds in the stomachs of the great blue herons he investigated. Audubon said that the great blue

always strikes its prey through the body, and as near the head as possible. Now and then it strikes at a fish so large and strong as to endanger its own life; and I once saw one on the Florida coast, that, after striking a fish, when standing in the water to the full length of its legs, was dragged along for several yards, now on the surface and again beneath. When after a severe struggle, the heron disengaged itself, it appeared quite overcome, and stood still near the shore, his head turned from the seas, as if afraid to try another such experiment.

I was hoping to catch a great blue trying to spear a pike or paddlefish on the lower Yellowstone, but I never did.

Audubon also talked of watching a great blue heron chase down a large hawk and lunge at it until the hawk dropped the fish it was carrying. Arthur Cleveland Bent writes, "There are very few birds or animals that dare to attack such a large and formidable antagonist as an adult great blue heron, for it is a courageous bird, armed with a powerful sharp bill that can inflict serious wounds. Even men must approach it with caution, when it is wounded and at bay."

At the same time that I was gaining respect for the birds of the Yellowstone, I was becoming fascinated with ornithologists like Bent and Audubon. One of Audubon's most famous trips was up the Missouri into Montana. These men belied the present-day view of bird watchers as reticent and gentle folk. Audubon approached birding the way others approach big-game hunting. He often went collecting with a shotgun and a fishing creel to hold the catch, as in "so we took our guns and went after Black-breasted Lark Buntings" (*The Missouri River Journals*, 1843).

I also wanted to catch the formidable great blue in its frenzied mating dance, but it was too late in the year for this paddling voyeur. Again, Audubon will do:

> The males walk about with an air of great dignity, bidding defiance to their rivals, and the females croak to invite the males to pay their addresses to them. . . . [W]ith little attention to politeness, [the male] opens his powerful bill, throws out his wings, and rushes with fury on his foe. Each attack is carefully guarded against, blows are exchanged for blows; one would think that a single well-aimed thrust might suffice to inflict death, but the strokes are parried with as much art as an expert swordsman would employ; and, although I have watched these birds for half an hour at a time as they fought on the ground, I never saw one killed on such an occasion; but I have often seen one felled and trampled upon, even after incubation had commenced. These combats over, the males and females leave the place in pairs. They are now mated for the season, at least I am inclined to think so, as I never saw them assemble twice on the same ground, and they become comparatively peaceable after pairing.

I was also interested to read that many big birds, such as herons and eagles, not just geese, tended to mate for life. Though I never saw them parry, thrust, and mate, after Billings I saw or overheard great blue herons almost every hour. For one of the most elegant-looking birds on the Yellowstone, it has the most unlikely voice. It sounds like a duck being slowly strangled or a chicken puking up a bad grasshopper. The first few times I heard the gravelly extended bassoon cackle of the great blue heron, I thought I must have the wrong bird. A loon stuck in the mud, maybe, with a coyote loping down the bank. But there was never another candidate in sight. In matters of the tongue, the great blue heron is like that beautiful star of the silent screen who opened her mouth in her first talkie, only to have the audience rolling in the aisles.

By dusk the river was covered with mayflies. Shad worked the water in boils all around me, and dozens of swallows skimmed the surface. Swallow nests sometimes lined the crevices of the sandstone cliffs that formed the sides of the main river. The nests looked like clay pots with holes in the bottom glued at an angle to the banks. The mayflies were strange little creatures, about three-quarters of an inch long, translucent white with tiny, jet-black eyes and upturned abdomens. They smashed into my face and found their way inside my kayaking helmet.

It was good to be back in the main channel. I was enjoying the big new touring kayaks we were using on the lower river. These Aquaterra Chinooks were a foot longer than the Spectrums we had paddled on the middle Yellowstone, and they were a new ride entirely from the little white-water Dancers and rubber duckies of Yankee Jim and the mountain stretch. The lines of the touring kayaks were less rounded. From above they looked like two elongated triangles stuck together. There were two holds, one fore and one aft, covered with waterproof hatches. An air bag was installed in the front hold, as a safety measure. Should the shell be punctured, the air bag would presumably keep the bow afloat. I always packed a smoke flare and a strobe light. The smoke flare would indicate our position in daylight. The strobe would flash every two seconds all night long. Both devices were smaller than my fist.

Unlike the smaller kayaks, the Chinooks came with a retractable metal rudder, about a foot long. Wires ran from foot pedals in the bow, along the transom, to the stern. When the rudder was cabled down into the water, the kayak could be steered with the feet, like a pedal car. In strong crosscurrents the rudder stabilized the stern, so that it was less likely to fishtail. In straight-ahead water the steering mechanism allowed me to fold my hands across the stretched spray skirt, with my paddle resting out of the water upon the coaming, and smile at the croaking of the herons as swallows clapped wings around my head.

These state-of-the-art touring kayaks were a pleasure to operate. In design, they resembled the original kayaks developed by the Aleut tribes of the Bering Strait, though ours came to more of a point at the front. Nobody knows when kayaks were invented. Archaeologists believe the Aleut came to what is now northern Alaska as long ago as eight thousand years. "The skin boat's biodegradable components left archaeologists with scarcely a trace," writes George Dyson in his history of the kayak, *Baidarka*. *Baidarka* was a Ukrainian river term applied to the Aleut's craft by the Russians who had come to kill sea otters in the seventeenth century, much as the mountain men would later come to the Yellowstone for the beaver.

The first person to describe these kayaks in detail was Georg Wilhelm Steller, the naturalist for Vitus Bering, the Danish navigator who explored for the Russians. The Steller blue jay and the Steller sea lion are named for this meticulous German, who wrote in 1741:

> The American boats are about two fathoms [twelve feet] long, two feet high, and two feet wide on the deck, pointed towards the nose but truncate and smooth in the rear. To judge by appearances, the frame is of sticks fastened together at both ends and spread apart by crosspieces inside. On the outside the frame is covered with skins, perhaps of seals, and coloured a dark brown. . . . [O]n top is a circular hole, around the whole of which is sewn whale guts having a hollow hem with a leather string running through it, by means of which it may be tightened or loosened like a purse. When the American has sat down in his boat and stretched out his legs under the deck, he draws this hem together around his body and fastens it with a bowknot in order to prevent any water from getting in. . . . The paddle consists of a stick a fathom long, at each end provided with a shovel, a hand wide. With this he beats alternately to the right and to the left into the water and thereby propels his boat with great adroitness even among large waves.

We were cruising the Yellowstone in native craft then, except that shiny red-and-blue plastic polymers had replaced brown seal skin, our spray skirts were foam and nylon rather than whale intestines, and our paddles were made of graphite, like tennis racquets.

The Yellowstone's banks were different here, from Billings. The soft, dark cliffs had turned to much harder sandstone and rim rocks, sparsely covered with juniper and pine. At one point I saw a burr of sticks high on a dead tree. I thought, what if that were an eagle's nest? A few hundred yards closer, two bald eagles stared down at me. According to the *Greater Yellowstone Report,* active eagle nests number ninety-five from the Tetons north through Yellowstone Park and down the river almost to the Clarks Fork. Ten years before, there were only thirty-eight. But I had seen about thirty eagles so far, just from the river.

The sun had set, though I could still read the water. I could feel it more than I could see it. The whirring and dipping swallows were my guides. Suddenly, I heard the sound of rapids. I stared but could see no white water, only the brown sandstone cliffs as the river made a turn. Then I realized that part of the cliff had long ago broken off and formed a small, treacherous rock island about fifteen feet tall, a dozen feet from shore. The water cut deep on both sides, running swiftly as it swept around the outside turn. As I came closer, I could make out that the hunk of sandstone was shaped exactly like a mushroom. Without stopping, I whacked the unexpected mushroom rock with my paddle for good luck and continued on.

I finished right at dark, which was an hour after sunset. The boys hopped up and down beside Ines. They were standing beneath a magnificent seventy-foot cottonwood. One side of the cottonwood's trunk was black and smoking slightly. A warm campfire lay in front of the tree. We covered the coals with dirt. Behind the cottonwoods was a bridge that led to the Bull Mountains. To the right of the bridge, a mile across a field of green alfalfa, was a massive tower two hundred feet tall, of ocher sandstone. It looked like a loaf of round rye bread with a corrugated ridge at the top and stove in at various places where the rocky crumbs tumbled down to the prairie. This was Pompey's Pillar.

Pompey's Pillar

FOR CENTURIES, the Crow had called Pompey's Pillar the Mountain Lion's Home, and had used it for vision quests, as they still at times use the recesses of the Crazies. The sandstone monolith is a stone island upon the flat prairie, the first great sign to travelers coming upriver that they are about to leave the plains and enter the mountains. It is also a sign for kayakers paddling down that they have begun the long slide toward Europe.

The steamboat *Josephine* tied up here in 1875 with Mark Twain's friend Grant Marsh at the helm and Colonel Grant, the president's son, a passenger. In 1873 Lt. Col. George Armstrong Custer camped across the river with much of the Seventh Cavalry and twenty companies of infantry under Gen. D. S. Stanley, about two thousand men in all. They had fought a battle with the Sioux twenty miles downriver. Sioux snipers hid themselves at the top of Pompey's Pillar. When most of the soldiers were down on the north bank, washing their clothes and frolicking in the river, the Sioux began to shoot. In his autobiography, Custer described the havoc with his usual gaiety: "The scampering of naked men up the hill was very comical."

Crow chief Arapooish stopped by Pompey's on his journey to wreak a revenge upon the Cheyenne, who had recently massacred a Crow village. Arapooish later claimed to have taken a thousand women and children prisoners and killed all the men. Sergeant Pryor had fashioned his two bison skin boats here after the Crow had stolen the rest of the expedition's horses.

But the important thing is that Pompey's Pillar is the only national historical landmark named after a toddler. Pompey, "My little Pomp," was the nickname Clark gave to Jean-Baptiste Charbonneau, the youngest member of the Lewis and Clark expedition and Sacajawea's son. Sacajawea, Bird Woman, was the sixteen-year-old second wife of Toussaint Charbonneau, the expedition's interpreter. Otter Woman was his first wife. Toussaint Charbonneau had won Sacajawea in a card game, or perhaps simply bought her. She was a Shoshone, which means "People of the Snake." As a girl she had been kidnapped by a Hidatsa warrior while picking berries along the Madison River. The Hidatsa carried her off to the Dakotas. The birth of Pompey was documented by Lewis, February 11, 1805:

> about five oClock this evening one of the wives of Charbono was delivered of a fine boy . . . her labour was tedious and the pain violent. . . . Mr. Jessome informed me that he had freequently administered a small portion of the rattle of the rattle-snake, which he assured me had never failed to produce the desired effect, that of hastening the birth of the child; having the rattle of a snake by me I gave it to him and he administered two rings of it to the woman broken in small pieces with the fingers and added to a small quantity of water. Whether this medicine was truly the cause or not I shall not undertake to determine, but I was informed that she had not taken it more than ten minutes before she brought forth.

Sacajawea was the heroine of the expedition. She guided the explorers over the western Rockies, where the Shoshone lived, to the Pacific Coast. Lewis and Clark needed her tribe for horses, and as it turned out, her brother had become a Shoshone chief in the years after her kidnapping.

This much is known about Sacajawea, and little else, except that she grew angry when she was prevented from looking upon the Pacific, after coming within twenty miles of the Oregon coast. The male leaders relented, and she saw a great whale beached near the mouth of the Columbia.

The Sacajawea myth was made up much later by Eva Dye, chairperson of the Clackamas County chapter of the Oregon Equal Suffrage Association. Dye was searching for a way to make her novel about the Lewis and Clark expedition, *The Conquest,* less male dominated.

I struggled along as best I could with the information I could get, trying to find a heroine. I traced down every old book and scrap of paper, but was still without a real heroine. Finally, I came upon the name of Sacajawea, and I screamed, 'I have found my heroine!' I then hunted up every fact I could find about Sacajawea. Out of a few dry bones I found in the old tales of the trip, I created Sacajawea and made her a living entity.

Clark carved his name just below the top of Pompey's Pillar, July 25, 1806. Today this carving is the only physical remains of the Lewis and Clark expedition. *Pompey* means "Little Chief" in Shoshone, and it had a nice double meaning, describing well the attitude of a confident toddler person.

Unfortunately, our own younger toddler person, Jack, got sick at about Pompey's Pillar. We retreated to the Northern Hotel in Billings, then to St. Vincent's Hospital, then to Bozeman. We lost two weeks on the river. I am not aware if Clark ever stopped for Jean-Baptiste.

When we returned to Pompey's Pillar, we were accompanied by David Schwartz, Isis Spinola Coury, and their two-and-a-half-year-old son, Anthony Schwartz, all of Muir Beach, California. They flew up to join the expedition for a few days. Our expanded party climbed the sandstone monolith, named after a pompaceous little boy, with not one, but three toddlers scrambling over the catwalks, attempting to vault the railings before they were rescued, shouting, stalling, running ahead, and in general disturbing the historic moment with their carryings on. Perhaps the ghost of little Jean-Baptiste had incited the boys.

After the expedition was over, Clark suggested to Charbonneau and Sacajawea that he be allowed to educate the young Pomp. The Frenchman and the Shoshone woman decided Jean-Baptiste was too young to leave home. Later, they brought the boy to St. Louis. Clark paid a Baptist minister and a Catholic priest to tutor him. In 1823, Jean-Baptiste joined an expedition led by Prince Paul of Württemberg, the German explorer, and then returned with him to Europe.

The son of Sacajawea soaked up the Continent for six years. When he returned to Montana, a half-century before Custer camped across the river, the young Charbonneau could speak German, French, Spanish, and English with ease. He was probably the most educated and traveled Native American of his time, at least in Caucasian terms. Back in the Rockies, he threw in with Kit Carson, the mountain man, and they trapped beaver together. He guided Col. Philip St. George Cooke in his campaign to loose the southwestern United States from the descendants of Cortés, and in 1860, according to several sources, he died in the California gold country. So that was the life of the original Pompey, abbreviated.

We sat on a wooden bench at the top of Pompey's Pillar with the cottonwood-lined Yellowstone to our backs, surveying, as Clark had two centuries before, three mountain ranges to the west, south, and north. Ever eastward was prairie. For the moment, our own toddlers were pooped.

From this perch, Clark had seen "emence herds of Buffalow, Elk and wolves." We saw none.

There was, however, a large cloud of what looked like gnats approaching from the southwest. The cloud took minutes to arrive but long before it did, Isis said, "Those are mosquitos. Let's go down."

Nobody believed her. The cloud was as big as a hot-air balloon. But she was soon proved right. Isis had grown up in Campo Grande, a city on the southern end of the Pantanal, a Brazilian marsh larger than France.

Under serious mosquito attack, we tripped down the hundreds of wooden steps to the parking lot and slathered ourselves with 100 percent DEET, a mosquito repellent that works well but is dangerous to children. The boys began to whimper as the mosquitoes dive-bombed them. We sparingly applied drops of DEET to the backs of their T-shirts so they would not get the repellent on their hands and into their mouths or eyes.

Clark called mosquitoes *musquetors,* as in, "Musquetors very troublesom this morning," or, "Last night the Musquetors was so troublesom that no one of the party Slept half the night."

We surveyed our camping options beside the river, on both sides of the Bull Mountains bridge. Over both the south and north banks, there was a ten-foot drop. Pompey's was judged unsuitable for toddler camping.

Cottonwood Alley

WE DROVE THE SHORT DISTANCE TO CUSTER. Sandwiched between the interstate and the railroad, Custer was judged too noisy. We consulted the map and drove a few more miles to the town of Bighorn. The town of Bighorn turned out to consist of one sagging, lapstrake wooden building. This was the post office, which appeared to have been built in Custer's time, if not Sacajawea's. We struck up a conversation with the postmistress, who said a person could have their own ZIP code if they moved to Bighorn. We drove back toward Pompey's Pillar along a river road. It was getting dark. The kids were hungry.

At the bridge that leads to the Musselshell River, which is named after the freshwater mussels one can still find there, and where Granville Stuart once hung immigrant homesteaders from cottonwood limbs, like strange fruit, we stopped to watch a farmer prepare silage. His farm was by the river, and I thought we might ask permission to camp.

The silage pit consisted of two long, parallel mounds of dirt "catted" up with a tractor. The farmer's wife was driving a massive dump truck piled high with chopped raw corn. As we talked, she raised the truck bed and the sliced-and-diced corn tumbled into the pit. She drove back for more. These people worked hard. She was about thirty, her husband a little older. Soon the corn would be sprayed with a preservative, and visqine plastic rolled on top. The bagged mess then ferments on its own. The old way was to pack silage in huge vertical metal containers, but plastic has made things cheaper.

I shook hands with the farmer.

"In summer, we raise corn, and in winter," he smiled, "we feed it to the cattle. That's what we do around here."

This farmer's name was Les Rough. Later, Dave Schwartz would say, "Did you ask Les if his brother's name was More Abrasive?" But Dave had the grace to hold his tongue until Les Rough had directed us to a fine campsite on a cottonwood bottom beside the Yellowstone. I believe it was in fact Les's brother's property. Mr. Rough was an intelligent man. I think he had already heard the More Abrasive joke a few times in his young life.

Many of the Montana farmers and ranchers we were meeting were in their thirties, a new generation. They were all interested in our journey. They especially liked to ask questions about the kayaks. Most said they wished they had the time to float the Yellowstone the way we were, the whole way. To some, this was the dream, they said, of a lifetime. These sheep and cattle ranchers, sugar beet and hay farmers, never struck me as too different from us. I imagined they listened to Merle Haggard, John Mellencamp, Prince, Izzy Stradlin and the Ju Ju Hounds, Sly and Robbie, and Midnight Oil, just as we did, as we drove from camp to camp, though I guess I'm not so sure about Prince, and I think they might have gotten up a little earlier than we usually did, too.

Schwartz turned out to be a camp wonder. He hoisted our dome tent as well as his own, then started a bonfire from the dried cottonwood limbs that lay all about the bottom. He had brought a big cooler from California packed with a dozen bottles of North Coast chardonnays and cabernet sauvignons from the Napa Valley, as well as imported cheeses. This was roughing it. Soon we were grilling steak as the boys roasted marshmallows. Owls hooted in the wood behind us. The Yellowstone swirled along in front. A planetarium sky rotated above our heads.

In the middle of the night Isis rushed out of her tent. "What was that?"

It took us a few seconds to understand what she meant. The noise was a train. Trains no longer awakened us. In fact, they soothed us. But in Muir Beach, California, few freight trains loaded with forty gondolas of low-sulfur coal rumble by, to Minneapolis and Chicago, from places like Colstrip, Montana.

When Clark stopped near here, he wrote, "Emence herds of Buffalow about our [camp] as it is now running time with those animals the bulls keep such a grunting nois which is [a] very loud and dis-agreeable sound that we are compelled to scear them away before we can sleep the men fire several shot at them and scear them away." I supposed Ines could have popped away at the coal trains with the .45, but this would have disturbed our California guests even more, and most likely would not have scared the coal trains one bit.

In the morning, Schwartz helped me rig up a trot line for catfish. I had brought along a hundred yards of fifty-pound test monofilament and a box of very large, 2-O fish hooks for the lower Yellowstone. I had once been on a large boat in the Galápagos. The deck was thirty feet off the water. I had ten-pound line on that occasion. Every time I baited the two hooks, two fish would latch on. As I pulled in the line, it would break from the weight. I was taking no chances on the Yel-lowstone. We baited the hooks with rotten chicken parts, chunks of road-kill rabbit, and hunks of prime rib from the Livingston Bar & Grill. What catfish could resist? Dave slung the line as far as he could into the current beneath the bridge, and I tied the spool to a drift-wood log.

The next day's float was unexpectedly fine. There was a following wind of about a knot, not enough to whip up waves or make things unpleasant, but enough to pick up the pace. We were making an aver-age of twenty miles a day now, half to a third of what Clark made, but not too bad for a family float. Sometimes Dave and I put our arms around each other's shoulders and held our two-headed paddles up at the same time. The paddle heads functioned as sails, and together we scooted along like a single outrigger.

The river bottom was wide between Pompey's Pillar and our campsite, but the Yellowstone was cut into many fast-running, deep channels. The curves were lined with more fallen cottonwoods, drift-wood jams, and snags than anyplace else on the river. I named this stretch Cottonwood Alley.

Schwartz's father was a cancer doctor. Dave religiously applied the highest number sunscreen and wore a double-billed hat that shaded both the back of his neck and his face. I laughed. This was the same hat I used. I call them Ozone Hats. A manufacturer in Oregon makes them.

Schwartz was a landscape contractor. He said when he launched his Boston whaler from the beach in front of his house early in the morning in search of salmon, he kept in contact with his landscaping crews from a cellular phone. We joked. I am sure that if a Disney executive ever careens down Cottonwood Alley in a touring kayak, she will sell fantasies over the cellular long distance. That time is fast coming, for better or worse. The Yellowstone is the best-kept river secret in America.

Because he understood plants and soil, Dave pointed out some obvious things Ines and I had missed in the floats of the last few days. The bank on the outside curves of the river was usually flat, composed of sandbars or gravel bars, covered, close to the water, by grasses or ground cover, soon rising with bushes, later young cottonwoods, and only then, if there was room before the sandstone bluffs, mature, old-growth cottonwoods. Outside curves are depository.

Inside curves are repository. The river lops off the bank. The plants there are old-growth cottonwoods, some sixty to eighty feet tall, shaped by decades of lightning strikes, beaver gnawing, and woodpeckers. When the bank is cut out from under them, the cottonwoods tumble into the water and create dangerous sweepers, which are long arms of deadwood, sometimes submerged. Debris piles up against these cottonwood sweepers and creates tricky logjams and eddies in the narrower channels. Twice in Cottonwood Alley we could not negotiate our turns quickly enough and we piled against logjams like logs ourselves. The water held us until we pulled ourselves hand-over-hand along the dead branches, unable to paddle, until we reached the end of the flotsam. There the current grabbed us and we whooped! for the snap.

I thought, two hundred miles upriver such danger would have frightened me so much that I might have beached the kayak and taken many deep breaths before I proceeded. Now, ripping round these sweeper bends in Cottonwood Alley was big fun. I thought, maybe we should come back in spring rise when the current was too swift to keep the sweepers horizontal and they tumbled end-over-end like Ferris wheels. Eeeh-ha! A watery rodeo.

Dave was a demon fisherman. In the midst of these slick runs, we still trolled with spinning rods held to the stern by the spider web of expedition bungee cords. I hooked a two-pound shad at one point. A shad is a hard-fighting silvery fish that migrates up the Yellowstone from the Missouri in the summer. To Montanans, utterly spoiled on trout, the shad is a trash fish, but in Florida the shad would be a major game fish, and in China its relatives are considered a delicacy. I whacked the shad's head against the combing and clipped a bow bungee over its body. The back of the shad is a favorite bait for large catfish.

Then Dave hooked a shad. But the current was especially swift and there were several sweepers to negotiate. The shad caught itself in a downed tree. The drag on the spinning reel screamed.

"Just paddle!" I shouted.

The snagged rod jumped off the bungees and we lost the rig, but at least Dave was not pinned against the downed cottonwood and overturned.

We proceeded. At other times the water was so slow we floated backward and talked of Brazilian women. It is rare that a couple of guys kayaking backward down the Yellowstone River in Montana are both married to Brazilian women. I wondered what sort of notes Isis and Ines were comparing on dry land.

When we pulled out at the campsite, we were early. Nobody was there. We went to check the trot line for catfish. I pulled the line in slowly, but I could tell from the lack of weight that we had come up empty.

"Careful," said Schwartz, then.

I slowly turned around.

In a hollow of the big cottonwood log that I had anchored the trot line to was a rattlesnake, about three to four feet long. The rattlesnake slithered out of his hole. I think he wanted to enjoy the warmth of the late afternoon sun. I do not know if he saw us, or cared if he did. I laid the trot line on the ground, and we respectfully backed away. Perhaps the rattlesnake would enjoy the prime rib fat from the Livingston Bar & Grill more than the catfish had.

That night we decided to dine out.

We found a country bar on Highway 47, the road from the Yellowstone south to the Crow Agency. It was a large stucco box. They were advertising twenty-two-ounce T-bone steaks for $7.95—soup, salad, and potatoes included. The restaurant had a few tables in the dining area, which was next to a small horseshoe bar that fronted the kitchen. The bar was full with locals. A Chinese-American couple from Hardin, which is the market town for the Crow reservation, sat at a table next to us. They had two little girls.

We ordered our steaks, and then the five toddlers took possession of the joint. First, they discovered the exit door, which led to the wheelchair-access walk around the side of the restaurant. The toddlers circled inside and out, screaming. Then they climbed the bar stools and ordered cups of ice. They tried to order pickled eggs. Their fathers told them they would not like pickled eggs. They conversed with the old farmers sitting beside them. They jitter-bugged to the country-western jukebox. They discovered the video poker machines. "Coins, coins! Give us some coins! Please."

The owner lifted little Anthony off his perch in front of a video poker machine and returned him to his mother, Isis. "Sorry ma'am, he has to be twenty-one to play those machines. He looks underage to me."

"Too bad," muttered someone at the bar. "Kid had a royal flush."

Isis did not know what a royal flush was. I thought the owner was about to ask us to restrain the troops or leave. But the man wanted to apologize for the delay in our order. "You get all those T-bone orders at once, they crowd the grill." To make up for this, he offered us a round of free drinks, which we accepted. After dinner, he provided extra homemade apple pie. We packed the sleepy savages into their car seats. We were missing someone's coat. I returned to retrieve it. The Chinese couple had left, too. The bar had recovered, and the regulars were nursing the experience.

"I was never much for child abuse," I heard one rancher in a pheasant hunting coat say, "until tonight."

Everybody laughed.

"What do you think about wife abuse?" somebody asked him.

"I guess that's OK under certain conditions, too," said the man.

"You don't got no wife," said the bartender, who was a woman.

"It ain't hard to see why," said the man, laughing at himself, and everybody laughed with him.

Dialogue was good on this part of the river. The next night we stopped for corn soup at the Hysham Hills Supper Club ("Where Friends Get Together, Pop a Cork, And Maybe Do a Little Eatin', Drinkin', and Dancin', Too").

"Hysham's a nice place," I said to the waitress.

"Very peaceful, except for the murders."

"What?"

"Oh, it's quiet most of the time, but people do get killed around here."

And she talked of how a rancher who had five thousand acres at the confluence of the Bighorn and the Yellowstone had been found in his pickup with a few bullets in his skull, on his own land.

"Who did it?"

"Nobody knows, and that was ten years ago. There aren't enough people in Treasure County that probably they eat here."

It was very good food, at the Hysham Hills Supper Club. I was especially impressed by the corn soup. I had never had corn soup before. This was made with fresh corn kernels, fresh peas, and local carrots.

It was great fun to camp with friends. The funniest thing happened on the morning our guests were to leave. The coffee on the stovetop espresso machine boiled over and clogged the gas burner. When Dave went to relight the stove, it caught on fire. The flames shot up three feet until we doused them with river water, everybody laughing.

Custer to Sanders: Languid. Spent much of the time traveling backward. Drone of cicadae passed over river like sound waves. No other waves at all. Current lazy.

Forsyth

WE MADE CAMP NEXT AT FORSYTH, where the Rosebud River of eastern Montana joins the Yellowstone. Forsyth is a congenial old river town with one street of frontier brick buildings. It is named for Gen. James W. Forsyth, who stepped off a river steamer here. He was also the officer in charge of the massacre of some two hundred Sioux men, women, and children at Wounded Knee.

Though our camp was completely hidden by thick trees, we could walk through the bower at night and watch the moon over the wide water created by the second of the three diversion dams on the river. (There is also a small weir at Waco.) At night the road was kept locked with a long iron bar, and campers were issued keys, as if at a hostel. We always slept well.

The sound of the Yellowstone tumbling over the short spillway was like the sound of gentle surf. In the morning fly-fishermen hooked fat carp for sport. At night, late, kids rodded up to the spillway in pickup trucks and made out. In the morning the caretaker at the Rosebud campsite dropped by to collect the state's fee. We always chatted. The caretaker's brother owned a ranch where the land was too dry for beets. To make ends meet, he charged for deer hunting.

We stayed for a week, while we covered the water between Custer and the mouth of the Powder.

We were beginning to experience a difficulty particular to the lower stretches of the Yellowstone. There were fewer bridges and fishing accesses, and the distance between was much greater than before

Billings. The good part was that we were meeting more farmers and learning more about Montana. The bad part was that much time was lost locating places to launch and take-out. Some farms, although bordering the river, had no roads leading to the water. At other farms, nobody was home. Not once, however, did a farmer or rancher ever refuse us permission to cross his land. For six hundred miles, people, on the river at least, could not have been more friendly.

On our first foray back upriver, we stopped at a pleasant ranch house with a tire swing out front and three or four small boys shooting each other with plastic weapons. Gina Assay came to the door. In a few minutes her husband, Bill, left his tractor and joined us. He was wearing a Holly Sugar cap. The Assays raised sugar beets, which would be boiled down at the Holly factories in Billings and Sidney.

Sugar beets are one of the best money crops in Montana. The industry was started by German-Ukrainian immigrants at the turn of the century. Last year, the Arctic front that had knocked us off the river had destroyed the crop as it was being stacked and loaded for market. Sugar beets need hot September or October days to sweeten, and the percentage of sugar in the beet determines the price. This summer, things looked good, indeed, but farmers were nervous that their record-sized crop could be wiped out by another strong storm.

Bill Assay also complained that the end of the Cold War meant Cuban cane sugar would be allowed into the United States, which would hurt Montana beet sugar. The Assays were political people. Bill Assay's father was the region's state senator. The elder Assay had just returned from the former Soviet Union. Completely on his own, he had organized an airlift from eastern Montana to aid farmers in Russia.

"Only 1 percent of Americans are farmers," said the younger Assay, "but we feed everybody else. We don't have the political influence we used to. There's too few of us."

He complained that things were changing in Montana. It was an election year, and Montana's congressional delegation had been reduced from two to one, for the first time in many decades. Montana was gaining people overall, but losing in relation to the total U.S. population. Consequently, a six-term Democratic congressman who had represented western Montana was running against a Republican who had represented eastern Montana for seven terms. In Montana, west versus east is as important as Democrat versus Republican, and is usually the same thing, since the ranching and farming regions of the east elect Republicans and the mining and logging west elects Democrats. New realities, mainly environmentalism, had thrown a soggy sugar beet into the old alignments, with union loggers and miners often voting Republican, and young city people in Billings, as well as newcomers from California and elsewhere, voting Democratic because the Democrats were perceived as pro-environment.

"Eastern Montana is already dominated by western Montana, and western Montana is dominated by the Californians," is how Bill Assay summed it up.

We talked so long with the Assays that we did not make it on the river until the next day. We ended up launching from the land of an old trapper, Jim Petty, an upstream neighbor of the Assays.

Mr. Petty was seventy-two, with remarkable blue eyes and a tall, sinewy build. "He must have been a very handsome man when he was younger," the Brazilian said. His face lit up when he talked but sagged when he was silent, as old faces sometimes do. He had about seventy acres, raised a few cattle. Mostly he was retired. There was an iron target in the shape of a turkey leaning against a cottonwood. Petty could sit on the bench swing in his yard and pop off a few practice rounds.

He showed us his trap room. He had dozens of traps for many animals—beaver, skunk, muskrat, coyote—everything orderly, hung on hooks and sorted—silent clinking chains, old leather straps, sharp metal teeth. But he complained that there was no longer any point. Environmentalists had made fur coats unfashionable. A coyote skin was worth too little to justify the effort of trapping, skinning, and tanning. "So coyotes are killing more lambs," he shrugged.

"You're getting on the river a little late," Mr. Petty pointed out, "but I wouldn't worry. Almost a full moon tonight."

And then, "Watch it son, Spook's not used to strangers." Spook was Mr. Petty's collie-Australian shepherd, and he was snarling at Cody, since Cody was patting him on the head a bit too hard with a leather strap from a skunk trap.

Next day, we drove back to Hysham for more corn soup, but the corn had been replaced by chicken gumbo, less exotic. Hysham was a town unchanged from the thirties. The movie theater looked like a museum, with turrets and cupolas. This section of the river was very peaceful, far enough from the interstate to be lost in time. Hysham was more of a farming community than a region of ranchers. Thousands of immigrant farmers had tried their luck around Hysham at the turn of the century. Few were left. All about today's working farms lay tumbled-down houses, some made of old squared logs, as well as abandoned churches and schools. The immigrants had dug in, failed, and moved on, always westward.

Hysham days were hot, sunsets late. A couple of evenings we played and swam in the slow eddies at the edge of the river outside town. The lonely prairie beach was disturbed only by the honking of geese or the occasional rumble of a sugar beet truck. The beet farmers worked into the night. They fastened spotlights to their harvesters and trucks. Driving back to camp, it was as if leprechauns with torches were mining the fields.

The country continued to change. The bottoms became more arid. The bluffs were streaked with muted color, violet and black and degrees of yellow. The mountains looked twisted sometimes, broken by the bottom of the ancient sea, which in the Cretaceous stretched from the Arctic to the Gulf of Mexico. But what I noticed most were the lines upon the land. They were horizontal without being flat. Here was a mystical landscape, so large it almost slowed breathing. We were coming upon the edge of the badlands, *makoshika*, which is the Sioux word for "bad earth" or "bad land." Wild gardens of strange shapes began to crowd the north bank, as I paddled on.

Johnny Woodenlegs's brother-in-law, Johnny Russell, invited us to a barbecue. We made a hurried side trip fifty miles south to the Cheyenne reservation. Rain pelted us along the road. Then the sun would dry the blacktop, and rainbows would appear over the rampart bluffs, always to the east, for some reason. Once we stopped the car to stare at a giant mule deer with an eight-pointed rack of antlers. Another time we stopped to take pictures of Colstrip I, the power plant that jumps out unexpectedly from the lonely hill country like a jumbo jet on a dirt runway. A slurry pipe taller than a person runs for miles carrying coal to the plant, which operates twenty-four hours a day. Much of the electricity is sent to Los Angeles.

In Lame Deer, we were told the barbecue had been rained out. We drove on to Birney, where a powwow was being held in a circular arbor of cottonwoods and white trellises covered by vines. Johnny Russell showed us the drum. A half dozen old men sat around a big base drum covered with hide. They smacked the skin rhythmically and with great force as women, and a few men, wailed endlessly. The rhythm was low and slow. The sound reminded me of humpback whales, heard underwater. The crescendos took half an hour to climax. When they did, people stopped whatever they were doing to listen. The drum took them by surprise.

The air in the bower was damp from the rain, and cool at this elevation. Many battles had been fought near here in the 1870s and 1880s among soldiers, and many more with Crow and Shoshone before that. We were the only white people that I noticed.

The Cheyenne men were tall, many over six feet, often six-five or better. In the last century, the Cheyenne were known as the Beautiful People by other Plains tribes. Now many of the men and women were fat, though still handsome. The favorite food this day was fry bread, which is a flattened circle of sweet dough heaped high with chunks of beef, mixed with green peppers and onions, and slathered with honey. Wrote an old Cheyenne woman, Iron Teeth, once:

> Any kind of meat tastes good to me if I am hungry. Young dogs or old pups are good enough if I cannot have anything better. Old dogs or full-grown wolves have a strong and unpleasant odor that I do not like. Buffalo, elk, deer, antelope and bighorn sheep used to be the favorite meats of the Cheyennes. The best of all was buffalo. We never grew tired of this food. The worst of all meats I know anything about is the kind the white people have in cans they buy at the trading store. I do not understand how they can eat and enjoy such food. There is no good taste in it. Another thing: I do not like the glistening appearance of that kind of meat when the can is opened.

The young women in the bower had thin, angular faces. They were much taller than Crow women. Girls and little boys wore purple makeup and red, white, and blue feathers in their hair. The arbor was draped with bunting. The Stars and Stripes flew everywhere from tall poles. It could have been a Veterans' Day ceremony, there were so many American flags.

The drum pounded on till morning. We could hear it from the Western-8 Motel. Then the giveaways began. We stayed for one. A Cheyenne girl had done well in school in California. To honor her, or rather to share her honor, and to show the tribe the parents were not

overly prideful, the family was giving away table after table of gro-
ceries, covered by expensive blankets of many colors in snowflake and
star designs. I looked under one blanket. There were five-pound cans
of MJB coffee, sacks of white sugar, and speckled blue enamel cook-
ware sets. An announcer droned on through an ancient public address
system. He spoke of the talents of the young scholar. His voice was
like the slow rhythm of the drum. I soon lost track of the words and
heard only the changes in pitch.

Wrote Iron Teeth:

White Frog's wife gained a high name for herself when a band of
Pawnees attacked the Cheyenne camp. The warriors of that tribe took
many of our women, at different times, but in her case they failed. She
was running away afoot and alone. A Pawnee man caught her. She
jerked her hatchet from her belt and struck him. His head was split wide
open, and he fell dead. After all of us got reassembled in quiet camp, she
was heralded as a brave woman. Young warriors led her on horseback
about the camp and sang songs in her praise, the same as was done for
the regular warriors. Her husband, White Frog, gave away all of his
horses and robes and blankets, to show how proud he was of her. . . .

Giveaways.
Late in the evening we returned to the Yellowstone. I thought
about myself as a white boy, a pioneer's grandson.

Powder River

WE TURNED OFF THE ROAD AT TERRY, named for one of Custer's commanders, Gen. Alfred H. Terry. We drove into the only private campground in the tiny town. There was a tidy green lawn, spaced with old trailers, occupied by retired agate hunters. Televisions shone faintly through the trailer curtains like cataracts. We did not want this, tonight. Already, we missed the feel of camping.

We drove the back river road to the Powder, crossed under the B&N railroad bridge, and followed a dirt track through the cottonwoods toward the Yellowstone, which lay a mile or two farther on. It was a black summer sky, with snowflake stars everywhere. Once, I got out of the Trooper and lay on my back underneath a tree to see if the ground was level enough for comfortable camping. Though it was after midnight I was not tired. The moon was strong. The moon was always strong on the lower river.

It was not scary here. It was breathable calm. Though many had camped here before us, over the centuries, there was not a living soul tonight. The children were strangely awake.

The place under the first cottonwoods was not right. We could still see the railroad bridge. It was too close to the interstate. I could imagine a serial killer driving from Minneapolis to Seattle, or Seattle to Minneapolis, sliding off the exit and doing to us what the Pawnee did to the Cheyenne and the Cheyenne to the Crow. For a family that floated, paddled, and camped the entire length of the longest free-

flowing river in the Lower Forty-eight, we were a pretty paranoid outfit, but there you are.

The road was terrible but not bumpy, and we had four-wheel
drive. The track rose and fell smoothly in hummocks. This was bottom
land. The earth was soft.

We came to the end of the track, got out, heard a rushing, got
back in and turned off the engine, got back out, listened. The Yellowstone was falling across a bar before us. We were on the lip of the
river, thirty feet from a nice turning rapid. The moon was over Sheridan Butte, to the north. Clark had camped across the river. A tall cottonwood whose upper branches had been stripped of leaves by lightning strikes stood just in front. The naked top branches thrust
upward like wooden spears. The huge weathered tree looked like an
umbrella that had popped its fabric. A little line of sandstone rocks
formed a windbreak behind the jagged cottonwood. This was an
excellent spot.

We set up the tent without talking. Setting up camp was rote by
now. The guys had finally fallen asleep in the back seat of the Trooper.
We placed them inside the tent and covered them with coats. We gathered cottonwood logs, which were everywhere, and built a campfire. A
bonfire. I poured white gas from the Coleman lantern on top of the
logs, no formalities here, and tossed on a match. No harm in piling up
a fire that would last to morning. Scare away the leprechauns.

We woke up late, and it was wonderful. The guys stumbled
around safely in the tall yellowing grass, though we had to start after
them in the middle of cooking the hash browns. They had crested the
ridge, where Pvt. William George had been buried after the Battle of
the Little Bighorn, or they had stumbled off the shallow bank to the
Powder, where Sioux had looted the supplies Custer had left behind
when he and Reno started their forced march. When the boys wandered for the Yellowstone, we ran after them. The river was swift
there, and the bank fell off. Sitting Bull and his tribe had wintered
here in the grove in 1868. General Crook had quartered four thousand troops here in 1877. They caught and ate thousands of trout,
while they awaited further orders. Later, there was a depot for
steamships, a rough bar and inn. Much earlier, ice age peoples had
cooked mammoth hereabouts, before they hunted them to extinction.

Even more so than in Carbella, we were camped in a bush of ghosts, though it took days for this to sink in.

We tried to put a family float together. It was impossible to hire helpers, though we tried. I had met a young woman paddling a canoe in a wet suit above Hathaway. She was a lifeguard at the public pool in Forsyth. She admired our kayaks and expressed interest in accompanying us to the confluence. The extreme lower Yellowstone is an exotic place, even to Montanans. I called her from the pay phone at the old Kenyon Hotel, in Terry. It was Sunday morning. After a wait of several minutes her mother put her on. The lifeguard had just won the Miles City Triathlon, a feat of jogging, canoeing, and, I think, archery, and she was, she said, in no shape to join us, after celebrating at the Olive, the Montana, the Bison, and around Forsyth. At least she was honest.

We always seemed to do things backward. After being refused by the triathlon athlete, we walked to the local Ace Hardware store and bought a tiny life jacket for Jack. A lady at the checkout stand was talking about her sister's garage sale. We walked up the street to the sale and purchased a children's book by William Saroyan, another about a little tugboat on the Mississippi, and a third, the back story to *The Rescuers Down Under*. We had been playing the video of *The Rescuers Down Under* in various motels. It struck me as odd, 9:00 A.M. on a Sunday morning in Terry, Montana, that the Disney corporation was recycling some British old maid for her original tale of mice in love. I thought of the original *Bambi*, another Disney video we were playing motel to motel as we traveled east, when the rain was too much for camping. *Bambi* is originally an allegorical novel by a Czech writer named Felix Salten. Salten was worried about the Germans, long ago. They gave him the Nobel Prize, though who, who has seen *Bambi*, knows this? Who knows that Forsyth commanded the troops at Wounded Knee?

Without help, we decided to abandon hope of a family float for the day. I would hop on the river and try to cover as many miles as possible. This early in the morning, launching from the campsite, thirty river miles might be possible. We had become obsessed. Whatever else happened we would cover every watery inch. And, though we always knew this from the maps, it was sinking in just how long the Yellowstone really was. We had come two hundred miles from Billings, alone. It was another one hundred miles to the confluence. Gardiner to Livingston had been less than that, and it had taken many weeks. Though we had momentum, we were running out of time, once again. If the snows came early as they had the previous summer, we might find ourselves frozen out once more. I recalled that one party of miners in the last century had simply left their boats locked in the ice below Terry, and walked to Glendive with nothing but their gold and their guns.

We started back for the Powder River campsite. The Brazilian said, "We forgot to buy milk."

I guess we were out of milk.

I whipped the Trooper around in the middle of the street, in front of Ace Hardware, and across from the bank. The back door of the Trooper swung open and everything fell out, Newman's spaghetti sauce, red raspberry jam, a Rubbermaid container of brown sugar for coffee, toys and sleeping bags.

We stopped the car and climbed out.

It was a pastiche upon pavement: glass shards, spaghetti sauce, a mess. There was no point in getting mad. We were beyond that. Obviously, thirty river miles was now a high estimate, with the central intersection of Terry, Montana, red and gooey.

Immediately, a man stopped his yellow pickup truck and started to help us. He had graying full hair, blue jeans, and a cowboy shirt. He said nothing. The disaster was so major, to us, we could say nothing ourselves.

"Heck," said the man, finally, "you can use my hose to wash off your things, if you want. I live over there across the tracks."

Another Terry person stopped. She was driving a late-1970s Cadillac, saffron yellow, about the biggest car an American manufacturer ever made, last of the behemoths.

The first thing she said was, "I like to see a couple that doesn't yell at each other when a disaster like this happens." Jack started crying from his car seat. Cody was bedeviling him. We intervened. Ines was shouting. "That's what little boys do," said the woman. "They fight and cry. I had two of them myself. I loved my husband. He treated me with respect all his life. I have a boyfriend now." Her voice dropped, and she seemed embarrassed by that. She was about seventy, and wearing a colorful brown-red-and-green dress, which she said she had made herself. She called it her Thanksgiving dress. "My son is an accountant in Bozeman. I only visit now and then. All those mountains! I get lonesome for flat spaces."

The calm man in the yellow pickup said, "You folks need anybody to ferry you around?"

"You know," I said, "we could use a boat. We're trying to get everybody on the river and we're between rafts."

"I have a boat in the garage," he said. "Come over, wash off your things, take a look at the boat."

Ines went to replenish our supplies, with Jack. Cody and I followed the man in the yellow pickup. He was an industrial mechanic. He maintained the big conveyer belts at the Colstrip plant. His wife was a chemist. They were in their forties. They lived in Terry and worked night shifts in Colstrip. (Later I looked at the map closely. It is 118 miles from Terry to Colstrip.) The woman had grown up on a farm on the north side of the Yellowstone between Buffalo Rapids and the Powder. The schoolhouse lay on the south side of the river. There was no bridge in those days. She had, I believe, seven brothers and sisters, and they all climbed into a gondola car outside their house and rode across the river on a cable, twice a day. I had noticed the cable and the two wooden towers on either side of the river when I floated under it the previous day. The cable was about forty feet above the water.

"Were you scared in the winter, when the river was frozen and you were suspended over it? Must have been windy."

She looked surprised. "I never thought about it," she said.

We went to the garage to see the boat. It was a heavy steel-and-fiberglass canoe full of old river water and decomposing leaves. The gunwales seemed shallow. But it looked wide enough to hold us all. We heard Cody screaming.

In the yard, Cody was pulling down his pants. He had already pulled up one of his pant legs. He was yelling bloody murder. A shovel lay before him on top of a raised ant hill. Cody danced and screamed.

"Poor little guy," said the man.

I pulled down Cody's pants and picked off the large red ants that were stuck to his flesh.

When Cody was mostly quiet, the man and I hoisted the heavy

boat on top of the Trooper. It was a cloudy day, one of those days when you wake up early and you know nothing will happen. But a lot was! A muddy day. If we were constitutionally calm people, I am sure everything would come to us. We were not. And so we usually had to remind ourselves that everything got done, just never in the way we planned. When circumstances conspired to knock us off the river, why, then the story was to be found on dry land.

We picked up Ines in front of the market. She had a barbecued chicken, nicely spiced by the market's butcher. We ate it on the hood of the Trooper, in the street, for lunch. The day was passing rapidly.

We drove back to the campsite on the Powder. The swirl of rapids looked too intimidating for a family float in a fiberglass-and-steel borrowed canoe. We drove a bit east to the old Milwaukee Railroad bridge, and attempted a launch. It took many minutes to rock over the gravel and cactus, no road, to the river, then to suit up the boys in life preservers, Jack in his new orange jacket, Cody in his spiffy blue preserver. We packed a lunch. We packed flashlights and emergency gear to be on the safe side. Meanwhile, the wind came up. The Brazilian became increasingly anxious. Cody attempted to hit Jack with a paddle. Jack succeeded in hitting Cody with a paddle.

We launched. When we had arrived, the Yellowstone here below the Milwaukee Bridge had been glassy. Suddenly, sixty feet out, it was crisscrossed with whitecaps, like a case of bad hives.

"If we capsize," I said, "I'll grab the baby. You grab Cody."

Saying this put things into perspective. A couple of waves lapped over the gunwales. We paddled hard for the south bank. The hell with it.

Much later, I read what Clark had said about the stretch, just below where we abandoned the family float, for this day:

At 20 miles below the Buffalow Shoals passed a rapid which is by no means dangerous it has a number of large rocks in different parts of the river which causes high waves a very good chanel on the Lar.^d Side. this rapid I call Bear rapid from the circumstance of a bears being on a rock in the Middle.

Perhaps the family could have scooted right past that old bear with only a minor anxiety attack and a lot of screaming.

It took two hours to loft and return the borrowed boat, dry out the toddlers, and regain the campsite at Bush of Ghosts II.

We sipped some hot chocolate. It was still early. All was not lost. *Batman Returns* was showing at the Prairie Drive-in Theater. We left at the part where Danny DeVito, as the Penguin, sends his minions to kidnap the firstborn sons of Gotham and throw them into a sewer vat. Traveling with a young firstborn, we thought that might be a little scary. But what a place to watch a movie. Our ticket was taken at the gate by Bert Lee, who with his wife Evelyn have owned the Prairie Theater for thirty-seven years. We were a little late. We parked the car in the middle of the grounds, next to a pole with two heavy metal speakers about six inches square. I was trying to recall how to work the speakers in a drive-in when a dozen cars started honking. There were only about a dozen cars in the lot. "Turn your lights off!" somebody finally shouted. Leaving your headlights on is the cardinal sin at a drive-in theater. We turned off our lights.

It was just as much fun to watch *Batman Returns* from outside the car. The little speakers blared from around the lot, and another, bigger, speaker was bolted to the roof of the concession stand above a small and rickety grandstand where all the kids were seated. We walked to the entrance of the concession stand. I felt tingles. I remembered the Sage and the Motor-Vu in Billings. I asked Evelyn Lee if there were many drive-ins left in Montana.

"We're it."

Evelyn was a short woman in a print dress. She wore black tennis shoes, and after she finished some sentences, she raised her eyebrows and shrugged her round shoulders for emphasis. She prepared us a feast of hot dogs, popcorn, and "real malted milks, not the powdered mix kind they give you at McDonald's." And then she said, having had time to think it over, "Maybe there's another drive-in in Scobey. We haven't been up to check it out." Scobey is a couple hundred miles north, along what's called the High-line, near the Canadian border. So most likely we were probably at the last drive-in in Montana, and for sure we knew the ice cream in the malts was real.

Through a window over the grill, we could see two men in another room running the projector. The carbon lamps were incredibly bright, and they used mirrors. We talked with the operators. They said this process hadn't been changed for forty years. They said it provided a better image than what you saw at the multiplexes in the big cities, like Los Angeles and Billings.

The next afternoon, we backtracked and I kayaked from a place we called Mosquito Point, to the campsite on the Powder. Mosquito Point looks onto Little Sheep Mountain to the north, and borders an alfalfa field on the south bank. It was a quick run. I was always paddling, rarely just drifting, and I had arrived an hour earlier than Ines and the boys. The mosquitoes were as thick as they had been atop Pompey's, only bigger, about as big as geese. I went swimming twice, to slough them off. The current was smooth and strong. Fish jumped all around me, for the mosquitoes and for the mayflies. We had secured permission to use Mosquito Point from a Mr. Becker, who had been out hunting birds in an old compact Ford, a field car, shotguns laid across the back seat. Mr. Becker was such a big man he seemed too big for the car.

"Sure, go ahead, use the river. Nope no birds yet," he said. "I don't know where they're keeping themselves."

The next day I kayaked from the campsite to the bridge at Terry. I passed over Clark's dreaded Buffalo Shoals, "by far the worst place which I have seen on this river from the Rocky mountains to this place a distance of 694 mountains by water. a Perogue or large canoe would with Safty pass through the worst of those Shoals, which I call the Buffalow Sholes from the circumstances of one of those animals being in them." No buffalo these days, and the rapids weren't spit, in a kayak, simply an underwater shelf of shale teeth protruding a hundred feet into the current.

Though still light, a full moon had risen as I took out under the Terry Bridge and dragged the boat through the sagebrush to the car. A jackrabbit ran from behind a rock and Jack toddled after it, squealing and cawing. The moon and the sun were both up. The moon lay like a polished Roman egg, high above a stone buttress to an abandoned bridge a hundred yards downriver. Upriver, the sun was shimmering amber. This was a landscape without time, with the sun and moon hung at opposite ends of the day.

The next morning I floated from Terry to the Fallon Bridge. There were no trees at all. It was like floating a desert with canyon walls.

*   *   *

The following day, we wanted to make it to Glendive, but there are no bridges between Fallon and Glendive. We took exits off the interstate with names like Bad Route Road, which led away from the river into the Big Sheep Mountains, and chatted with farmers to find a good place to put in. On the roads we sang "Old MacDonald's Farm" to keep the boys occupied. They loved that song. You feel a little silly the first twenty times you sing "Old MacDonald's Farm," with an oink-oink here and an oink-oink there, but after only about two hundred more times, the tune grows on you.

"Old MacDonald had a farm! With a what?"

"An alligator!" shouts someone from a car seat.

"OK, with a *grrrrhh-grrrrh* here and a *snap-snap* there—" Just what sort of sound would an alligator, on the old MacDonald place, make?

Farmhouse after farmhouse, nobody was home. They were in the fields, bringing in the sugar beets. Women were as likely to drive harvesters and giant trucks as the men.

We found an elderly lady home at one place. She had lots of cats in the yard.

"How many cats do you have?" asked Cody.

"Seven."

"What are their names?"

"Kitty Kitty."

"What's that one's name?"

"Kitty Kitty."

"What's that one over there's name?"

"Kitty Kitty."

"What's that one's name?"

"Kitty Kitty."

"Oh. What's that one's name?"

"What do you think?"

"Kitty Kitty," said Cody.

The old farm lady laughed and Cody laughed with her. They had a joke going.

The next farm was more of a dog kind of place. A bull mastiff and a large Chesapeake Bay retriever with chocolate-brown eyes ran to meet us. We did not get out of the car. We rolled up the windows. The mastiff stood on his hind legs with his front legs against the driver's door and stared in at me. He had hepatitic yellow eyes. He slobbered on the glass.

"That's a big dog," I said to the farm lady when she came out.

"Oh, he's just the neighbor's pup. Down dogs! C'mere, Shiloh."

Shiloh was the name of the retriever, which was hers. Everybody got out. The lady invited us in for cookies. She was taking care of her granddaughter, who was wearing green pedal pushers and black high heels, a bit big for her. She was four.

"Cody, you want to race across the barnyard?" asked the little girl.

They went outside and lined up with Shiloh and the neighbor's puppyish brute as the race judges.

"Oh, first, I must take off my high heels," said the little girl.

Cody was taken with this girl.

(I had the impression, though I could be wrong, that either the girl's mother or father had left this child to be raised with the grandparents while the parents put their lives together, separately, in some city far away. This was true of another small child at one of the farms where we had stayed upriver. Like some ghetto grandmothers, these farmers, though much better off economically, believed it was their Christian duty to take care of their own, and they did it, as far as I could tell, with great love. These sorts of things were never stated, of course, and we never inquired.)

"What happened to Shiloh's neck?" asked Ines, after we had finished the cookies and gone outside again, and the lady was pointing out a low place on the river about a mile from the house that would be a good place to take out the boats.

"Rattlesnake bit Shiloh, I think over there in that corn field. His neck blew up big as a basketball. They lanced it in the vet's office. Slime and pus flew everywhere. Oh, it was awful."

She told us about two boys who had been bitten by rattlesnakes and were just then in a Billings hospital learning how to walk again.

We were impressed.

"Those snakes were over by Glendive, though," she pointed out.

Glendive was only fifteen miles downriver.

"It's worse in August, cause the snakes are molting then and they don't have their rattles. You can't hear 'em so well."

This farm was in Dawson County. Here is an account of rattlesnake infestation in old Dawson County from Montana historian Roberta Carkeek Cheney:

One of the biggest rattlesnake dens found was near a school house on Little Breed Creek. In 1929–30 there were nine children attending this school. The snakes were in a "dog town" right at the school house, and the children hunted snakes from the first day of school until cold weather drove the snakes down the prairie dog holes. No estimate is available of the number killed, but the record for one noon hour was 116 good rattles. Rules set up by the youthful snake hunters did not permit counting "buttons" or broken rattles.

The farm lady stared back at the place on the river that she had recommended as a good take-out. "No," she said, "I wasn't there the day Shiloh got bit. My husband told me about it. It was down on the river."

"The place there, where you think it'd be a good place to take the boats out?"

"Think so."

One time in northern California, I shot a rattlesnake that was menacing my two malamutes. I skinned the snake and fried it in butter, out of curiosity. The dogs refused to eat it, and these malamutes rarely refused anything, especially a butter-fried delicacy. It was not bad, I thought, though maybe it needed a sauce.

The next farm, a little farther downriver, was called the Cottonwood Lane Ranch. To reach the ranch house, we drove through lines of cottonwoods, for two miles. They were so beautiful, these cottonwoods, that we had to stop the Trooper and walk among them. These bushy-bearded soft monsters are the aspens of the bottom land, and they were turning from green to chartreuse to russet. If you compared them with their mountain cousins, the aspens, you might imagine aspens as minimalist brush strokes, and cottonwoods as wild blotches of color run amok in willy-nilly gnarliness. Cottonwoods worked in this landscape. In the mountains, aspens were usually hemmed in by bigger spruce and pine. Delicate yet tough, there was nevertheless something punctilious about those narrow, symmetrical aspens. Here on the prairie, the lumbering cottonwoods knew they had the sky and earth to themselves. They could flop out and stretch. They didn't have to dress for dinner, like those upriver aspens.

For three hundred miles I had been falling in love with birds. Now I found myself rhapsodizing about trees.

I understood why the little old lady in the wild homemade dress in Terry felt cramped in the lush bowl of Bozeman, to the west. I also understood that to live here in eastern Montana, it might help to be a little crazy of mind and a lot pure of soul. In this landscape, some men had fallen in love with the wolves they had killed. Some women went mad in sod huts, and others flowered, like Evelyn Cameron, the famous British photographer who started the Eve Ranch near Terry a hundred years ago. Cameron preferred the hard living of *makoshika* and prairie to the pretensions of the lesser English royalty to which she had been born.

Cottonwoods provide the only living color on the lower Yellowstone, save for the blue feathers of the herons and a few rouge-painted cliffs. Cottonwoods require an untrammeled river to reproduce. The banks of their river must be flooded for the seedlings to take root in the repository curves. Real impoundments that stop flow and lower the water level cause cottonwoods to die out, as they have on the tamed and despoiled Missouri to the north. Here, on the Yellowstone, cottonwoods are the ancient forests.

I had never thought about cottonwoods as ancient forests, like baobabs or banyans, or the ipe and mahogany of the Brazilian rain forest. Twelve years old, I used to walk out on the river flats with a BB gun and shoot cicadae droning high in these cottonwoods. When hit, the cicadae sputtered to our feet like winged fighters in a history-book war. Now I thought about those old cottonwoods the cicadae made their music in.

First I had fallen in love with the birds, and now I was in love with trees.

There's no accounting for taste.

I was turning into a redneck druid.

I guess I was home.

It was time for a final family assault on the Missouri.

Mrs. Holden, of the Cottonwood Lane Ranch, was harvesting a field close to the house. Mr. Holden showed us the chickens and the animals, and explained how to crisscross the roads bordering the corn, beet, and alfalfa fields to reach the bottom acres, which he used for the sheep. By the time we finally found the river, it was too late to drive back to the Fallon Bridge and launch. The air was so dry and yet languid that we put on bathing suits and lay down in the shallow

current over a gravel bar. We did not think to worry about the rattlesnakes. The water was about ten inches deep over the bar, and
swift. Our backs and the bottom of our legs lay on the stones, while
our heads and toes arched out of the river. The water was much
colder than the air. A fall bite was coming into the river. I tied a strip
of orange tape to a branch of a cottonwood on the bank so that I
would be able to spot this place the next day, and we lazed back to
the mouth of the Powder.

By Terry it was raining hard, so hard we had to slow down. The
guys were hungry and we were out of cheese, milk, and bread. We
stopped at the Sinclair minimart, and loaded up in the rain. It was
turning colder. The Brazilian said that since it was raining we should
stay in Terry. We had been camping at the Powder for six nights. In all
that time, we had seen nobody there, except for a couple of sauger
fisherman, early one morning. I said I didn't think it would be raining
over the campsite. The western horizon looked clear, if dark. Even
though it had been a wonderful day, we were all a little ragged by the
time we reached the turnoff from the old river road, and started the
slow drive through the cottonwoods along the Powder to the Yellowstone.

By the time we reached the end of the road and the dome tent
flashed in the headlights, the boys had fallen asleep, and it was twenty
degrees colder, though the rain had stopped, as I had predicted.

It is a funny thing about camping. Mood is everything. I have
tramped through snow with extreme ebullience and been bummed
out in perfect summer weather, and over the same trail. It is easy to
become spooked, too. We cooked up some fish we had caught. Of
course, there had been a lot of shadows in this lengthy grove for six
straight nights, but tonight there were more, and we read them differently. Or else the ghosts had turned against us.

"What if it rains later?" Ines asked.

"It probably will," I said. "I mean, it has a couple times. We've
got the tent. We could tie down the blue tarp over it if you think it's
really going to rain hard."

That is not what Ines meant. She didn't know what she meant.

Cottonwood burns differently from pine or oak. Cottonwood
burns fast, and cottonwood flames are higher. When you're in a
rousing beach party summer mood on the Rochejhone, a cotton-

wood fire leaps, and you are cheered. When the mood has suddenly dampened, and the heebie-jeebies are slinking amongst the underbrush where the frumulous bandersnatch lurk, when all of a sudden at the edge of the Coleman's buzzy glow, you can imagine a Ted Bundy dropping off the interstate for a night of sleep, then coming upon you, already asleep, or you can imagine some local hired hand a little hard up for cash, though you instantly remind yourself that the people around Terry have struck you as being about as honest as Americans get, you do not harvest sugar beets at two in the morning with portable lamps unless an honest dollar is about the only way you can call it, right then you hear an unexpected noise, and you tighten up all over. You do not jump and laugh about it, as you might have days before.

"What was that?" said Ines.

"I don't know."

"It sounded like a person."

"It couldn't have been a person."

We turned away from the fire and surveyed the shadows and the broken limbs of the cottonwoods. The moon was burning the bluffs across the river. It was light over there, compared with here in the trees. The big cottonwood at the edge of the river with the dead spikes at the top, a tree more dead than alive, I had noticed at breakfast, since only the lower left side still supported a bush of green leaves, this beautiful tree caught our attention for some reason. A long *who-who* came out of it.

"It's an owl."

The sound turned to a moan.

"It's a person trying to sound like an owl."

That sounded crazy to me. We stood and listened. The *who-who-who* came again, and then the goofiest human moan, more than a little scary.

"No owl sounds like that."

"Well, let's just pack up the car and leave," I said. I knew we wouldn't get any sleep now. This was it. I have been afraid in the woods before, and there is no point to it. Just get out of there, if you can.

"Let's put the guys in the car and grab a few things, quick."

"Where's the gun?" asked Ines.

"In the bag in the tent."

Ines left the circle of the fire and came back with the Colt .45 semiautomatic. I put Jack in his car seat and propped up Cody beside, with my down coat over him. The back door of the Trooper was open, and I stood on the ledge above the bumper, feeling upward with my hands to make sure the kayaks were securely fastened. I could see Ines in the circle of the fire as she held the .45 in proper position and popped off two rounds at the old tree by the river.

"Jesus!"

She let off a third languid round. Slow and easy the way she pulled the trigger and kept her crouch. They make Ipanema girls tough. I swiveled my head around and across the entire grove of cottonwoods and only then stared back at the big tree by the river. Only then did the big bird jump from the top and cross toward the Powder.

"It is an owl!"

"An owl," said Ines.

I was thinking, maybe the guy heard the owl the first time, or saw the owl, so he imitated the thing. Though I knew that was ridiculous, my adrenaline was still charging. I didn't have to ask Ines if that was also what she was thinking. We stuffed the down bag and the down quilt in the car, and started off.

"It was just an owl," said Ines.

"You never know," I said. "And who cares? We never would have slept a minute after that."

"I wouldn't have slept a second," said Ines.

Of course, we didn't sleep much that night in Terry, either, in a place called the Kenyon Hotel, which was on the main street, because some enormous delivery truck came off the interstate to deliver beer, or something, to the bar across the street, and the truck left its refrigerator motor running for what seemed like an hour, and the thickly furnished room smelled of cigar smoke, from some old retired guy. Maybe the old guy had lung cancer and he could not sleep for thinking about it, and smoking soothed him. Once you're back in a big city like Terry, Montana, you think neurotic city things.

We came back to the Powder after breakfast and broke camp. I made the river from the Cottonwood Lane Ranch to Glendive. The water was unexpectedly fast. Few islands divided the flow. Here and there were some of the oldest houses on the river. They were built of brown brick and clay. They looked to be from the 1860s. Tucked in cottonwood clearings exploding with color were old-fashioned oil rigs, the rocker arms gently pumping away like toys, fossils left over from the Sand Creek oil boom decades before.

From Glendive to the confluence with the Missouri, it is only seventy-five miles. We had made five hundred. It was hard to believe, at least for us.

But I think we were also losing patience.

Glendive: Sir St. George Gore

GLENDIVE TAKES ITS NAME FROM GLENDIVE CREEK, which was originally named Glendale Creek by Sir St. George Gore. I envied Sir George of Glendive, originally of Sligo, Ireland. He made camp early in the afternoon, he traveled in style, and he never lost his patience. In 1854, decades before the rude Custer rode out to the West like a Michigan carpetbagger, Gore hunted the Powder and the Yellowstone with an entourage unequaled before or since. Sir George did not stay in motels. He traveled with forty servants, 112 horses, twelve yoke of oxen, twenty-one French carts (all painted bright red and pulled by two horses each), three milk cows, and fourteen dogs. There was one wagon for the seventy-five rifles, the fifteen shotguns, and the pistols, and two more wagons for the fishing gear. One of his retainers was a professional fly tier. When Sir George went hunting, a man handed him his gun. He shot, handed the discharged weapon back, received another loaded weapon. Sir George brought dozens of bottles of French wine, and each night after dinner, he would read Shakespeare to his guide, who was Jim Bridger, the mountain man who later would spin those tales of geysers and petrified forests in Yellowstone Park that nobody believed. Bridger said that for him Shakespeare was "a leetle too highfalutin." Bridger preferred the fantastic exploits of Baron Munchhausen, which Sir George also read aloud around the campfire. Munchhausen's adventures were no more unreal than his own among the Blackfeet, said Bridger.

Of course, one of Sir George's wagons unfolded into a four-poster bed, by means of cranks at the corners, and he had a linen tent, too, with red stripes. The short, ruddy, bald and paunchy Gore, with his mutton-chop sideburns, was no tenderfoot. He toughed out Montana weather. Above Glendive, where the Tongue slides into the Yellowstone at what is now Miles City, he had a small cabin built for himself, and there he spent the winter, alone with his favorite horse, a gray thoroughbred from Kentucky.

Nobody trifled with Sir George of Sligo, not Indians, nor trappers, not the army, because nobody trifles with a spectacle, in Montana or anywhere else, then as now. Sir George was as safe cloaked in Irish lunacy as Ferdinand Hayden, the Man Who Picks Up Stones While Running, was cloaked in scientific obsession. Hayden collected fossils near Glendive the same year Sir George butchered the living animals, though no record exists of their ever meeting.

The aptly named Gore "slaughtered the enormous aggregate of forty grizzly bears, twenty-five hundred buffaloes, beside numerous elk, deer, antelope, and other *small* game," complained Alfred J. Vaughan, the Indian agent for the upper Missouri.

Lacking Gore's four-poster bed, which we could not have all fit into anyway, and a bit camp-shocked by the psycho owl of the Powder, we stayed the night at a Glendive motel. Glendive was a rough old Western town, bisected by the interstate. The place was interesting enough for a night or two, but we found we did not like motel life any longer. It was hard to tell whether we had become too soft or too hard, by this point.

Interstate motels all look alike. The same white plastic modular bathrooms, the beds built on platforms so that nothing can be forgotten underneath, the carpet rising to the mattresses, to make vacuuming easier, the chip-board furniture, the early 11:00 A.M. checkout time. Staying in these American motels is like watching too much television.

I hoped we were not growing cranky. A friend of mine once wrote a book with the subtitle *Around the World in a Bad Mood*. I did not want our last days to turn into that. I wanted to smooth along like Sir St. George Gore.

Well, so, we were footsore, so to speak, and whining just a little. What was happening to us? Completion anxiety? I recalled that I used to stand with my father at the luncheon meetings of the Billings Kiwanis Club and we would all sing "Home on the Range": "Home, home on the Range / Where the deer and the antelope play / Where seldom is heard a discouraging word / And the sky is not cloudy all day." Quitters never win and winners never quit. I hoped our attitude problem was only the residue of too much urban living. Onward we paddled.

Crack of noon, I hit the river below the interstate bridge. I felt better with the first stroke. The river sopped up my anxiety. On the water I thought less and observed more. At Glendive the interstate rolls on to Minneapolis. I was glad to leave the road behind. The Yellowstone turned north. The land became more isolated.

There were herons and cottonwoods, but what I noticed most here was the coal. It was everywhere, stretched out in long black and yellow stratum lines, cupped in exposed caverns, chunked along the banks like tar at a New Jersey beach. At a convention of environmentalists in Billings, it might seem madness that anyone would want to turn the Yellowstone into one giant coal slurry to provide power for blow dryers in St. Louis and L.A. And it is. Let those people towel off.

But the vastness of the resource cannot be understood until you kayak through it, over it, and below it. I recalled two newspaper articles. I had read them both in McDonald's restaurants. (We often stopped at McDonald's because the glass-enclosed play rooms provided instant babysitting.) The first article, which I perused at the Livingston McDonald's, was in the *Wall Street Journal*. It said that with all America's talk about new energy sources, solar and the rest, and our studied revulsion with foreign oil, the bottom line was that something old had become something new. King coal was replacing nuclear. The article said the problem with coal was that it polluted, but that the Department of Energy was pumping hundreds of millions of dollars into new technology to clean up coal-fired plants and, also, that the low-sulfur coal that polluted least was concentrated in Montana.

Geologists often become excited discussing Montana's coal. "Its astronomically large coal content makes the Fort Union formation the most valuable body of rock in the state, one of the most valuable in the entire world," write Professors David Alt and Donald W. Hyndman. "The actual amount of coal is unknown, but certainly staggering, probably something more than 50 billion tons, an unbelievable reserve of fossil fuel." What I was seeing was called Ft. Union lignite. The original Ft. Union overlooked the confluence.

The other article I read was in the Glendive McDonald's. The Billings *Gazette* said the counties of eastern Montana had lost as much as 40 percent of their population in the 1990 census, and that hundreds of people had met in Powder County to talk of ways to bring in tourists and high-tech light industry.

So there was lots of coal here, and people badly needed jobs at the same time. The pressure to use the Yellowstone would grow in the years or decades to come, or perhaps the big river could be kept pristine while the region mined its coal correctly. But something would happen. You did not need a full moon to see that.

As I came around one barren hill of clay and coal, I saw out of the corner of my eye a coyote drinking from the river on the right bank. The animal stared at me as I paddled closer. I stopped paddling and froze, but I kept the edge of my paddle in the current. The coyote was fixated on the slight gurgle made by the edge dragging in the water. Then the animal dropped its head. The coyote turned and trotted off with a lope and a lark. It was the first coyote I had seen right along the river. It disappeared into a ravine that was neon yellow, with turning cottonwoods, on one side, and black, with crumbling coal, on the other.

What a strange thing, that bodies compressed long enough make good fire.

Intake

A T THE LIP OF THE INTAKE DIVERSION, the river is flat as a lake. A bald knob of earth rises on the left, and a channel about thirty feet wide is diverted there into an irrigation canal. There is still a tremendous amount of water left for the Yellowstone. You have to be almost on top of the hedge of boulders that stretches across the river to see below the crude dam. I beached the kayak on a muddy sandbar and inspected the drop. It was about ten feet.

I checked the curtain of water through the boulders for several minutes. The dam was formed in about 1905 by dropping jagged lumps of sandstone from gondolas pulled over the river on cables. The water formed a series of slanted waterfalls, like foaming split teeth, before it reached the huge churning pool below. I decided it would be hard to execute an Eskimo roll in the narrow sluices, and by the time I reached the pool it might be a little late. The boulders were close together. I would have to do some paddle whacking to keep my balance, not much chance for real stroking. I thought, well, what the hell, it's a hot day, and I have my helmet on. This is probably the last white-water thrill on the river. I'll do it.

I started back for the boat. I looked up. At the campsite, far across the roiling river, the gang was waving and cheering. One hates to go down wrong and come up bloody in front of the family. Sets a bad example.

So I dragged the boat to the right, over the thirty-foot embankment of earth, broken cottonwoods, and boulders piled high to contain the river in spring rise. It took half an hour of huffing and puffing. It was the closest to a portage I had made in five hundred miles.

Intake is an ugly name for a beautiful place. In name, Intake reminded me of Iceland. I once had a conversation with a local in the Hollywood Bar in Reykjavík. He claimed the original settlers had named Iceland as they had because there was little ice there and the warmish ocean current that surrounded the island kept the temperatures not so bad. The name served to discourage folks from sailing there. The old Vikings then named the truly cold and desolate island Greenland, to encourage immigration. Of course, that was the view from the Hollywood Bar in Reykjavík.

We camped in a wide grove of cottonwoods a few feet from the river, at Intake. Each day the leaves turned a deeper yellow, until they began on the russets. The branches rustled softly at night. They smelled good and crisp as they turned color. The churning water a few hundred yards upstream below the diversion was like the sound of surf. We wore bathing suits and sandals, and here it was already October. The air was as dry as a desert. There was nobody around. The river and prairie seemed ours, most of the time.

We slept in close quarters, but we had decided camping was better than any motel. At least we did not have to share the dome tent with a Kentucky thoroughbred, as Sir St. George Gore had shared his cabin.

Intake was a place for fishing. In this it was like the stretch of the Yellowstone through Paradise Valley, but the fish were very different. There, black-spotted cutthroat trout, chunky German browns, and sleek rainbows hit nymphs and dry flies. Here the fish were big and brown: sauger, walleye, channel cats, Northern pike, sturgeon, and paddlefish, and the fishing methods were downriver.

In May, three thousand mad Montana anglers descend upon Intake to snag spawning paddlefish. Paddlefish are prehistoric. They have been in the river for seventy million years. They are big, forty to ninety pounds, and with a two-foot-long spatula of a nose they look a bit like goofy swordfish, yet they are more closely related to cartilaginous sharks. They taste like sturgeon, which were also said to be swimming in front of our campsite. Paddlefish strain plankton. Their bill is a sensory organ for locating microorganisms. They do not take flies nor lures and must be snagged with treble hooks about four inches across, while they spawn, then pulled to shore with deep-sea tackle. I would hate to be snagged with a four-inch treble hook while in the throes of mating. The roe is sold as caviar in restaurants in New York, L.A., and Paris.

There were also schools of shad, which were very easy to catch. I would toss out a lure, hook into a one- or two-pound shad, and hand the rod to Cody. Cody would jam the butt in his belly like a marlin fisherman and crank away, the drag on the reel hissing. After the first morning, we knew where to find the boys after breakfast. They were up by the diversion, telling the locals how to catch sauger and shad.

Next morning I hit the river early and paddled hard. Strobel had left a message on our phone machine that he wanted to see the confluence. He would drive down from Bozeman. We would meet him at a place called Elk Island, twenty miles farther downriver. This was good timing because we had acquired a new raft. With Strobel on hand to help set up shuttles, we could finish the river as a group.

I made six miles an hour, my best time so far. When you paddle hard for hours without stopping, the endorphines take over. Your head becomes calm and clear, your vision stronger. I had with me a navel orange and a Cherry Coke. The orange fell over in a turn. I sucked down the stinky muck of black water and preservative, and it tasted like dessert.

Ines drove back to Glendive to pick up the new self-bailing raft. We inflated it at Elk Island, using a tiny electric pump that ran off the Trooper's battery. The pump was a genie of unlimited lung power. The raft was more than we needed for the lower Yellowstone. But the walls were high and safe and it was painted a jolly blue.

Strobel drove up just as we were about to drive to the little town of Savage and shanghai a teenager or friendly farmer in a truck to set up a shuttle to Seven Sisters, the take-out. Strobel was wearing some Japanese art hat, and his hair had grown. He held it in a knot behind the hat. He was shirtless, in Teva river sandals, with his usual wraparound Oakley sunglasses. We were in business.

Even so, the shuttle took longer than we thought. It was all dirt roads through bottom land at both ends. We hit the river a little late.

A mile into the float, Jack vomited, but we had come too far to turn back. He immediately fell asleep and woke up half an hour later with a cherubic smile on his face. Neither seasick nor sunstruck, he was probably just getting something off his chest, with drama.

Ines swam behind the raft, for temperature control. It was ninety degrees. We took turns rowing, even Cody. When the boys became too antsy, we stopped to play see-saw on some downed cottonwood log. I waded into the current until I was standing on the bottom with just my fingers holding my sunglasses above the surface. Time ran over the hill like a band of wild horses.

"We're not going to make it before dark," said Strobel.

Both boys fell asleep against the pneumatic walls of the raft. The sun set. Darkness was swift. Here we were, finally caught on the river at night, as Persis and I had been long ago at Carbella when we had jumped on the water for a test spin in new rental kayaks and quickly managed to feel something between heady excitement and raw panic. This time we enjoyed the dry beauty of the evening. There was a sliver of a moon. We listened carefully for the whisper of the snags of the downed cottonwood sweepers. We kept close to the left bank. The danger lay in missing the car. The next bridge was at Sidney, and we wouldn't make it until the middle of the night should we miss the take-out.

After a while, we could see almost nothing. Still, it was a fine night. Then, like a little miracle, a car turned on its headlights a hundred feet from Dave's Accord. It was probably the only car besides ours to visit this isolated place all day. If the driver had chosen to leave five minutes before, we would have slid past into the night.

Back at Intake, the boys were laid in their sleeping bags. We built a fire of cottonwood logs and watched the crescent moon rise above the brown churning water where the ancient paddlefish slithered about and strained their zooplankton with their noses. We dined on grilled sauger and russet potatoes and retired.

The float between Seven Sisters Recreation Area and the town of Sidney was as peaceful as Elk Island to Seven Sisters. We had seen less than a dozen other people on the river in the weeks since Billings, mostly fishermen in aluminum boats around Miles City. We saw nobody at all on the river these days. The Yellowstone and the territory on both sides were as isolated as any stretch since Yellowstone Park. The wildlife recreation areas were full of deer, grouse, ducks, and beaver, though the beaver were hard to catch out, except at dusk.

Mostly we gazed upon the banks and lost ourselves looking into the current. What a gorgeous piece of wetness the Yellowstone was.

Sidney proved to be a hopping little town, unexpectedly so. We were getting a little weather cocky, I think, expecting we could laze on down to the confluence in the comfortable blue raft, dangling our feet over the edge and musing upon paddlefish and crescent moons. Two or three days more and we would be in the sites of restored Ft. Union where Clark, Lewis, Colter, Shields, Sacajawea, Pomp, Charbonneau, and the rest had gotten so excited to have reached the Yellowstone that they broke out the rum (one dram per person) for the first time since St. Louis and fiddled and danced round the campfire into the night.

We decided, since we were in Sidney already, to celebrate with steaks at the old Pyramid Club. With its western swing band, large dance floor, dark wood walls, white tablecloths, cordial cowgirls, and old waiters, the Pyramid could have been a set for a Patsy Cline musical. The boys ran around the dance floor and the dining room and nobody cared. An older woman offered to dance with Cody, and did. "That boy's too young for you, Lil!" admonished her old girlfriend.

Then we hit the Cattle-Ac Bar & Grill downtown. The Cattle-Ac had just opened, and it entertained a younger clientele. People looked very good in Sidney, the Brazilian pointed out. They were thin and tall, animated. There was a furniture factory in Sidney, and a railroad yard, but what was really going on was that the beets were coming in, and the sugar content was high this year. High sugar content! This was enough to make a farm girl kick up her heels on Thursday night at the Cattle-Ac. A farmer reminded us that last year, mountains of piled beets had been frozen in the yards by the same Arctic storm that had knocked us off the river and kept us holed up at the Olive, the Northern, and the Eagle Nest Ranch.

So we partied with the beet farmers of northeastern Montana, and returned to the camp at Intake perhaps a little late. Next morning we had a sauger brunch. Then we sauntered back to Sidney to pick up the raft. We had stashed it behind a fallen cottonwood in a field beside the Sidney Bridge, the night before. We lofted the raft and drove the vehicles down to Fairview, the last river town in Montana. We would skip the Sidney-to-Fairview stretch for a day, so that Strobel could cruise into the confluence with us. A literary ending. He had been with us in the beginning, at Gardiner, and would be with us at the end.

But skipping twenty-five miles down to Fairview with the thirteen-foot raft inflated and flopping on top of the Trooper was slow going. A southerly wind had come up, though the temperature was still in the eighties. We left Ines and the savages below the bridge with the raft. There are two bridges at Fairview. The car bridge crosses over to Cartwright, North Dakota. It is a high, upwardly sloping bridge. The river is at least a hundred feet below. But the railroad bridge is even more spectacular, a four-section, wrought-iron drawbridge crossing into a black hole of a prairie tunnel on the North Dakota side. The light below these bluffs was always an exquisite amber throughout the afternoon, like burning ships in a Turner painting.

We sped down to the confluence. Several times along the farm roads, pheasants burst out of the corn or beets, and almost smacked against the windshield. We parked the Trooper under a bridge, and raced over to Ft. Union in Dave's car to ask about the river from the park supervisor.

I was very excited to be inside a replica of the most historic fort of the fur trading era, resurrected on the original plot. Here Audubon stayed, and Prince Maximilian, and the artists George Catlin, Carl Bodmer, and Rudolph Kurz. The commanders of the American Fur Company, Denig and Culbertson lived like prairie princes in a white lapstrake house complete with glass windows, inside the fort. We stood inside a replica of the house of the bourgeois. But we had no time for Ft. Union's history today. The supervisor, who was also the fort's historian, informed us that we were in the wrong place. We were not at the confluence. We were a couple miles above it. The river we saw out front was the Missouri. The Yellowstone joined a few miles east, at old Ft. Buford. We had the wrong fort and the wrong river.

We shot back, picked up the Trooper, and placed it near the boat ramp that overlooks the joining of the two rivers, close to old Ft. Buford. Then we drove 85 mph through a few more startled pheasants and dodged the big sugar beets that had fallen off harvesters' trucks, to the Fairview Bridge, where the usual crisis ensued.

The final section was supposed to be full of downed cottonwood snags. It would be unsafe to put the children on the river this late. We did not want to risk being caught on the water at night, if it were swirly and snag-filled. We consulted the maps and spoke with a commercial catfish fisherman named Preston, who happened by, and realized that, once again, we had been whipped by logistics. Or maybe it was that late sauger-and-Heineken brunch.

There was some point in self-flagellation, since Strobel needed to be at Montana State University in Bozeman at eight the next morning for midterms. He could not stay an extra day. But being Montanans, at least neotropical-migrant Montanans, self-flagellation was not permissible. We were made of sterner stuff, and so we repaired to the Cattle-Ac Bar & Grill in Sidney to celebrate the fact that we had at least come within a cactus hair of a literary ending.

After dessert, we all walked outside to say good-bye to Strobel. A storm had come up, a hard and cold rain. Sheets of the disgusting, camp-wrecking, river-ruining stuff.

"I hope it isn't snowing on the Bozeman Pass," said Strobel, understandably thinking of the three-hundred-mile drive he had ahead of him. And then he laughed, "Good luck, guys."

Within an hour the temperature was in the low forties, and the rain would not stop. Instead of driving an hour back to Intake, we decided to stay in a motel. This motel was a pleasant one, across from a park, and equipped with a kitchen. The rain quit after a day, but the temperature stayed cold, and the southerly wind was twenty to thirty miles an hour. We watched the Weather Channel the way California anorexics count calories. We did not want to take the boys out in weather so bad it might give them pneumonia. We wanted a happy ending.

One night I called up the commercial fisherman we had met at the Fairview Bridge. He took me cat fishing at dawn. We started at the elusive confluence in his eighteen-foot aluminum outboard, and slowly motored across the Missouri, then up the Yellowstone, dodging sandbars, to the place he had set his hoop net. I wore long underwear, heavy jeans, and a down coat. Notboom wore two stocking caps, rubber boots, and a cloth coat he had sewn together with big canvas patches.

Here is how he talked: "I was workin' construction. Bucket of hot tar poured down my arm. I had first-degree burns. I'm in the hospital. Boss drops by. He wants to know when I'm gonna work again. He didn't give a s— about my arm. I ain't never going to work for nobody again. Oh, this is a nice mess of catties!" We had heaved up about 250 small channel catfish from his carefully placed hoop net. In the center of the squirming, croaking mass of catfish was what looked to be a five-pound salmon. "What is that salmon doing here?" Notboom kept asking, of the rain, the mud, and the fog. "I prefer cats, though. They be better eatin'. The cattie is a beautiful fish once you get over how ugly they are. Take care now sonofabitch don't horn ya. They have stickers in the fins up by the head. Grab 'em like this. There was a girl I knew, one of them horned her and she almost died from the poison. Shit, my hands are so cold poison doesn't bother me, or maybe I've got enough in me. Whooeeh! lookety these cats! I'm a happy man today!"

Afterward, I toured the graves of Ft. Buford, which, unlike Ft. Union, was an army fort. Here are some of them:

Little, Robert, Citizen, Dec 5, 1878, Alcoholism
Newton, Allen, May 9, 1880, Mumps
Shane Baptiste, Interpreter, Feb 10, 1881, Suicide
Durrand, Emma, Feb. 14, 1881, Pneumonia
Argarra, Fernando, Scout, March 24, 1881
Jones, Henry, Citizen, April 15, Suicide by Poison
Left Handbear, Scout July 11, 1881, Consumption
Morrison, Sylvia Aug. 7, 1881, Meningitis, Age 2
George, Morrison, Aug. 17, 1881, Cholera, Age 1
He That Kills His Enemies, Scout, Jan. 18, 1870, Died of Wounds
Coonrod, Aquila, Sgt. Company F7 US Cav., May 14, 1880, Killed by
     Road Agents
Son of Owl Headdress, Jan. 5, 1870, Disease
Owl Headdress, Died Feb. 8, 1870, Beat to Death
Aldrich, Theon, Citizen, Sept. 9 1870, Killed by Indians
Going Eagle, Mandan Chief, Sep 1870, Killed

It was a cold, windy day. The sun was poking about, far to the west and south, in the direction of Terry, but the rest of the large sky was black and racing with squall clouds. The trees were bare. The cottonwoods looked like the skeletons of large men. I went down to look at the confluence. I stood in my down coat. I was in despair. I wanted to finish that river.

By the third day I was so antsy, I put on wool gloves and a couple of sweaters beneath my paddling jacket and launched at the Sidney Bridge by myself. I could at least kayak the river miles to Fairview. Then as soon as the weather warmed, we could make the confluence as a family in the big blue raft.

As we pulled out of the motel parking lot, the proprietor was loading shotguns onto the gun rack of his pickup. He was going after grouse. He smiled at the kayak.

"Hey, buddy, it's hunting season now."

"I agree," I said.

But, though "coolish," as they say in Montana to cover any weather between fifty above and zero, it was, nevertheless, a fine fall float.

The river was muddy and delta brown from all the rain. The cottonwoods had lost most of their russet-colored leaves in the strong winds. The grass on the flats was dead. Even the rocks on the bluffs looked battened down and ready for winter.

But that amber eastern Montana light, and the feeling of paddle pulling through water! I could not stop stroking for an hour. To be back on the river was such a pleasure, and a relief. The rains had also put a lot of water into the Yellowstone and the old man was pumping.

I thought of a very different spot back before Forsyth, when the water was still blue and the cottonwoods green, the sugar beets still in the field. I had come around a flat turn, and there standing on a gravel bar to my left were seven magnificent horses, five chestnuts and two as white as the snow on the Beartooths. They stared at me and I watched them. The sight of the frozen horses left me breathless, but the current swept me past them, and then I was around the next turn, and the howl of a close freight train suddenly took over. The train was hauling forty gondolas of coal somewhere east, to power those blow dryers. And then within a mile came the geese, flocks of fifty or more, honking away at me, until at the last moment they rose off the river in their sputtering *V*s, still highly annoyed with the strange polyethylene creature paddling toward them. I had not forgotten the geese in these last days, but by now I was taking them for granted.

This far downriver, the outside banks on the bigger bends were sometimes piled high with car bodies. This was the old way to keep the Yellowstone from jumping her banks. Upriver, it seemed, junked cars had been mostly pulled out or covered over. When I was a kid, these tangled layers of cars fascinated me. They were like dinosaur bones—a Packard from the thirties, a DeSoto from the forties, and, once in a while, underneath everything, a vintage Model A, pitted and rusted. The cars lay in datable strata like fossils from different geological eras, a jolly charnel house of metal history, with perhaps a muskrat swimming out of a glassless window.

But this moment, car bodies on the banks reminded me sweetly of bodies in cars. Back seat dreams, the stuff of late adolescent reality in a rural state where most people are married before they reach twenty.

We used to cruise along the old river roads between Billings and Huntley in a red 1960 MGA convertible that I had bought for $500. The top never worked. In the winter anybody riding in that car put on two coats. We would take the thing out on an icy parking lot late at night when the cops were likely to be spread thin, get up some speed, turn the wheels, and slam on the brakes. The car swirled around the lamp posts like a ribbon on a fan. We laughed so hard, we never thought we could crash. We were young.

That roadster sat so low that in the summer we would lay out quart cartons of milk, or beer cans, rev her to 40 mph, and try to pick the containers up without stopping. It was a good game, though if you did not grab that can of Great Falls Select just right, your fingers might sting for minutes. Other days, or on moonlit nights, we would drive out to watch cows make love, the way kids today go "cow-tipping." Watching the cows make love was a guaranteed goofy thing to do. It served sometimes to break the ice in a budding relationship. Later, though later to us still meant only sixteen or seventeen, we might end up sleeping beside the river together, before we woke up and drove home to the houses of our respective parents. One prom night in June, I remember staying out all night, waking up beside my date, her hair still piled high from an hour at the beauty shop, but her face encrusted ever so thinly with a layer of frost. She looked beautiful. Though strange.

The river flows on. That was then and this is now. Now I am sliding down the river of return with a new wife and two new kids. To be frank, I think the real reason I left Montana after my father died was for the sex, a poor expatriate, adrift and agog on the times, randy times that will never return. Until very recently, when Montana became fashionable, women were always in somewhat short supply. Though they were a wild bunch, those Montana girls. It is rare to meet their equal.

Montana women seem stronger than their bicoastal sisters. In fact, one could argue that feminism in America was not begun on the East Coast by descendants of patriarchal Mediterranean cultures but rather out in Montana, Wyoming, and the West, where the vote was first granted to women. Everybody recognized, as the independent film *Heartland* later showed, that a ranch could not be run properly by a man, at least alone, that it always took two to resist drink and the elements.

Western macho is largely an eastern myth, just like the myth of the nonexistent Montana outlaw. For instance, America's first congresswoman was a Montanan, Jeannette Rankin, born south of Glacier National Park. For years Rankin was Montana's sole representative. "I have my work cut out for me," the laconic rancher stated upon her election, and she introduced the first bill to grant women citizenship independently of their husbands. But Representative Rankin was perhaps a bit too Montanan. She voted against U.S. entry into both world wars. The first time, the state's populist voters agreed there was no point in spilling blood to retrieve J. P. Morgan's bad loans to Britain, but to question FDR's judgment after Pearl Harbor, that was puzzling and a bit persnickety. Rankin was defeated and went back to running her ranch.

They say you can't go home again, but they couldn't have been talking about Montana. George Webber in Thomas Wolfe's novel could not go home, true. But Webber's small town refused to change, while Webber, who had become a successful novelist in New York, had changed irrevocably, even embarrassingly. I could come home to Montana, because Montana had changed with me. These days you could wear a wet suit into the Blue Cat, and nobody would pick a fight. They only wanted to know how the river was.

*　　*　　*

The river split below Sidney and I took a west channel because it looked faster. The left bank was high and undercut. I could see exposed the roots of cottonwoods that would slip into the river to become sweeper snags in next spring's rise. Would they tumble end-over-end like Ferris wheels? I would miss that.

Another side channel cut the bank into an island. The deep current swirled the boat along. My eye caught a glimpse of white in the brown grass on top of the high little island. It must have been a bone, that slash of white. But the current was fast. The bone was quickly behind me. It must have been a big bone, I thought, for me to be able to spot it from the river. I tried to stop myself, which was difficult. I made an eddy turn and paddled hard upstream. I could not make any real headway. I beached the boat and climbed up the steep bank of the little island.

What if the bone were from a dinosaur? A Triceratops, the three-horned monster every child plays with in model form, had been found near here. So had a *Tyrannosaurus rex,* whose bones now stand in an East Coast museum.

But the bone was a skull, more dirty brown than white, up close. It was the skull of a buffalo, not a dinosaur, though it appeared a little old, perhaps a hundred, perhaps two hundred years. The shifting river bared these old skulls each season. How had it died, this old gangue, as Clark called buffalo? Trampled by ten thousand running mates spooked by a grass fire? Run down by wolves, like the one that had bitten Sergeant Pryor's hand while he slept, after the Crow had stolen his horses? Wounded by a mountain man's flintlock, a cavalry officer's Springfield repeater, a Cheyenne's arrow, a superbly smithed French rifle held infirmly by Sir St. George Gore after a night of red wine drinking?

I was no expert in skull dating. It might have been downed by a spear thrown by a Neanderthal. Or was the animal taking a peaceful swim under the moon, only to be caught by spring rise, and drowned?

The Yellowstone, like no other river, is a many-layered journey: dinosaurs to buffalo, Neanderthals to gold miners, Cheyenne to Custer to beet farmers, trout to paddlefish, cattlemen to kayakers, Gardiner to Sidney.

This summer there was a plan ashore to turn an immense chunk of the Great Plains into a Buffalo Commons, where the buffalo would be free to roam as they had in the time of the Indians, as Clark and Lewis had seen them. A part of Montana bigger than most of New England was being proposed for this scheme, as well as much more land in drought-cursed parts of Wyoming, South Dakota, and the Great Plains states. The upper and middle Yellowstone and the beet- and wheat-rich borders of the lower Yellowstone were spared in this clever vision advanced by an academic couple from Rutgers University, in New Jersey, of all places. But Montana counties within miles of the old buffalo skull would be included, and counties above the Missouri, and a vast tract south and east of Miles City, too. Naturally, cattle ranchers throughout the West were up in arms, Indian tribes politicized, and restoration environmentalists were excited.

All across Montana, however, it seemed folks were intrigued. Even some cattle ranchers saw the merits. Stock quotes on buffalo meat were rising, while beef prices were stagnant, though hardly depressed. The Europeans loved Montana beef. Still, eastern Montana was hurting, the ranching often subsidized. The people in the town meeting in Powderville treasured their way of life, but some were already savvy enough to realize that their children might be selling insurance in Denver or writing software in Seattle unless something bold was done to save the eastern region.

I had listened to some pissing and moaning about East Coast intellectuals in Miles City at the Montana Bar, which sports a stuffed head of a Texas longhorn on one wall. ("Why not turn New Jersey into a Toxic-Dumping Commons?" "Why not turn all of Manhattan into a walled prison, like in that Kurt Russell movie?") People who owned and worked cattle ranches were hardly unsophisticated. They pointed out that the new buffalo herd in Yellowstone Park was already overgrazing the native grasses. They had read their Lewis and Clark, like most literate Montanans. They knew that some range scientists, in rebuttal to the Buffalo Commons idea, believed that massive herds of gangues had depredated the plains in Clark's time, so that much of the land near the Yellowstone was then blanketed with prickly pear cactus. This land was better off now, with cattle, they said. And what of lost property taxes, if the government bought out cattle operations and stocked buffalo? But these ranchers were intrigued, at the same time. They could grow cattle if cattle was in demand, buffalo (or beefalo, which is a tasty mix) if not.

If my own brother could decide to convert one of his cattle

ranches in Australia into a bird-watching preserve sanctioned by the Audubon Society, build bungalows in the trees, and rent them out to German tourists, his cousins in eastern Montana could not be that far behind.

I had nothing particular against cows, myself. That is, I did not mind barbecuing their tasty skinned and carved flesh over a hot grill and eating it with onions. At the same time, I thought my environmentalist friends in San Francisco made a strong case for banning the subsidized cattle raising that caused rain forests to be cleared for American hamburgers. I guess, having just returned to Montana, I was a bit betwixt and between, a redneck ecologist, if you will. In six weeks, I would go deer hunting, and also chop down a Christmas tree from the national forest. It hurt me more to cut down the tree than to kill a deer, which did not hurt me at all but rather excited me. That, I suppose, is a good working definition of a redneck ecologist.

Perhaps my family is a little more eccentric than most, but in my experience Montana ranchers are a little different from their brethren in South Dakota or Wyoming. What counts here is money and fun. Eco-tourism was both. If Dave Drum could launch Kampgrounds of America from Billings, it was not surprising that other Montana entrepreneurs were already proposing to turn the Big Open north of Billings, slightly east of where I was paddling today, into what they called a new Serengeti, wild with antelope, elk, and buffalo, wolves, too, perhaps.

What will Montana look like in twenty years?

It will be a mix. There will be cattle ranches, big mines, wheat and sugar beet spreads. But timber will be reined in to make way for ski resorts, clear trout streams, and newcomers. Those newcomers themselves will be reined in, since subdivisions loose the family dog upon the deer and septic tanks seep into the Yellowstone's feeder streams. A good-sized trout might be worth as much as a cow, measured by the money trout fishing brought to the state. Hunting will not die. It will flourish. Newcomers come to Montana to hunt. But elk and buffalo will be allowed, in fact encouraged, to wander the migratory routes they have trod for a thousand years. There will be buffalo underpasses on the interstates. The Japanese and the French will drive out in tour buses, and Montanans will put them up in places like the Grand, the Murray, and Chico Hot Springs Resort, as they once set out spreads for dudes traveling to Yellowstone Park in the heyday of the railways.

Trout, pheasants, geese, wolves and grizzlies, sulfur-eating hot springs bacteria, and butterflies will all find themselves far more protected than they are now, because they will come to mean as much to Montana's coming new power structure as they do now to the Montana breed of ecosystem environmentalist.

The old power structure in Montana has been quicker to see the possibilities of clean coal or a new Serengeti than it has the worth of another new development, high-tech industry. But this solution will be forced upon them, too, because those who make their living this way are coming to Montana on their own, attracted by the mountains and the beauty of rivers like the Yellowstone. Some people in Silicon Valley would rather write programs in a place where they could cast a fly line after work, or ski, and where their children stand less chance of being kidnapped or shot accidentally by gangs. The products of these newcomers are shipped to market not by cattle car but through modem, and the deals are cut by fax. Bozeman was not yet Boise, the high-tech center of the northern Rockies, but younger Montanans had taken notice, and they did not want to have to leave the state to find work.

The key to change in the next century will be protection of the environment, as change was dictated by its manipulation in the last. The new approaches will be ecosystemic. They will follow the old patterns of moving fauna and growing flora across interstates and county and state lines, not to mention down rivers. The vision of a Buffalo Commons presumes an ecosystem, as does a view of a Greater Yellowstone.

Our river, too, is an ecosystem, a wild and woolly one, grizzlies, sauger, beet farmers, and Heineken drinkers. If buffalo could be reintroduced to its banks, then the black-spotted cutthroat trout could certainly be restored to its pools. The Yellowstone is the watery soul of Montana. It joins mountain to prairie. It is also a historical, archaeological, and geological rarity. There is nowhere else like it.

Why not designate the Yellowstone a wild and scenic river? Why not make it the Yellowstone River National Park? This could be done for the entire length, from Yellowstone Lake to the confluence of the Missouri. The Yellowstone is the longest free-flowing river in the lower forty-eight. Why not celebrate it? Even with pesticide and fertilizer runoff in the lower stretches it is still remarkably pure, a lost and enchanting world, yet one easily accessible.

For starters, the Yellowstone could be sanctified in its blue ribbon stretch, the Paradise Valley from Gardiner to Livingston. Or, extending this preserve a little farther, from Livingston around the old Great Bend, along the base of the Beartooths, to the Clarks Fork, the Lodge Where All Dance, as the old ones called the tributary.

The Lodge Where All Dance—this was a name for the Yellowstone itself, or could be. Montana was called the Treasure State, but in twenty years, that nineteenth-century treasure might more obviously be seen reflected in the Yellowstone's currents, pools, and flowing beauty. The river was a national treasure, as well as the pride of Montana.

To think that a trout might be worth as much as a cow. In this vision, kayakers might be the new pioneers.

I laughed at that. But best not to look too long into the full moon of the future, become blinded, and tip over. Ruminate too long and the old Rochejhone might freeze on us, once again. The Yellowstone lacked all patience for dawdlers. As did Montana weather. It was time to get the hell out of Dodge.

We decided to bundle the boys like caterpillars and pray for warmth. It was time to finish.

Without Strobel, a shuttle was more difficult. The attendants at the gas station in Fairview, and at the minimart, could not leave work. The farmers were working into the night, with those portable arc lights, to get the crop in. They were as spooked by last year's freeze and the probability of this year's freeze as we were. Anyone else who could drive, pretty much, was working for a beet farmer that week in Richland County. What else was there in Fairview? The live bait shop.

We offered to pay the woman who owned the shop. She agreed. We set up noon the next day to meet. In the morning we went to set up the raft. For safe keeping, we had moved the raft from a sand hollow below the Fairview drawbridge to a retired couple's lawn half a mile away. With the old farm couple, who were remodeling their garage and had moved our raft to the backyard, we entered into a discussion of cats versus raccoons as preferable pets on a farm, whether Mormonism was the new Catholicism or a silly upstart religion or both, and whether William Clark hunted on the property, long ago. These sorts of discussions had been making us late for six hundred miles, and they made us late for the bait lady.

When we pulled up to the bait shop an hour after lunch, the bait lady was in the middle of doing her nails. She seemed a little out of place in a bait shop, a young buxom blond in a bouffant hairdo and a miniskirt, painting her nails a darker red than the cottonwoods had turned, but, then, it was her bait shop. She owned it, as she said more than once. I wondered if she had chipped her nails pulling crayfish from the bait tanks, but I held my tongue. We needed this woman.

"I can't now. Might get a customer on their lunch break."

"It's after lunch."

She didn't look up.

"I think everybody's out bringing in the beets."

The bait lady did not reply.

"Could you help us, please," Ines almost begged. "We're afraid the weather will snow."

"That'll be good for sauger fishing, won't it, honey?"

This was low, unnecessary comedy. But I knew we would make it now, because one thing I had learned about the river gods was that they had a sense of humor, just not always a very sophisticated one.

"You have nice nails," Ines said.

"Thank you," the bait lady said.

We tried the bars. Fairview is not Roscoe, or else the bartenders were also out driving the sources of this nation's sugar to the Holly factory in Sidney. The first two bars were closed. We went to the Stockman, which looked small from the outside but opened to a cavernous room with a dance floor, an overhead projection TV, pool tables, and a horseshoe bar, with grill and soup counter to the side. We had some homemade minestrone. It was very good. Above the bar was an aquarium. It housed a single fish. His name was Fat Boy and he was a puffer from Thailand. Customers paid a quarter to buy Fat Boy a goldfish, from a water bag behind the bar. We gave the waitress a quarter. Fat Boy was much quicker than his name implied. He swam the poor goldfish into the aquarium grass and sucked it inside his mouth without bothering to chew.

Except for us, there was only one other customer in the Stockman. He was a kid of about twenty eating a steak so large it flopped over the sides of his plate. We told the bartender what we needed, and she waited until the kid had swallowed a few pieces of steak, before asking him. We all watched him eat. He ate with his knife raised in one hand

and his fork poised high in the other, between bites. I think he thought the steak might try to get away.

We offered him $10. I would have paid $20 in a second.

"Sure, but lemme finish my steak, 'K?"

The kid drove his pickup like a bat out of hell, which was good since those wild horses were running over the hill, as usual.

"How come you're not driving a beet truck?" I asked him.

"I'll be driving my uncle's beets all night, like I done last night, and the night before. I'm the night shift. I just got up."

So the steak was breakfast. He was a good kid. He kept talking about how the police in Washington and Texas had falsely arrested him for this or that, but Montana cops let a working guy alone. I didn't say anything funny. I just wanted to get on the river. An oil roughneck on his day off, fishing for the wily sauger below the bridge, waved us off.

It started to rain within a mile, that cold rain that wrecks everything. We started to argue how stupid it was that we were on the river in such weather. In another mile, the sun poked out. Cody was allowed to row. Jack grew cheerful with the wood ducks floating beside us. The bluffs on the east bank seemed lost and beautiful. We thought of Lewis. The first thing he did when he saw the Yellowstone tumbling into the Missouri was cross the river and climb those bluffs for a good long look at the coming centuries.

It was a river older than time. Lewis and Clark had given their names to it: Pompey's Pillar, Clarks Fork, Buffalo Rapids, Wolf Rapids, Shields, Pryor, the tributaries. We, too, had found names for the parts of the Yellowstone we had made over in our own image: Front-of-the-Boat Rapids, Day Care Rapids, Dead Nurse Rapids, Mosquito Point. We smiled at the memory. It had been hard, at times, but it beat living two thousand to the city block by a sharp, pointed stick in the eye.

I had begun the float in search of my father. I had not thought about him for several hundred river miles, though perhaps I loved him more. The reason for this was that I had become more of a father myself, regulating the savages as they grew into toddler bruisers, trying to make them laugh as frogs jumped out of the reeds and their mother popped away at psycho owls in the trees. You still are what you are, even when you get away from it all. That is an old truth. Outside of Montana we had always been Montanans, at heart, and that is why,

I suppose, we had returned. We were happy enough with what we had become, because we knew we were lucky to be here at all, paddling downriver through a landscape that had enthralled our kind for centuries. This was a place, the Yellowstone, to be at peace and, also, to avoid being killed, if you could help it. That was the central tension, over the centuries, that seemed to impart giddiness to the river's adventurers.

Magpies spun and landed in the willows that lined the river on the west bank, flat delta land. The boys loved magpies. They're a boy's kind of bird—loud, squawking, colorful, usually fighting, and always doing the unpredictable. There were no bends at all in this last stretch of river, which is hard to tell from looking at a map. It was a straight shot. We knew we were going to make it. Then the sun retreated. The wind came up. Cody fell asleep on the bottom of the boat and was covered with a down coat. Four days before, he and his brother had been splashing in the river naked. We reached the steep bank where Preston had heaved up his net full of croaking catties, along with that one badly lost salmon. Others had told us, "When you reach the confluence, paddle hard for the far bank of the Missouri. Otherwise, the big river will sweep you downstream."

This was ridiculous. The Missouri was a kitten to the Yellowstone's cougar, even if there were three hundred yards of crosscurrents. Besides, those not asleep on the floorboards were shouting. It was half an hour past sunset. Everybody was wearing gloves or mittens. The rain was a couple degrees from snow. If we had not been jumping up and down onshore, finally, we might have frozen. The original plan of pouring champagne over our heads was scrapped since we did not want to pick sheet ice out of the children's hair. They refused to leave the Trooper for pictures, anyway. Sweet God Almighty! the Missouri at last.

We threw the big blue raft on top of the Trooper, and rumbled back to the Stockman in the rain. After clinking hot chocolate glasses all around, the adults clinked a couple of double iced bourbons. The enormity of the feat sank in. Any twenty-five-year-old world-class kayaker could shoot the Nile or the Boh. That was easy. He or she had not met anybody they wanted to have children with. Probably nobody would put up with them that long. Either way, support logistics were minimized.

We had run America's longest free-flowing river as a family float in the American way, bitching and moaning the whole distance like pilots on a Mississippi flatboat.

But here we were, in the last river bar, in the last river town in Montana, forking over quarters to feed an imported celebrity puffer fish from Thailand named Fat Boy. We had run the rapids, and strolled the shallows. We had made it. Braggarts, we ordered a single glass of champagne and drank it slowly together. Outside, the rain turned to sleet. Summer, it appeared, was over.

Again.